Digital Fashion

Digital Fashion

Theory, Practice, Implications

Edited by
Michael R. Spicher,
Sara Emilia Bernat, and
Doris Domoszlai-Lantner

BLOOMSBURY VISUAL ARTS
LONDON · NEW YORK · OXFORD · NEW DELHI · SYDNEY

BLOOMSBURY VISUAL ARTS
Bloomsbury Publishing Plc
50 Bedford Square, London, WC1B 3DP, UK
1385 Broadway, New York, NY 10018, USA
29 Earlsfort Terrace, Dublin 2, Ireland

BLOOMSBURY, BLOOMSBURY VISUAL ARTS and the Diana logo are trademarks
of Bloomsbury Publishing Plc

First published in Great Britain 2024

Cover design: Adriana Brioso
Cover image © Parallel Universe
threeASFOUR X PLACEBO

Photographer: Petros Kouiouris @petros_koy
Styling: Altorrin @altorrin
Hair: Cassie Carey @cassiecarey.hair
Makeup & Nails: Stephanie Hernandez @clawedbylacreme
Talent: Charlotte Kemp @charlottekempmuhl
Cover edit: Brit Shaked @brittshaked

A catalogue record for this book is available from the British Library.

A catalog record for this book is available from the Library of Congress.

ISBN: HB: 978-1-3503-5961-1
        PB: 978-1-3503-5962-8
        ePDF: 978-1-3503-5963-5
        eBook: 978-1-3503-5964-2

Typeset by RefineCatch Limited, Bungay, Suffolk
Printed and bound in India

To find out more about our authors and books visit www.bloomsbury.com
and sign up for our newsletters.

To Hannah, Craig, Itay, Ari, Irén, Ferenc

Contents

Part Two Practices and Applications of Digital Fashion

Part Three Issues and Ethics of Digital Fashion

Part Four Looking to and Hoping for the Future of Digital Fashion

Figures, Tables, and QR Codes

Figures

Table

QR Codes

Contributors

Idit Barak is a fashion designer specializing in digital fashion and new media. As a senior lecturer at the prestigious Fashion Design Department at Shenkar, Barak introduces and promotes the study and research of digital tools and new methodologies to the next generation of fashion professionals. Barak earned her master's degree from the Interactive Telecommunications Program at NYU. In her thesis, she explores the capabilities of augmented reality technologies using AR to revolutionize the future of fashion retail by allowing designers to curate content-driven immersive experiences. She is a co-founder of the Fashion X Games Research Group at Shenkar in collaboration with Browzwear, focusing on exploring fashion's role in representing identity in digital environments. Barak is also a co-founder of FT—smart fashion tapes, winner of the 2017 We Work Creator Award, a technology-based textile-to-textile range of innovative adhesion products. Barak's work has been shown in numerous exhibits including, most recently, The Ball, Design Museum Holon, Israel. Her work 11:59pm, a dress made using 10,000 meters of fiber optic strands, dealt with the topic of unattainable fantasies and a fleeting moment. She is a fashion and design content curator of conferences and exhibits focusing on emerging technologies driving responsible growth in the fashion industry. In 2021, she co-managed Jam Week Shenkar in collaboration with five NPOs to tackle the problem of loneliness. Jam Week brings 750 students and professors from the Design, Engineering, and Art Faculties to create a framework for creative interdisciplinary thought and a "hackathon" mentality.

Sara Emilia Bernat, Ph.D., is a sociologist and brand strategist. She graduated with a M.PS. in Branding from the School of Visual Arts in NYC, before pursuing a Ph.D. at Humboldt Universitat-Berlin in Sociology, specializing in consumer motivations behind sustainable luxury and fashion. In tandem with her research, Sara advises private and public organizations on strategic branding and development at Gemic, a global strategy and innovation consultancy, and regularly contributes to academic and industry publications, such as *In Pursuit of Luxury*, *Fast Company*, and *Glamour*. She splits her time between Europe and the United States.

King Debs is a Cape Town-based South African artist who works primarily in 3D digital art, animation and his self-developed calligraphy. He creates a unique aesthetic to transpose his ideas on identity and Afrikanism, with his work spanning multiple media including textiles, graffiti, large-scale murals, CGI and augmented realities, and more. The work King Debs creates is centered on themes of identity, socio-political commentary, life and death, and the human condition at large. He is inspired by "trans-humanist" ideology and the dystopian convergence of man and machine. King Debs was born in the North-West Province town of Mafikeng and grew up in Tshwane, where he graduated from the Tshwane University of Technology with a Bachelor's Degree in Multimedia Design, in 2010. He has exhibited locally and internationally, with his first solo exhibition, *Bokamoso (Future)*, held at the AVA Gallery in Cape Town, South Africa, in 2020.

Erica de Greef, Ph.D., is a curator, author, academic, and co-founder of the African Fashion Research Institute (AFRI), the South African Fashion Journal, and Refashion Lab. Her work spans museums, creative platforms, educational institutions, and grassroots projects. De Greef works collaboratively to prompt critical and creative attention to the possibilities of redress and imagination. In 2018 she curated *21 YEARS: Making Histories with South African Fashion Week* at the Zeitz Museum of Contemporary African Art in Cape Town. With an ongoing commitment to develop the field of African Fashion Studies, de Greef's Ph.D. in African Studies at the University of Cape Town, "Sartorial Disruptions," explored the stasis within fashion collections and exhibitions at South African museums in post-apartheid democracy. She has also lectured and contributed to curriculum development and supervision in fashion institutions for many years. She co-edited *Rethinking Fashion Globalization*

(Bloomsbury, 2021), and has published widely with chapters in books, articles, zines, and online platforms. De Greef is an editorial board member for the *International Journal of Fashion Studies* and a Research Fellow with UNISA (2023–6), and since 2020 has co-convened a monthly online *Conversations in Decoloniality and Fashion*.

Doris Domoszlai-Lantner is a New York-based fashion historian and archivist. She holds an M.A. in Fashion and Textile Studies: History, Theory, Museum Practice from the Fashion Institute of Technology (FIT). Domoszlai-Lantner has founded and developed several private and corporate fashion archives and presented her research at numerous international conferences, including those at Oxford University, the University of Lille, France, and Columbia College Chicago. Her study "Fashioning a Soviet Narrative: Jean Paul Gaultier's Russian Constructivist Collection" was published in *Engaging with Fashion: Perspectives on Communication, Education and Business* (Brill, 2018). Her co-authored study in *Vestoj*, "Tamás Király: Hungary's King of Fashion," is the only English-language history study available on this avant-garde Hungarian designer. Domoszlai-Lantner's work has been published in both academic and public platforms, including *Fast Company*, *Glamour Hungary*, and the Intellect journal *Fashion, Style and Pop Culture*. She is the co-founder of Fashion Forward and is currently an adjunct instructor at Massachusetts College of Art and Design, and Boston Architectural College.

Matthew Drinkwater is a world-renowned expert in emerging technologies and their application to the creative industries. A specialist in immersive technologies (XR/MR/AR/VR), he and his team are building pathways for a truly digitized world. Named as a "fashion-tech trailblazer" by Draper's, a "pioneer and a visionary" by Wired and the "OG of Digital Fashion" by RTFKT Studios, Drinkwater has delivered groundbreaking experiences and a stunning range of projects that have captured the imagination of both the fashion and technology industries, including what Forbes described as "the first example of truly beautiful wearable tech." He was also named as a "Digital World's Influencer" by Stylus for 2020. In 2018, Drinkwater worked alongside Lucasfilm's immersive entertainment division ILMxLAB to bring their new performance-driven augmentation technology, LIVECGX, to London Fashion Week—an iconic project that set the scene for real-time digital fashion and the future metaverse. A regular speaker at technology conferences, Drinkwater can usually be found on stage talking about the convergence of fashion and tech as well as updating on his latest projects. He has presented at the Internet of Things Summit, Wearables Europe Berlin, Web Summit, South Summit, Unbound Digital, Dubai Fashion Forward, Wearable Technology Show, DigitalK, Fifteen Seconds, London Technology Week, SXSW, The Virtual Reality Show, Decoded Fashion, Millennial 20/20, Innovation Fashion Summit Madrid, Arab Luxury World, World Retail Congress, the V&A's Future Series, Tech. and Wired Retail. Drinkwater is currently working on the DeFine Project, a European Commission-funded initiative aimed at growing the fashion technology sector across Europe. He is also heading up the innovation strand of the London College of Fashion's ambitious Fashion District project, which aims to position East London as the world's leading hub for fashion technology. Drinkwater sits on the advisory boards of the Centre for Fashion Enterprise (CFE), the Stockholm Fashion Tech Talks, and the Independent Fashion Advisory Board (IFAB), and is a judge for LVMH's DARE intrapreneurship program.

Petra Egri, Ph.D., is a fashion researcher and an Assistant Professor at the Department of Applied Arts at the University of Pécs, Hungary. Her research interests and publications are in deconstruction and fashion. Egri has published her research in professional journals and edited books in English, Hungarian, and Russian, serving as a co-editor of three books about theatrical performances. Her paper, "The Allegorical Deconstruction of Socialist Style," on late socialist neo-avantgarde fashion performances, was published in *Russian Fashion Theory* in 2019. Egri has lectured at numerous international conferences (Reykjavik, Washington, DC, Milan, Pontevedra, Belgrade, Moscow, Manchester, and Roubaix) and in May 2023 curated an exhibition of fashion illustrations by Lúcia Mészáros at the Republic Gallery in Pécs. In October 2022, she was a co-curator of *SOCIAL_EAST*, an exhibition on the Kádár era and fashion presented in New York City. Egri's book on radical fashion performances, *Fashion Theory, Theatricality, Deconstruction: Contemporary Fashion Performance*, was published by SZIF Publishing in 2023.

Leslie Holden is co-founder of The Digital Fashion Group. Founded in 2020, TDFG is a European-led collaboration between fashion academics and industry innovators. Working with industry leaders, TDFG equips fashion education professionals and brands with the relevant skills, mindset, and strategies for tomorrow's workplace. Previously, as Head of Fashion at the Amsterdam Fashion Institute (AMFI) and a member of the AMFI board for over fourteen years, Holden was responsible for the redevelopment of the international curricula focusing on digitalization and sustainability in fashion. As design director and entrepreneur with over twenty years' experience in the fashion industry, he worked for companies such as Dunhill, Stefanel, Byblos, Burberry, and Liberty. Holden sits on the Steering Committee of the EU Worth Partnership Project and is a mentor for the Farfetch Incubator program. He was for many years an Executive Board member of the International Foundation of Fashion Technology Institutes (IFFTI) and a trustee of the UK Graduate Fashion Foundation. Holden is an experienced keynote speaker and moderator and was recently nominated by Brytehall in the top 100 of the most influential leaders in digital fashion.

Siviwe James is a researcher, arts practitioner, and archivist who speaks to a sort of visual and sonic archeology, a reconstruction of time, place, and meaning. By researching and creating visual and sonic imaginaries-as-landscapes that acknowledge the rites of passage and lineal spaces of Xhosa peoples (black peoples), he is able to insert fragments of time that speak into the void. Archival audio/visual materials (personal and public), and collated interviews in the form of everyday conversations, are merged to form (k)new knowledges of history, encouraging audiences to shift their position in what Rolando Vázquez speaks of as changing the way in which we relate to other realities, other ways of thinking. Through sonic and visual assemblages, James proposes that there is a form of growing (to know) with others. His work offers archival and ancestral knowledge-fragments as new sites of visibility and accessibility.

Mingjing Lin, Ph.D., is a Senior Lecturer in Textile Science and STEM Practice at London College of Fashion. Previously, she held the position of Senior

Lecturer for the MA Digital Fashion program at the University for the Creative Arts. Lin's teaching spans Digital Fashion and Textile Design, Fashion Gamification and Metaverse, Parametric Design, 3D-printed Fashion and Textiles, and Ph.D. research supervision. In 2020 she earned a Ph.D. degree from the Textile Department at the Royal College of Art (UK). Lin's practice-based research focuses on body-oriented parametric design and Parametric Thinking 2.0 for 3D-printed fashion and textiles. She has been involved in various research-oriented commercial projects, such as contributing to the WISP sensual Jewellery project in 2017, which was funded by EU Horizon 2020 Wear Sustain. In 2019, Lin co-founded L-UP-L-DOWN wearable-tech studio and in 2015 established the non-profit UK–China design platform ABOUNDARY. Her works have been presented internationally since 2011, including exhibitions at the V&A, London Fashion Week, Disseny de Barcelona, Taipei Biennale, and the National Museum of China. Lin embraces the STEAM approach by exploring the creations of digital fashion, delving into the possibilities of wearable technology and smart textiles.

Daniella Loftus is a digital fashion founder, influencer, and investor. Beginning in 2020 as the first digital fashion content creator, she was one of the original movers in the digital fashion space. Over time, Loftus's writing about digital fashion's future has led her to become a leading voice in the industry, with insights featured across global media, including the *New York Times*, CNBC, Bloomberg, and *Vogue*. In October 2021, Loftus's ecosystem expertise led her to become a founding member of digital fashion investment vehicle RED DAO, with over $6m of digital fashion assets under management, including the Dolce & Gabbana DOGE crown. Loftus is the founder of DRAUP—a Web3 native platform for the next era of luxury fashion. Under the belief that digital fashion should become an economically democratizing force, DRAUP endeavors to push the bounds of what digital fashion can be for its creators and consumers.

Lesiba Mabitsela is a South African interdisciplinary artist and fashion designer based in Johannesburg, South Africa. Mabitsela's design practice incorporates critical fashion and performance studies in his exploration of fashion histories from the African continent, using performance, video, textiles, and immersive technology to explore a concept or feeling expressed by what he terms "cultural homelessness." His work critiques postcolonial perceptions of blackness, masculinities, and the symbolic underpinnings of Western aesthetics and notions of beauty. Mabitsela is a former recipient of the Andrew W. Mellon Foundation scholarship, contributing to the completion of his studies at the University of Cape Town's Drama Department within the Faculty of Humanities. He worked as a Research Assistant at Zeitz Museum of Contemporary Art Africa, before co-founding the African Fashion Research Institute (AFRI) in 2019. Mabitsela's creative research projects include Reinstitute, the Cutting Room Project, and Be Your Own Punk, and his work has shown locally and internationally, including the V&A and the Central Museum in Utrecht.

Mindy Meissen is a writer and consultant based in New York City. Her master's thesis, "Material Conditions: Fashion in the Bitstream," explores the material and cultural significance of computing in fashion. Most recently, she has worked with consumer startups on brand identity, positioning, and storytelling—including a company revolutionizing fashionable high heels with biomechanics-based comfort, and a menswear brand made for the active (and work-from-home) entrepreneur. Meissen has written for *Document Journal*, *Fashionista*, and the newsletters *FashionREDEF* and *Think Fashion*. She has presented her research at the Costume Society of America's annual conference and LIM. Meissen holds an MA in Fashion Studies: History, Theory and Museum Studies, and a BFA in Graphic Design.

Virginia Rolling, Ph.D., is an Assistant Professor of Fashion Merchandising and Apparel Design at Georgia Southern University. As an Auburn University graduate, she received a dissertation best paper award from the International Textile and Apparel Association in 2019 for her neuroaesthetics research on wearable technology. This cutting-edge research at the Museum of Design Atlanta examined the beholder's neuroaesthetic responses to a wearable technology garment using both eye-tracking technology and electrodermal skin sensor responses in conjunction with Shimamura's I-SKE model. The methodological significance of this study remains unparalleled in various fields such as neuroaesthetics, museum research, and apparel. Furthermore, the results from this study remain beneficial for various disciplines such as fashion, fine arts, and performance arts. In addition to this research, Rolling's publications encompass other topics such as 3D-printed digital fashion. In 2022, she was an invited guest speaker at the Manchester Fashion Institute's 3rd Digital Fashion Innovation E-Symposium to discuss her research on wearable accessory designers' perceptions of 3D printing, which was published in the *International Journal of Fashion Design, Technology and Education*. Rolling's research has also been published in various other journals, including *Dress, Social Responsibility Journal*, and the *International Journal of Consumer Studies*. Her research interests include neuroaesthetics and digital fashion.

Idiat Shiole (Hadeeart) is a Web3 startup founder and accomplished 3D designer specializing in digital fashion and XR technologies. With a deep passion for the intersection of art, technology, and fashion, she has established herself as a prominent figure in the industry. Hadeeart's expertise in creating captivating 3D virtual garments has led to recognition in renowned publications like *Quartz Africa*, the *Guardian*, and *Fashion Network*. She has also made significant contributions to shaping digital fashion in Africa through her work with Hadeeart Atelier and her startup, MomentumX. Driven by her desire to push boundaries, Hadeeart has honed her skills in virtual and augmented reality, utilizing software such as Spark AR, Unreal Engine, and Snap ML. Her dedication to innovation led her to pursue a fully funded Masters of Art in Fashion Design and Theory at Zhejiang Sci-Tech University, China, where she incorporated immersive technology to advance digital fashion. Notably, Hadeeart has been awarded the prestigious Global Talent Visa, recognizing her as a tech talent of international acclaim. Through her groundbreaking work and visionary approach, she continues to redefine the possibilities at the intersection of technology, art, fashion, and games.

Sihle Sogaula is a Cape Town-based material culture researcher and photographer who uses the curatorial to meditate on relationships between the embodied, memory, and garments, both in archives and the quotidian. She is currently pursuing a MAFA at the Michaelis School of Fine Art at the University of Cape Town, specializing in fashion curation and critique, fusing her interests in film photography as a meditative practice and fashion as emancipatory and embodied ritual. Using found photographs, image-making, and garment-construction, and drawing on unconventional research methodologies, Sogaula explores how material and immaterial objects become keepers of lived experiences, and how these records can be read, interpreted, and engaged. More broadly, her work is interested in the relationship between the index and the referent, lived experiences and memories contained within objects of significance, the thing we see and the thing we remember. Using film photography, writing, and making, Sogaula's work explores the ways in which material things can hold many truths at once and how memory objects are invocations of the present as much as they are invocations of the past.

Michael R. Spicher, Ph.D., writes and speaks about aesthetics, beauty, taste, and digital fashion, especially how theories connect to different practices. In 2016 he founded the Aesthetics Research Lab, which brings together different sectors engaged with aesthetic questions and solutions. Drawing from his perspective as a philosopher, Spicher addresses professional and general audiences, including contexts like fashion, business, and architecture. He has written academic articles about aesthetics, but has turned his attention to more public contexts and is a regular contributor to *BeautyMatter*, a resource for the beauty industry. Spicher is also the aesthetics area editor for the *Internet Encyclopedia of Philosophy*. Based in Boston, he teaches at Massachusetts College of Art and Design and Boston Architectural College.

Jonathan Michael Square, Ph.D., is the Assistant Professor at Parsons School of Design, having previously been a lecturer in the Committee on Degree in History and Literature at Harvard University and a fellow in the Costume Institute at the Metropolitan Museum of Art. The recipient of numerous fellowships and grants, Square's work considers histories of enslavement through the lens of fashion, and his research has appeared in numerous scholarly and public-facing venues. Currently, he is working on a book manuscript tentatively titled *Negro Cloth: How Slavery Birthed the Global*

Fashion Industry. Square has curated exhibitions at Harvard University and the Herron School of Art and Design in Indianapolis.

Beata Wilczek is a Polish-born fashion and emerging technologies researcher, educator, and consultant, now based in Berlin. In 2021, Wilczek founded the consultancy and education lab Unfolding Strategies, and in 2021–2 served as a Head of Impact at fashion tech start-up The Dematerialised. Her clients include Nike, BMW, H&M, and Vorn Hub. Wilczek holds an MA in Social Psychology from SWPS University of Social Sciences and Humanities, Warsaw, and an MA in Culture, Curating, and Criticism from Central Saint Martins, University of the Arts London (UAL). She is currently pursuing her Ph.D. in Fashion Studies at the Academy of Fine Arts Vienna (AKBILD Wien) and Aalto University, Helsinki, with an expected completion in 2024. With over a decade of teaching experience, Wilczek has been a design and fashion studies lecturer at the School of Form in Poland, Akademie Mode & Design (AMD) Berlin, and ESMOD Berlin. She has also taught at various universities worldwide, served as a Guest Professor in Digital Design at the University of Virginia and co-authored an MA program in Social Design and Sustainable Innovation in Berlin/Beirut.

Julie Zerbo is a lawyer, legal analyst, and the founder and Editor-in-Chief of *The Fashion Law*. With a background in international business, economics, and law, she has practical experience working with companies ranging from early-stage brands to publicly-traded retail giants and well-known luxury goods purveyors, giving her a dynamic understanding of the fashion business and global consumer culture. Zerbo is regularly relied upon by fashion and consumer goods brands, world-renowned law firms, non-profit organizations, trade groups, and educational institutions to speak about cutting-edge legal and commercial issues facing the retail industry.

Foreword

In an era defined by rapid technological advancements and a growing consciousness towards sustainability, the fashion industry finds itself at a crossroads. Traditional practices are being challenged, and a new wave of innovation is reshaping the way we perceive and engage with fashion. We are honored to present this pioneering academic book on digital fashion—an exploration into the forefront of fashion's digital revolution. As the founders of DRESSX, we are excited to witness the profound impact this innovative concept has had on the fashion industry and beyond.

DRESSX has emerged as a visionary platform, offering a "metacloset" (digital fashion closet) of digital-only clothes, NFT fashion items, and augmented reality (AR) looks. Our journey commenced in July 2020 when we recognized the urgent need to address the adverse environmental consequences of the fashion industry. In response, we embarked on a mission to develop a sustainable alternative—one that would eliminate waste, carbon footprints, and harmful chemicals from the production process. Thus, DRESSX was born.

Collaborating closely with accomplished traditional and 3D fashion designers, we have created a vibrant community that thrives on innovation and sustainability. Through DRESSX, users can try on and wear digital garments in their photos and videos across various digital domains—an exciting and environmentally conscious way of self-expression and content creation. With the advancement of technology, augmented reality, and artificial intelligence, and the rise of fashion for avatars in social media and the metaverse, the possibilities of digital fashion are truly limitless!

Since our inception, DRESSX has become the biggest platform for digital fashion, boasting an impressive line-up of over 400 designers and more than

4,000 digital looks available for purchase, as of today. The DRESSX app launched in 2021 provides a platform that seamlessly integrates AR technology, enabling users to effortlessly try 3D looks to their real-time videos and photos. Through strategic collaborations with renowned fashion and lifestyle companies such as Meta, Roblox, Snapchat, Google, Coca-Cola, FARFETCH, and more, DRESSX has not only provided the technological infrastructure for digital fashion dressing and a new way of marketing and self-expression in the contemporary world, but has also showcased collections from the most popular brands in their digital form, including Burberry, Balenciaga, Off-White, and Dolce & Gabbana. Our signature AR digital hat has become an iconic symbol of the digital fashion movement, adorning the heads of millions across our app and various social media platforms.

While DRESSX has made significant strides in shaping the landscape of digital fashion, we recognize the need for rigorous academic exploration of this burgeoning field. This book represents a significant contribution to the scholarly discourse, as it delves deep into the implications, possibilities, and limitations of digital fashion. We are delighted to introduce the esteemed editors of the book—Doris Domoszlai-Lantner, Sara E. Bernat, and Michael R. Spicher—whose extensive qualifications and experience researching both physical and digital fashion make them uniquely suited to curate this pioneering publication. These three editors bring interdisciplinary backgrounds from the fields of fashion history, sociology, and philosophy to unpack this remarkable new segment of the fashion system that is unraveling before our eyes.

From addressing the solutions and limitations of digital fashion for the LGBTQIA+ community to exploring the depiction of identity in the digital realm, the editors have demonstrated their commitment to understanding and shaping the future of fashion. In order to provide a diverse understanding of the scope of digital fashion, this volume includes essays and interviews by designers, journalists, curators, educators, and historians. The first of its kind, *Digital Fashion: Theory, Practice, Implications* seeks to provide a foundation for the future growth of this new area of fashion without offering a rigid definition that is restrictive or will be outdated in the near future.

Together, let us embark on a profound academic journey as we unravel the transformative potential of digital fashion. We invite you to engage with the rich insights presented within these pages, challenging conventional paradigms, and forging a path toward a future where creativity, innovation, and sustainability converge.

Daria Shapovalova and Natalia Modenova
Founders at DRESSX, 2024

An Introduction to Digital Fashion

MICHAEL R. SPICHER, SARA EMILIA BERNAT,
AND DORIS DOMOSZLAI-LANTNER

Overview

Digital fashion, as of this writing, is still in its nascent phase. People have just begun to hear about it more widely in popular media, and academia has yet to catch up. For some, digital fashion sounds like science fiction. The thought of wearing digital fashion strikes people initially as strange, since, by definition, they cannot physically wear these clothes. However, most new technologies evoke suspicion at first; many people were confused about the concept of "e-mail" when its use was popularized amongst the general public in the 1990s, and now email is a mainstay aspect of our daily lives. While your IRL (in real life) body, or self, may not wear digital garments, your digital self, in the (near) future, may wear a variety of digital garments. Like IRL fashion, digital fashion encompasses more than just digital garments themselves; it also involves creation and projection. In other words, digital fashion infiltrates all aspects of the fashion system, from production to consumption, from the industry to whole communities, as well as individuals.

People spend an ever-increasing amount of time online, in front of a variety of digital devices and screens. Many predict the future of the internet will consist of three-dimensional virtual spaces, rather than the flat websites we have so far experienced. If this is true, and the internet morphs into something more akin to a video game, then one's digital self will surely want more than a default outfit. After all, we will want to present ourselves, albeit digitally, in particular ways for the same reasons we dress a particular way in the physical world; these digital selves represent and are an extension of human beings in those virtual spaces. We use fashion to imitate others, differentiate ourselves, and express meanings, oftentimes in more symbolic ways than through physical fashion. Digital garments find no boundaries in physicality, opening up new dimensions in symbolic expression.

Approaching the Concept of Digital Fashion

While we will clarify the main aspects of digital fashion in its current or near-future iteration, we acknowledge that the future is open and highly dynamic. What we call digital fashion now may change substantially in the next ten years or more. What we hope to achieve in this book is not a rigid explanation of the nature of digital fashion nor an exact statement that depends on current technology. While we will refer to current understandings and technologies, the emphasis will be to provide a guide for the future development of this industry. Our attempt to define digital fashion and its attendant components provides some theoretical and practical explanations for the next wave to build upon.

Other noteworthy factors in our approach to digital fashion include the following two considerations. We use the broad sense of the term fashion to refer to most kinds of adornment, including clothing, accessories, make-up, body modifications, and jewelry. Although the term digital fashion is interchangeable with virtual fashion, most stakeholders (users, journalists, scholars, designers, etc.) use the term digital fashion the majority of the time. Thus, although there are instances in this book where a contributor uses the term virtual fashion, the title and focus of the book is on the term that is more prevalent: digital fashion.

Defining Digital Fashion

Fashion, at its core, is concerned with clothing and accessories. However, there is no singular definition for the concept of fashion. Rather, it has come to encompass things like self-expression, group identification, social capital, artistic pursuits, sources of financial profit, and more. Just as we don't have a singular definition of fashion, we do not have a singular understanding of digital fashion either. In fact, defining digital fashion presents some difficulties, not only because as a subset of fashion, it has been around for a mere fraction of the time that fashion itself has, but also because the concept must remain flexible enough to allow new-use cases that we cannot yet imagine.

Thus, rather than trying to offer a rigid definition of digital fashion, it seems more fruitful to present the dominant contexts with which contemporary practitioners and researchers are working. Thus, under the umbrella term of digital fashion, the contributors to this book refer to fashion that can be either semi-digital and fully digital, in the form of wearables and phygitals, photography and videography, and found on platforms as varied as video games, social media, virtual try-on experiences, CAD/CAM software, augmented reality (AR), virtual reality (VR), and mixed reality (MR), the last three of which fall under the heading of extended reality (XR). In 2022, Abu Sadat Muhammad Sayem proposed a four-part breakdown of digital fashion, into which he grouped the above, yet also intriguingly included the processes used to make them, as well as the post-production marketing.[1] Unlike Sayem's framework, the chapters in this book are focused more on the output—the digital garments and their use cases—rather than the paths to take to make and market them.

Indeed, the definitions and understandings of digital fashion vary from author to author in this book, and in some cases, may even seem contradictory. Daniella Loftus takes a broad lens to the term, noting that digital fashion refers to "any garment created in a digital realm." Julie Zerbo notes that there is currently no set definition for digital fashion in the law, although through recent cases, it seems to be understood as "virtual and/or 3D garments, apparel, and accessories that are designed for a medium that is different than the 'real,' or the physically-tangible world."

Through the concept of "wearing," Doris Domoszlai-Lantner provides an overview of the various kinds of digital fashion and the platforms on which we find them. Although her analysis harkens back to eighteenth-century looming innovation *en route* to discussions on *Roblox* and Instagram, she does not address wearables, leaving that to Virginia Rolling, who categorizes them as a subset of digital fashion. Idit Barak, on the other hand, posits that wearables are related to, but *not*, digital fashion. Leslie Holden takes a hybrid approach, defining phygital as a blend of the physical and digital, while exploring the implications of digitalization for the industry. The varied approaches to defining and interpreting digital fashion reinforce the infancy of the field and its media and academic coverage, as well as its relationship to the general field of fashion.

Types of Digital Fashion

The most common idea of digital fashion consists of garments that only exist digitally. These adornments clothe characters and avatars—digital versions of ourselves—in video games such as *Fortnite*, and in personalized emojis, such as Memojis, but they do not exist in the physical world. This does not mean that they must always be fantastical, made with wings of fire, or space exploration-inspired metallics; they might, for instance, look exactly like something worn in the physical world. It just means that this particular garment exists only in a digital realm, in either a 2D or 3D format.

For 2D images, a person buys a digital garment and uploads a specific photo, onto which the design team fits the garment onto the person in that photo. The main limitation to this type of usage is that the garment exists only in that single photo, and the person cannot switch the garment to another photo without getting the design team involved again, which presumably comes with an additional charge.

For 3D formats, there are at least four basic types of use: pre-made animations; "live" animations with avatars in a digital space controlled in real time; pre-recorded people in a physical environment with digital clothing added at some stage in production; and "live" people being filmed in a physical environment with digital clothing covering their bodies. People in "live" video, whether in a physical or digital space, are able to wear digital fashion, but there is often a noticeable lag in movement, especially the arms and legs, as the garment has to catch up with the person's motion. The bigger issue with 3D garments is not being able to bring your digital wardrobe into every platform; most platforms have been programmed to feature and support their own avatars, characters, and skins, which by and large are not transferable to other platforms. Since technology is evolving, there is a strong chance that these issues will be resolved in the near future, especially if the movement towards centralized experiences and a singular metaverse continues.

Perhaps, for some people the thought of wearing a digital garment seems strange. After all, it cannot keep you warm, protect you from rain, or shield you from the sun. If someone opts out of virtual world experiences, then it may seem like digital fashion does not apply to them. However, digital fashion, as an umbrella term, extends beyond garments that exist only as pixels on a screen or in a headset. Aside from video games and social media posts, there are other uses for digital fashion.

Phygital is a combination of the physical and the digital, which can occur in a variety of ways. Spanning the entire consumer fashion journey, phygital clothing appears from inspiration through consideration to purchase, and beyond. Over the last few years, designers have applied digital tools in a variety of different ways in the manual-design process. This approach has also been seen in the operational phase, notably through the use of blockchain to improve supply-chain solutions. Retailers are also applying hybrid solutions through the use of AR and VR, or through QR codes. These instruments are crucially impacting both production efficiency and the consumer experience.

When it comes to wearing garments, we again observe novelties. Hence, people can see each other wearing phygital clothing in several ways. One can use a smartphone's camera in conjunction with an appropriate app to interact with garments that they are not wearing in the physical world; as such, these garments can only be seen through the medium of an electronic device. Another idea would be for clothing to be added to either live or pre-recorded video of people in the physical world. This process bears a similarity to filmmakers using CGI to transform an IRL actor into a digital character in a movie; for example, turning actor Mark Ruffalo into the Incredible Hulk (Marvel Studios, 2008). Another possibility that some speculate about is that, despite Google Glass' failure, people will eventually wear smart eyewear on a regular basis, which could add digital garments to other people in the user's line of vision, in the viewfinders's lenses, in real time.

Uses for Digital Fashion

People increasingly purchase physical clothing online. Once a niche category, ecommerce for fashion is a segment that was worth $700 billion in 2022,[2] and shows no decline in sight, even though it duplicates many of the pitfalls of brick-and-mortar retail. Sizing, for example, can be hard to navigate in an online store, providing consumers with items that they cannot physically try on until after it arrives at their physical location. Digital fashion presents an opportunity to alleviate the pressures and impacts of purchasing physical clothing online. Imagine if you could see an article of clothing on your own body before buying it. Further, let's say you need a shirt. You could match a shirt with the rest of your wardrobe, so that you can see, for instance, that it works well with most of your pants. Digital fashion, in the form of virtual try-on, makes this possible.

The idea is that you could see yourself, similar to looking in a mirror in a physical dressing room, but you can also move your digital self around, so you can see different angles. It's likely that future versions can show what it looks like to walk or sit, rather than only seeing you stand still. Additionally, modifications might be possible. If you wanted the pant legs to be a bit longer or shorter, then maybe these adjustments could be made.

In other words, digital fashion may mark the emergence of tailor-made garments on the mass level. These designs can be also understood as designer blueprints that can be customized for any type of body, at no extra cost, unwanted attention, or public stigmatization. Hence, we seem to be entering into an era that combines master design on the one hand, and accessible DIY on the other. The result is a medium that is flexible, creative, and seemingly democratic. This is crucial, as it brings up another key aspect.

Imagine that for some clothing, your decision to buy something is made after seeing and manipulating a garment on your digital self, as discussed above. But this time, you make any adjustments that you want, likely with some limitations. After you finalize all these choices, then—and only then—the company makes the garment. This process would necessarily take longer, which is why stores—both online and brick-and-mortar—would still need to exist. But this could potentially reduce a lot of unwanted garment purchases, resulting in landfill. Overproduction is one of the leading reasons for exorbitant waste coming from the fashion industry, and digital aspects of fashion offer a solution, even if only a partial one.

Other, more niche media is also shaping and molding the fashion system. Artists experiment as they try to get their work just right. Painters and sculptors may make a string of sketches. Architects make models. Fashion designers often use fabrics to design and then send out to possible buyers. Architects have begun to make digital versions of their buildings for clients to "walk through," and fashion designers have also begun doing similar things with their work. As the technology has gotten better at demonstrating how a particular fabric will move or hang, designers have been able to present more accurate renderings of their ideas. In addition to the process of creation, another common cause of pollution is overproduction. Instead of companies making clothes hoping people will buy them, they can now send their digital designs out for testing before production. From the consumer side, people can see how garments fit the digital versions of their bodies in digital dressing rooms, perhaps even being able to make minor adjustments, so that people only buy what they know will basically fit and look good on them. And the garments might even be made only after a person orders it, which would drastically cut down on overproduction. This process would also lessen online returns, which most often end up in landfill rather than back on the shelves.

Physical garments with a digital component have been predicted to arrive, such as temperature control, music playback, or flexible, cloth-like screens to change images or colors. The 1989 film *Back to the Future: Part 2* contained "smart" clothing in their imagined version of the year 2015: sneakers laced themselves up to fit the foot perfectly; a jacket that dried itself after getting wet. These things did not appear in the real 2015, but that doesn't mean smart clothing doesn't exist and won't continue to develop. However, just because we can do these interesting things with digital clothing does not mean that these are good or useful ideas.

What is the Metaverse?

While the metaverse is not necessary for digital fashion's existence, a connection between the two certainly seems inevitable. If the metaverse develops into something more viable and widespread, people will begin to use it the way they did with the other iterations of the internet. In a succinct explanation, Cathy Hackl, Dirk Lueth, and Tommaso Di Bartolo explain the three eras of the internet so far. "Web1 was the Internet of the 1990s and early 2000s. Web2 added social networks, eCommerce, user content creation, and the sharing economy. Web3 is about more immersive experiences."[3] Web3 is what enables the metaverse to exist. Meanwhile, Matthew Ball offers a comprehensive definition of the metaverse:

> A massively scaled and interoperable network of real-time rendered 3D virtual worlds that can be experienced synchronously and persistently by an effectively unlimited number of users with an individual sense of presence, and with continuity of data, such as identity, history, entitlements, objects, communications, and payments.[4]

This definition comprises many facets, which Ball discusses in greater detail. For our purposes of focusing on digital fashion, we will highlight only a few of these concepts. First, the notion of interoperability needs to be explained as it relates to digital fashion. Someone could upload a photo to Twitter; then, someone else could copy that photo to Instagram; another person could then download that photo and text it to a friend. The reason this is possible derives from the fact that people accepted certain types of files (in this case probably a JPG or PNG), and they built various different platforms to allow users to display or share images made in those file-types. Imagine if every platform or system accepted a different image file; we would likely give up on sharing as many photos as we do. Interoperability, a major tenet of the metaverse, will eventually allow us to use the same avatars and their digital garments in all of the different virtual spaces in existence. In order to achieve interoperability in digital fashion, practitioners will need to agree on the use of certain universal file formats and functions

Next, we can discuss the idea of "real-time rendered 3D virtual worlds." If you go into your kitchen and move a glass, then that glass is in its new location when someone else comes into the kitchen five minutes later. Early video games would have people start in a default location with a default set-up. The metaverse, people predict, will remain in real-time. If someone wears a garment, then they will continue to wear it until they decide to change into another garment. And this garment will be seen by everyone else in close proximity (from all directions) to the wearer.

Ball explains that from the individual's perspective there will exist "an individual sense of presence." When wearing the appropriate headset, an individual will gain that first-person perspective that they possess in the physical world. It will be immersive. Rather than looking at a flat screen, the individual will feel as though they are inside this virtual space. Rather than playing a character in a video game, one's avatar or digital self will become an extension of their physical self. This significant change in the digital experience will influence our identity as we proceed.

As the metaverse continues to develop, fashion (and adornment more broadly) may be one of the driving forces because people care about how they appear to others. But, as deeply social human beings, we also care about how we appear for our own sake too. For other people, we express something with our fashion. What is projected in the metaverse will surely change compared to what we do in the physical world. For example, people generally wouldn't wear a three-piece suit to work on a farm or perform an oil change on their car. Since real oil can't stain your clothes in the metaverse, people's clothing choices are not necessarily contingent on their activities in virtual spaces.

On the larger level, fashion, as we know it, is one of the leading industries of the world, valued at $1.7 trillion in 2022.[5] In addition, "the global digital transformation market size was evaluated at USD 731.13 billion in 2022 and is anticipated to witness a CAGR of 26.7% from 2023 to 2030,"[6] while "the global digital fashion market size is expected to expand at a CAGR of 187.88% during the forecast period, reaching USD 195071.83 million by 2028 [and] was valued at USD 342.71 million in 2022."[7] In other words, digital fashion goes beyond a niche segment of social scientists. It is a category that has massive implications for the economy, productivity, sustainability, and welfare, too.

Overview of the Book

We divided the chapters in this book into four parts: *Theories and foundations of digital fashion*; *Practices and applications of digital fashion*; *Issues and ethics of digital fashion*; and *Looking to and hoping for the future of digital fashion*. Each part comprises a selection of topical essays by a mix of academics and industry professionals, bringing a unique, hybrid lens to the issues broached, questions raised, and solutions offered regarding the history and advancement of digital fashion. Each part concludes with an interview that complements the discussion through a first-person perspective.

1. Theories and Foundations of Digital Fashion

The first part of this book draws from history, philosophy, and neuroaesthetics to create a theoretical foundation for the study of digital fashion. Some of the questions raised by these authors include: What is the nature of digital fashion? Where did digital fashion come from? These kinds of questions are crucial in helping to shape the future of digital fashion, to guide it in a positive direction.

Doris Domoszlai-Lantner draws from the history of fashion and computers to tell the story of the origins of digital fashion, and its progression to where it stands today. Beginning with the use of punch cards in textile weaving as far back as the eighteenth century, Domoszlai-Lantner identifies some of the main points in computer and software history that form the backbone of digital fashion's development. In this backstory, she provides a more recent history of digital fashion through a framework that explores the ways in which digital clothing and accessories can be worn in both static and dynamic imagery and videography, and platforms such as video games, social media, and virtual try-on experiences.

Michael R. Spicher draws from philosophy to probe into questions about the nature of digital fashion. What does it mean for digital garments to exist? The existence of reality is a perennial question in philosophy, but digital objects add another context to these discussions. Spicher explores what it could mean for digital fashion to exist in light of functionality, utility, and longevity no longer being important, or even relevant. If garments cannot be touched, their movements heard, or creases felt, do they really exist? If their entire value is in their immateriality, lacking the ephemerality of physical garments, then can they possess a real function? These questions guide his analysis about what digital fashion is and is not, and how, without practical functions, digital fashion exists for people to ascribe meaning and present a particular aesthetic.

Virginia Rolling explores wearables as a subset of digital fashion by tracing the development of spools which began as a seemingly simple device for physical garments, but became the basis for binary code in a process called S.P.O.O.L., paving the way for digital fashion to become a possibility. Rolling provides examples of wearables that allow users to interact with music and arts, mimicking phenomena such as synesthesia, and in doing so, introduces us to neuroaesthetic considerations and research regarding digital fashion.

In her interview with editor Doris Domoszlai-Lantner, Julie Zerbo discusses the implications of digital fashion (and other digital objects or assets) in a legal context. Zerbo addresses the ways in which digital assets, such as digital garments, have been characterized and litigated in US and international law, while analyzing the cases that have major implications for the future of digital fashion in the years, if not decades, to come.

2. Practices and Applications of Digital Fashion

Part Two examines some of the practices of digital fashion, in terms of making, teaching, and applying techniques. Rather than focusing on technology, which is always changing rapidly, these chapters focus on ideas about the practices that transcend the specific cultural and historical framework, providing models for future work in culture and education.

As a bridge between the foundation laid in the first part and the practice-based chapters in the second, Petra Egri analyzes the collaboration between luxury fashion brand Balmain and the toy brand Mattel, in which they created a collection of Barbie NFTs. In this case study, Egri focuses on the NFT Barbie and explores what it means for it to be made; specifically, whether it is a reproduction of something in the real world or a new thing in itself. Her inquiry has implications for how people create and use digital objects, whether in conjunction with, or in lieu of, physical ones.

Mindy Meissen catalogs the history of online sneaker culture, going back to its early days in basketball culture in New York City and its infiltration into the world of Web2 to the present, Web3. Rather than representing the burgeoning market for NFTs—in which digital fashion, such as digital sneakers, plays a major part—this chapter illustrates that the collector mindset has existed for a long time. Instead, digital sneakers and NFTs are the next evolution of that historical progression.

Idit Barak explores the relationship between wearable tech and digital fashion. Barak outlines the promises of, as well as the many barriers to, the advancement of wearables, and juxtaposes her findings with the emerging category of digital fashion. Her criticisms are vital: while extraordinary funding is being channeled into new categories in early stages, this does not translate into immediate success. Understanding potential hurdles in adjacent categories may help us gain a deeper understanding of digital fashion's viability to succeed long-term.

Mingjing Lin discusses the challenges that have arisen in education and research where fashion departments and game design departments are often working in isolation from one another. While that may not have mattered in the past, the current movements in both fields and industries require closer collaborations, which begin in education. Using examples from her research and educational contexts, Lin demonstrates and proposes a model that could be followed for the development of a more collaborative learning environment.

In an interview with editor Michael Spicher, Idiat Shiole discusses her transition from physical illustration to digital fashion design. Shiole addresses the barriers she faced on her road to becoming a digital fashion designer, and the unique challenges and opportunities she now encounters as a member of the industry.

3. Issues and Ethics of Digital Fashion

Many people assert (or at least speculate) that digital fashion can solve or reduce several of society's woes, including climate change and equity. The chapters in Part Three seek to highlight some of those possibilities while tempering hopes with the realities of what would be needed to bring these potential benefits to fruition. What ethical considerations does digital fashion raise? Can digital fashion solve or lessen some of the problems with the fashion industry?

Daniella Loftus takes an economic perspective to assess the impact of digital fashion. Considering the new supply chain framework that underpins the creation of digital fashion, Loftus focuses on the economics of producers. She considers digital fashion to be the marker of a new industry revolution, and spotlights novel considerations, such as digital tooling, algorithmically generated exposure, or royalties in the cloud.

Sara Emilia Bernat takes a more sociological lens to issues of inequality. Focusing on consumers, Bernat takes into consideration how digital fashion may assist or undermine vulnerable populations. Notably, she argues, the unique needs of LGBTQ+ and disabled communities tend to be unconsciously ignored in real life, resulting in further marginalization. Digital fashion, accessible from the comfort and safety of one's home, may offer safe spaces, but they do not come without their own pitfalls.

Although digital fashion is most often approached from a Western angle in current discourse, Erica de Greef, King Debs, Siviwe James, Lesiba Mabitsela, and Sihle Sogaula showcase a new generation of South African digital creatives who intertwine heritage, technology, and business. Depicted through eight case studies, this chapter reassesses the meaning of authenticity, belonging, coloniality, and mythology, through the lens of digital fashion. Rather than treating digital fashion as a destination, the authors consider it as a hybrid tool to search and assess deep identity.

Beata Wilczek explores a paradigm shift in the fashion industry, in which new forms of consumption and production, as well as language, have appeared in the past few years. Wilczek acknowledges how digital fashion is touted as a revolutionary way to make fashion more ethical and sustainable, yet she also examines these claims and offers suggestions on how to move the industry forward. Wilzcek justly notes that by being a little critical now, we can steer the field towards better results as digital fashion progresses.

In an interview with editor Sara Emilia Bernat, Jonathan Michael Square reflects on some of the most pressing social issues facing both the IRL and digital fashion industries today. Square raises questions about, and provides examples of, issues such as inequality, cultural appropriation, and capitalism, suggesting that digital fashion may open a pathway for reform.

4: Looking to and Hoping for the Future of Digital Fashion

This concluding part takes an optimistic look at what the future of digital fashion may hold. Rather than acting as an exercise in utopian prototyping, the chapter by Leslie Holden, interview with Matthew Drinkwater, and the editors' Afterword imagine future-facing scenarios by drawing on the current state of affairs in the field of digital fashion.

Leslie Holden explains several innovative digital fashion projects and the considerations and technology they used to achieve their vision. Holden acknowledges that while the metaverse is not fully realized, it holds the potential to change our relationship with clothing and the fashion industry. He sagely notes that a phygital model, which prioritizes digitalization, and streamlines Web2 and Web3 technologies, will allow the fashion industry to evolve.

In an interview with editor Sara Emilia Bernat, Matthew Drinkwater discusses the current state of digital fashion, assessing both the areas where digital fashion currently falters, and where it will likely grow and advance. In particular, Drinkwater highlights the changes that occurred as a result of the Covid-19 pandemic, but points out that there is a need to set standards and expectations in order to move the industry forward in a structured yet conscious way.

In the Afterword, the editors Michael Spicher, Sara Emilia Bernat, and Doris Domoszlai-Lantner address some of the most recent, major developments in trends and technology, which impact the field of digital fashion. They conclude that even though society might still be trying to ascertain their relationship with new, contemporary buzzwords and products that are part of the greater discourse on digital fashion—such as the metaverse and NFTs—some parts of this field have existed for decades, in video games and tech packs, for example, and will likely continue to not only exist, but to thrive.

Digital Fashion Studies

Digital fashion, like IRL fashion, does not exist in a vacuum. It is shaped by developments in tech and design, environmental and social climate, and by personal and group preferences alike. Although some types of digital fashion have been around for longer than others, this is still a relatively new field, especially in comparison to its parent genre, fashion itself. The past few years in particular have been a very exciting time for digital fashion, heightening the need for an academic book such as this one—the first of its kind—to establish the field of digital fashion studies. It is our hope, as the editors of this volume, that the essays presented here will not necessarily answer but rather spark further questions and curiosity, and ultimately move the field forward.

Notes

1   Abu Sadat Muhammad Sayem, "Digital fashion innovations for the real world and metaverse," *International Journal of Fashion Design, Technology and Education* 15, no. 2 (June 2, 2022): 139–141, DOI:10.1080/17543266.2022.2071139.

2   Statista Research Department, "Fashion e-commerce worldwide–statistics & facts," Statista, https://www.statista.com/topics/9288/fashion-e-commerce-worldwide/.

3   Cathy Hackl, Dirk Lueth, and Tommaso Di Bartolo, *Navigating the Metaverse: A Guide to Limitless Possibilities in a Web 3.0 World* (Hoboken, NJ: John Wiley & Sons, 2022), 35.

4   Matthew Ball, *The Metaverse: And How it will Revolutionize Everything* (New York: Liveright Publishing Corporation, 2022), 28.

5   Sky Ariella, "28 Dazzling Fashion Industry Statistics [2023]: How Much is the Fashion Industry Worth," Zippia, June 15, 2023, https://www.zippia.com/advice/fashion-industry-statistics/.

6   Grand View Research, "Digital Transformation Market Size, Share & Trends Analysis Report By Solution, By Service, By Deployment, By Enterprise Size, By End Use, By

Region, And Segment Forecasts, 2023–2030," https://www.grandviewresearch.com/industry-analysis/digital-transformation-market.

7 TheExpressWire, "How Digital Fashion Market are made: An Overview to The Future Opportunities Over the Globe," January 30, 2023, https://www.digitaljournal.com/pr/news/how-digital-fashion-market-are-made-an-overview-to-the-future-opportunities-over-the-globe-114-report-pages.

Part One

Theories and Foundations of Digital Fashion

1

A History of Digital Fashion: Critical Theories and Turning Points

DORIS DOMOSZLAI-LANTNER

Introduction

The concept of creating and experiencing fashion digitally has existed for several decades, although the indirect history of the computing technology behind digital fashion experiences stretches back to the creation of the Jacquard loom. The multifaceted, complex field of digital fashion as we know it today encapsulates established and burgeoning digital experiences, such as the creation of digital samples in the production process of physical clothing, virtual try-ons, dressing avatars in video games and simulations, the use of filters on social media, and wearing customized, digitally rendered garments. Despite its multitudinous nature, however, as of the late 2010s, the term "digital fashion" has been used in popular culture mainly to refer to digital garments used in gaming, social media, and, most recently, in "the metaverse" and through the medium of NFTs.

Digital fashion can be understood, to some extent, through two historically significant, interrelated concepts that are built on the prefix "hyper," indicating that something is too much, excessive, and more than the normal: hyperreality and hypermodernism. Coined by philosopher Jean Baudrillard in 1981, the term hyperreality refers to what Baudrillard describes as the inability to differentiate between something real and its simulation: "the hyperrealism of simulation is translated by the hallucinatory resemblance of the real to itself."[1] Hypermodernism refers to the period in which we are living, which is understood/described by Gilles Lipovetsky in 2005 as characterized by overconsumption.[2] Digital fashion integrates a plethora of technological advances—such as 3D modeling, body tracking, real-time rendering, computer-generated imagery (CGI) and even artificial intelligence (AI)—all of which effectively blur the lines between the real and the hyperreal, and has taken consumption not only to extreme highs, but also to hyperreal spaces, such as online shopping outlets, digital gaming sites, social media outlets, and the metaverse.

The (his)story of digital fashion takes us from what computer historian Doron Swade calls the age of "pre-electronic computing"[3] to the hyper spaces of the contemporary era, from mechanical and analog devices to electronic, digital ones. As such, it is a rich and complex narrative with far too many nuances to adequately cover all of it in a single short essay. Accordingly, this chapter assesses the key points and theories that aid in our understanding of this rapidly-changing segment of the fashion system.

Digital Fashion's Foundations

From the Jacquard Loom to Modern Computing Technology

The foundation of all digitally-created and digital fashion lies in technical innovations of the eighteenth and nineteenth centuries. In 1728, a weaver with the surname Falcon invented a loom that operated with a system of punched cards.[4] In the 1740s, Jacques de Vaucanson created a loom that included a mechanism that lifted the warp threads, replacing the manual labor of the drawboy, who would otherwise be stationed at the top of the loom to operate them.[5] It was during the Industrial Age, when the textile industry underwent a massive wave of mechanization, when the Lyons-based weaver Joseph Marie Jacquard invented a loom that combined the processes and concepts behind

Figure 1.1 *As a precursor to modern computing technology, punch cards can be seen on the backside of this model of a Jacquard loom (Scale 1:2) from 1867. United Kingdom, November 2010. Photo by Science Museum/SSPL/Getty Images.*

Falcon and de Vaucanson's work to create something that not only revolutionized textile production, but also became known as the precursor to twentieth-century computing technology. In 1804, Jacquard patented a mechanized attachment, which, when added to a loom, became known as the eponymous Jacquard loom. This attachment consisted of a series of punched cards that

> . . . would be pressed once against the back of an array of small, narrow, circular metal rods . . . the precise array of raised or stationary rods (and corresponding raised or stationary warp threads) could be different for every single line of weaving . . . every single row of weaving would have a new punched card to govern it, and of course the punched cards would all need to be processed in the right sequence. But the beauty of this system was that once all the punched cards had been made and strung together in the right sequence, that chain of punched cards would always produce the same design.[6]

The Jacquard loom formed the basis upon which mathematicians Charles Babbage and Ida Lovelace designed the Analytical Engine, a general-purpose computing machine, which went through a series of developments and construction from as early as 1837 until 1871, and "was essentially the same as that which has dominated computer design in the electronic era."[7]

The Development of 2D and 3D Design Software

In a study of the role of computers in the fashion industry, Mindy Meissen notes that "computers were put to use for broad purposes across textile and apparel manufacturing, retail, and design from the mid-1950s onward."[8] In the 1960s, the now ubiquitous, early models of 2-dimensional Computer Aided Design (CAD) and Computer Aided Manufacturing (CAM) drafting and design software were introduced to the garment industry, increasing efficiency in both the design and production processes of a garment's lifecycle. IBM (formally known as the International Business Machines Corporation) was instrumental in developing the first CAD software used for textiles, DAC-1, in conjunction with General Motors Research Laboratories in 1960, and was also the financial backer behind the creation of Gerber Technology's IBM/Pattern Generator, which automated the process of pattern cutting in 1966.[9] In 1963, a Ph.D. student at the Massachusetts Institute of Technology, the now world-renowned engineer Ivan Sutherland, laid the framework in his doctoral dissertation for CAD/CAM software that one could control not with written language, but with an electronic pen (stylus), calling it Sketchpad. In his final chapter, "Examples and Conclusions," Sutherland noted under the heading "Artistic Drawings," that Sketchpad's uses extended well beyond engineering[10] and that "the methods outlined in this report generalize nicely to three dimensional drawing."[11] The technology in Sutherland's dissertation was a major step forward in human–computer interaction (HCI), the stylus technology that many fashion designers employ today, and most importantly, modern computer graphics and 3-dimensional CAD/CAM.

The list of technological developments that Sutherland's Sketchpad directly impacted is long, but there are several noteworthy software products that have been used widely in the fashion industry that can be linked to his work. French company Lectra, a popular CAD/CAM brand used and taught in many fashion schools to this day, was founded in 1973, after which they added Modaris Classic, their fashion-specific software, to their product range in 1984.[12] The Israel-based OptiTex was founded in 1988; their OptiTex 3D Runway has been used in schools such as Cornell University and Parsons School of Design. Tim Gunn, the former Parsons chair of Fashion Design and host and mentor on the popular TV shows *Making the Cut* and *Project Runway* called OptiTex a "remarkable tool for our students … Not only does it provide them with an invaluable resource, but it gives them a clear advantage as young designers entering the professional world."[13] TukaTech disrupted the industry in 1995 by offering an open system that could read other software files, and had a more intuitive user experience (UX) that did not require the extensive training that their competitor companies did. In 2022, founder Ram Sareen noted that TukaTech:

> … became the darling of all the factories and vendors because it was a problem they needed to solve. We are not very big with designers and brands. But we do control most of the big countries who are exporting countries, 90% of Sri Lanka uses my technology and they all had different technologies, 75–80% of Pakistan and 75–80% of India, and Bangladesh have invested in TukaTech software solutions.[14]

Another company founded in Israel in 2000, Browzwear, started off as virtual try-on software;[15] in 2012, they were bought and restructured by a Singapore-based investor.[16] Although it was founded considerably more recently, CLO Virtual Fashion has commanded the discourse with their MarvelousDesigner (2009) and CLO (2010);[17] *Wired* magazine singled them out as industry leaders by stating that "to create digital fashion, the only tools required are a computer and the right form of design software like CLO3D or Marvelous Designer."[18]

Digital Design Technology and Digitally-Designed Fashion

One major step in the shift of CAD technology from being a relatively obscure tool to becoming the industry norm was Yves Saint Laurent's 1980 "Peruvian" collection of knitwear. Designed on an Apple II PC with CRT display, and woven on a digital, computer-controlled Jacquard loom, using a record-breaking number of rainbow of colors, the YSL Rive Gauche collection brought a new level of innovation to an otherwise tradition-based, luxury market.[19] By the 1990s, CAD technology had become not merely accepted, but widespread; Gucci, for example, has been designing all of their leather goods, the mainstay segment of their product offerings, on computers since 1995.[20]

That same year, Jean Paul Gaultier debuted his "Cyber" Fall/Winter collection, which included his widely recognizable "Cyberdot" pieces, designed digitally to simultaneously capture the essence of Victor Vasarely's optical art, while posit ing the clothing of the future and the burgeoning era of an open internet, or Web2. *Vogue* magazine's Laird Borrelli-Persson deferentially notes that "Jean Paul Gaultier was one of the first designers to grasp the importance of technology to the future of fashion; he presented [this] collection far in advance of full-blown Y2K hysteria."[21] An October 1995 *New York Times* article, which discussed Gaultier's "Cyber" alongside collections by Anna Sui, Marc Jacobs, and others, explored the effects of digitality on color in fashion: "[D]esign work on computers is introducing a new palette of off-colors into designer's collections. Colors as they appear on a computer screen with light shining through don't look like true primaries, and designers are working to capture what they see on the screen," wrote journalist Amy Spindler.[22]

Today, digital design software is widely used to design and draft physical textiles and garments. Technical packages, commonly referred to in the fashion industry as "tech packs," are files containing digital illustrations and patterns that are made in digital design software, in conjunction with other vector-based software, like Adobe Illustrator. Tech packs have become an integral part of a global fashion system in which design may take place in one country, sampling in another, and production in yet another; different spoken languages necessitate the use of tech packs for streamlined communication and ease of manufacturing. Faculty from the BGMEA University of Fashion and Technology (BUFT) in Dhaka, Bangladesh underscored the importance of tech packs:

> A technical package integrates all information that a manufacturer needs to produce the entire garment. It ensures manufacturer and apparel brand are on the same page. Tech packs significantly reduce the time and afford [sic]

required producing the garments. A well-developed tech pack saves time and money by way of systematic construction detailing and improves efficiency and productivity. It protects against misinterpretation on style detailing.[23]

The digital garments in tech packs can be considered omni-virtual examples of digital fashion, a term that is discussed in greater detail in the following section.

From Digitally-Designed Fashion to Digital Fashion

The Quest to Define Digital Fashion

Digital fashion is a segment of the fashion system that has developed as a result of invention and advancement of 2D and 3D design software, by way of the electronic computing technologies that were a product of an innovative machine in the field of physical fashion production, the Jacquard loom. Taking this extraordinary developmental path into consideration, it should be of no surprise that the history of digital fashion encompasses an abundance of fluidly evolving use cases as well as the vocabulary to describe it.

When the Scandinavian brand Carlings debuted a digital fashion collection in 2018, it was not referred to as such by the online streetwear magazine *Hypebeast*, but rather as a "digital only capsule collection" that "exists only digitally," suggesting that the publication did not yet possess the now more commonly understood term for what they were witnessing. Readers did not take lightly to the article's byline, "is this the future of fashion?" A user named "RIP FREDO" declared "yall [sic] must be mad if you think im [sic] paying for fucking digital clothes," while "FunkPhD" disparagingly stated "digital assless chaps available for purchase. That's the world we live in." Another user, "Steve Joseph," replied to the byline by writing "'is this the future of fashion?' Now imagine Donald Trump pointing at you. 'What an utterly stupid question.'" Pithily, "Kevin Ma's Burner Account" simply asked, "what in the FUCK," without bothering to use a question mark.[24]

The first time *Hypebeast* used the name "digital fashion" was in their 2021 article, "NFT Platform Bitski Teams Up With PLEASURES for Digital Fashion Collaboration."[25] Since then, the fashion industry has grappled with the term "digital fashion," sometimes referred to interchangeably as "virtual fashion," trying to define and ascribe meaning to it. In 2022, *i-D* magazine contributor Rosalind Jana facetiously asked, "WTF is Digital Fashion?" as she described a variety of digital garments as part of the "vast and relatively confusing—umbrella [term] currently known as 'digital fashion.'"[26] Around the same time, Randy Ginsburg at Kiplinger, a business forecasting digest, described digital fashion as "virtual 3D clothing designed with both humans and digital avatars in mind. Rather than using fabric and textiles, digital garments are created with special 3D computer programs like Blender and CLO3D."[27] Likewise, in a market overview written by the global shopping platform Lyst and the digital fashion marketplace The Fabricant, digital fashion is described as "part of a cross-section of disciplines in the digital world, which includes gaming and crypto art. Our digital-only couture creations will never physically exist, waste nothing but data and exploit nothing but imagination."[28] FabriX, a Hong Kong-based initiative in 2022, which turned twelve designers' ideas into virtual collections, asserts that "the future of fashion will not be sewn with threads and textiles, but woven by pixels and programs. As technology continues to bring down barriers and distance, digital fashion presents designers with boundless freedom for creativity, instant global visibility and the opportunity to set the runway ablaze with truly imaginative, trend-leading styles."[29]

An early use of the term "digital fashion" in an academic context was in Louisa Stein's article "Playing Dress-Up: Digital Fashion and Gamic Extensions of Televisual Experience in Gossip Girl's Second Life" in *Cinema Journal* in 2009. Stein describes experiencing the virtual Gossip Girl space in the popular game, noting that

> ...participants new to *Second Life* may explore other neighborhoods as well, or they may choose to stay in the virtual Upper East Side, settling their avatar into the verisimilitude of spaces only previously imagined. Indeed, as I write, my avatar lounges on the digital couch in the extravagant sitting room of one Upper East Side bad-boy, Chuck Bass.[30]

Although she mentions digital fashion in her paper's title, she only refers to it somewhat diminutively as "digital dress-up" further in the text.[31]

As a burgeoning field of academic inquiry, few researchers—with the exception of the essays by contributors to this book—have attempted to define digital fashion thus far. In her essay "Conserving Electronic Textiles and Digital Fashion," Leanne Tonkin uses the term, but does not define it with a fully digital end goal in mind. Tonkin states that "digital fashion, in the context of this work, is fashion that integrates electronics small enough to wear on the body, referred to as wearable technology."[32] As further evidenced in this book's chapters, Idit Barak considers wearables to be adjacent to, but not the same as, digital fashion; Virginia Rolling, however, classifies them as a subset of the field. In 2022, two of the editors of this volume, Sara Emilia Bernat and Doris Domoszlai-Lantner noted that "as opposed to 'In Real Life' (IRL) clothing and fashion—the physical garments and accessories that people wear—the term 'digital fashion' refers to garments that were designed using computer software and intended to be worn on digital platforms, such as social media and video games."[33]

Also in 2022, Abu Sadat Muhammad Sayem proposed a four-part breakdown of digital fashion, into which he grouped the following:

– Digital Human and Metaverse: 3D Body Scanning, Virtual Avatar, Animation for Fashion
– Digital Design and E-Prototyping: 2D CAD [Illustration, Pattern Cutting, Marker Making], 3D CAD [Virtual Simulation and Fit Analysis] Artificial Intelligence for Design and Prototyping
– Digital Apparel and Smart e-Technology: Design Apparel with Embedded Electronics, Smart Electro-Clothing Systems (SeCSs)
– Digital Business and Promotion: E-Commerce and Social Media, Block Chain [sic] and other e-tools, Big Data Analytics, Artificial Intelligence for Business, Product Life Cycle Management (PLM)[34]

Instead of focusing on the digital garments themselves, Sayem included actions and technologies used to create them, as well as the post-production promotion used to market them, creating a definitional framework that is a strong foundation for the analyses in this book, but is arguably too broad.

Another major contribution to the field came from Judith Brachem and Lucas Stübbe, who classified digital fashion into three main categories: assembled, simultaneous, and omni-virtual. They explain each "way of wearing" as the following:

> The first term, assembled, describes the way a virtual piece of clothing is subsequently applied as an additional layer to a preexisting digital image, may it be a photo or a video. The second approach to dressing virtually is the real-time integration of virtual clothes. Instead of two consecutive operations—taking the photo/video and applying the digital garment layer—it is possible to wear the garment through a camera filter or a prosthesis like Augmented Reality glasses. This allows for a simultaneous perception, combining both the physical and virtual view. The third way of virtual wearing is to completely dismiss the physical realm and constitutes an all-virtual encounter. Instead of a photo, a video, or a physical live situation, the virtual garments are donned by our avatar, making this form of wearing omni-virtual.[35]

An oral interview with Roei Derhi, the founder of Placebo Digital Fashion House (renamed Placebo Phygital Fashion House in 2023), added an important layer of nuance to Brachem and Stübbe's framework. When speaking about the processes involved in the creation of digital fashion, Derhi noted that there is a "tension between the new generation and technology" that is manifested in the output of digital fashion designers and brands.[36] This tension can be seen on a foundational level in the types of files and programs that are used to make assembled, simultaneous, and omni-virtual digital fashion. In order to make assembled digital fashion, Derhi points out, designers create a 3D mesh file of the garment and a basic avatar on which to place it, then take the 2D flat file of the person to whom the garment will be applied and add its photographic elements to the mesh of the 3D file to produce the final instance of a person "wearing" a digital garment. Whereas applied digital fashion flows from 3D to 2D and back to 3D files, omni-virtual digital fashion is made up only of 3D files; these two categories are what Derhi deemed to be the less challenging types of digital fashion to make. Simultaneous digital fashion, conversely, is arguably the most difficult to create, as the garments must follow the movement of the person in real time, which necessitates the use of additional technologies such as body tracking and real-time rendering, which rely on complex algorithms that must be calculated on the spot.[37]

Omni-Virtual Digital Fashion

Omni-virtual has the longest history of these three categories of digital fashion, and is strongly related to the concept of avatars. Although the modern term "avatar" is derived from the ancient Sanskrit word *avatarah*—referring to a Hindu deity's incarnation in human or animal form—our contemporary usage of the word as a "label for digital representations of humans in online or virtual environments" dates back to "as early as 1984 in online multiuser dungeons, MUDs, (role-playing environments)."[38] These early games were text-based, therefore one's avatar moved about and completed actions in the game via text commands. MUDs were part of what Richard Bartle, the creator of the first MUD (MUD-1 in 1978), calls The First Age of virtual worlds (1978 to 1985). In his seminal book, *Designing Virtual Worlds*, Bartle notes that by 1993, several major internet companies, such as CompuServe and AOL, had appeared on the market, creating a price-war that caused prices to fall, ultimately creating greater accessibility to the internet and services such as video games. In 1995, millions of users joined the online world, in what became known as Web2, an era of internet connectivity characterized by shared experiences and the building of online communities; this ushered in the "Fourth Age" of video games, which lasted from 1995 to 1997.[39] The "Fifth Age" of gaming began in 1997 and is ongoing to the present day;[40] this is when omni-virtual digital fashion in the context of video games flourished, and when computer graphics advanced from real to hyperreal and into the metaverse.

Gaming: *The Sims, Roblox*

The Sims's long-standing presence has had a strong impact on digital fashion. The game's maker, Electronic Arts (EA), has strengthened their official sartorial offerings through key partnerships with several global fashion brands throughout the years. The true source of their strength, however, is due to a vast network of independent custom-content creators who exponentially widen in-game fashion. Meanwhile, another popular game, *Roblox*, only sells their own in-house digital fashion, some of which is made in special collections as collaborations with major fashion houses, developing what appears to be a long-term partnership with Gucci.

The Sims

SimCity, the simulation game in which users could build virtual communities, was first released by Maxis in 1989. After several popular iterations, in February 2006, EA released the spin-off game *The Sims*, in which users can create characters, families, and societies; according to GameSpot, in 2006, the game was "the best-selling PC game of all time."[41] It is not surprising that in June of the very next year, *The Sims* teamed up with fast fashion magnate H&M to release an expansion pack, *The Sims™ H&M® Fashion Stuff*, in which players not only could buy pre-made items from the store's collection, but also use the files in the pack to create their own digital garments for their Sims. The success of this first pack prompted the later release of *The Sims 3 Diesel Stuff* pack in collaboration with the Italian brand, Diesel, in 2012, and *The Sims™ 4 Moschino Stuff Pack* in 2019, both of which are still available for purchase on the EA website.[42]

Although *The Sims* collaborations with major fashion brands are the ones that tend to make headlines in popular media, there are plenty of small businesses and individual creators who make and sell custom fashion content, also called "mods" (modifications), for use in the game. Established in 1999, The Sims Resource (TSR) is the self-proclaimed "very first fan site," "offering an extensive back catalog of downloads for ALL Sims games that ever existed—all the way back to *The Sims 1* from 1999."[43] TSR's business model is to provide free, downloadable content for all users that is created by individual artists; paid subscribers to the website can access downloads faster, without ads. As of March 2023, for the latest *The Sims 4* game, TSR had nearly 75,000 creations in the "Clothing" category, nearly 20,000 in "Accessories," and over 3,000 in "Shoes"; body customizations were also well represented, with nearly 12,000 creations in "Hair," 1,300 in "Skintones," nearly 4,000 in "Eye Colors," and almost 21,000 in "Makeup." Both The Sims Resource and The Sims Catalog are independent of EA, which explains why there is such a strong product offering on these as well as other similar websites: independent creators essentially have the green light to make "customs" based on their clients' demands and the latest fashions, faster than can EA and its developers.

It logically follows that in a digital system that is largely modeled on the physical, the sociocultural issues that emerge in one realm also occur in the other. Although the proliferation of garments seems to have a positive effect on players' experiences, it also brings up the issue of counterfeiting. Many independent custom-content creators who have no affiliation or relationship with major brands are crafting garments that are digital counterfeits of major brands' physical and digital products. Take, for instance, Rose Bergdorf (it is unclear if this is her real name) who uses the Instagram handle @bergdorfverse and operates a Patreon page on which users can purchase custom garments made by her and various other independent artists.[44] Her Patreon essentially functions as an unauthorized, digital version of the famous Bergdorf Goodman department store, in that she sells files that contain digital counterfeits of items such as Coperni boots, what she calls a "Teddy Kelly Bag" (the name is meant to reference the Hermès Kelly bag without using the brand's name), as well as vintage pieces from Issey Miyake, and more. In many parts of the physical world, counterfeit sellers would be shut down, and their goods taken away, yet this has not been the case with *The Sims*. Mods sellers were largely free from legal ramifications until late in 2022, when EA debuted a policy that prohibits the use of EA and *The Sims* logos on mods, as well as the paywalled model of distribution, only allowing the free distribution of mods from then on.[45] Some sellers like Bergdorfverse continue to flaunt the rules, although it is not clear how widely EA has enforced them.

Another largely successful simulation game that has a strong history of integrating digital fashion is *Roblox*. Originally founded in 2004, Roblox Corporation describes itself as a "project [that] straddles several rapidly-developing aspects of internet entertainment: virtual worlds, casual gaming, and player-constructed content."[46] Like the field of digital fashion, *Roblox* experienced a surge in usership during the Covid-19 pandemic; global lockdown orders had a particularly heavy effect on youth usership, contributing to a 40% increase in players from February to March 2020, when many countries declared lockdowns.[47]

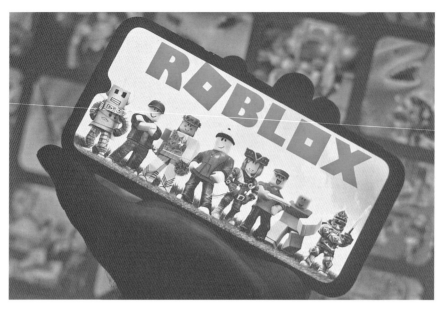

Figure 1.2 Roblox's *millions of daily users can customize and dress their avatars and characters in a myriad of digital fashion garments. Brazil, March 30, 2021. Photo Illustration by Rafael Henrique/SOPA Images/LightRocket via Getty Images.*

Roblox and Gucci: Building a Long-Term Partnership

Roblox has partnered with Italian luxury house Gucci several times since the lockdowns. In March 2021, they released a pair of virtual sneakers, The Gucci Virtual 25, created by the AR marketing agency Wanna, which could be worn by avatars in *Roblox* and VRChat. In their case overview, Wanna notes that the goals of the Gucci sneaker project were to "position Gucci as the most innovative brand in digital space, engage Gen-Z customers with Gucci brand and products, boost product activation for new releases."[48] Gucci's desire to be a digital leader has led them to offer increasingly broader product offerings, as well as virtual spaces in which they can be used. In May of 2021, they opened up the temporary *Gucci Garden Roblox* space, a digital counterpart to the physical *Gucci Garden Archetypes* interactive exhibition that took place at the same time in Florence, Italy. In this virtual environment, users experienced a transformative process that focused on the concept of rebirth. Gucci and Roblox explained the process as such:

> As they enter the *Gucci Garden* experience visitors will shed their avatars becoming a neutral mannequin. Without gender or age, the mannequin

symbolizes that we all begin our journeys through life as a blank canvas. Wandering through the different rooms, visitors' mannequins absorb elements of the exhibition. With every person experiencing the rooms in a different order and retaining different fragments of the spaces, they will emerge at the end of their journey as one-of-a-kind creations, reflecting the idea of individuals as one among many, yet wholly unique.[49]

During the two weeks in which *Gucci Garden* was open, one major digital fashion object made headlines for surpassing price points ordinarily set for IRL garments. In an act of sheer hyperconsumerism, a digital Gucci Dionysus Bag with Bee, which was retailed for 475 Robux (*Roblox*'s in-game currency) or $6, resold for 350,000 Robux, or $4,375, significantly more than the physical bag's price of $3,400.[50] Reddit co-founder Alexis Ohanian tweeted about the sale, emphasizing the ostensible conundrum between the two versions of the same bag, declaring "remember: this 'Roblox' purse is not an NFT and thus has no value/use/transferability outside the 'Roblox' world—yet it's worth more than the physical one. Watch this space."[51] Having welcomed nearly 20 million supposed visitors in a two-week timeframe, it is no wonder that Gucci wanted to replicate, and potentially top, the successes of *Gucci Garden*; almost exactly a year later, Gucci solidified their presence with their permanent space, *Gucci Town*.[52]

Applied Digital Fashion, and Simultaneous Digital Fashion

Applied Digital Fashion

Brachem and Stübbe refer to digital fashion that has been applied to a photo or video as "assembled," but the verb "applied" is a stronger, more specific name for this category. Carlings' 2018 collection is an early example of applied digital fashion. *Hypebeast* writer Jack Stanley explained the process: "[T]he collection works by users uploading a posed picture of themselves. Once the picture has been uploaded, and the digital pieces purchased, Carlings' team of 3D designers fit the clothes to the image to make it appear that the user is wearing the pieces in real life."[53]

In 2019, digital fashion retailer The Fabricant made headlines by selling what is considered to be the first digital blockchain dress. "Iridescence," which sold for $9,500 as an NFT on the Ethereum blockchain, was created in conjunction with AR designer Johanna Jaskowska and Dapper Labs, the makers of the CryptoKitties NFT collection. Once it was sold, Iridescence's new owner was given twenty days to send The Fabricant a photo on which they wanted the garment to be applied.[54] After the process was complete, Mary, the new owner, recounted her experience, including what she considered to be its shortcomings:

> I had to imagine what it would look like to wear the dress. There was a huge element of surprise that you wouldn't get with physical garments. It is like a green screen, you have to imagine what it will look like since the dress will be added in post production.
>
> Of course this was the first of its kind, but I would love to be able to use the dress more often, and wear it wherever I like, not just limited to the pictures I got, but it should be something I can endlessly use over the pictures being taken so I can wear it in different situations.[55]

Iridescence was sold as an NFT; as such, the file that was transferred to Mary contained a piece of omni-virtual digital fashion. However, because Mary sent The Fabricant an image on which they applied Iridescence, the final file that she was given is an example of applied digital fashion.

DRESSX, the largest digital fashion retailer, offers a plethora of applied digital fashion in their marketplace. Much like the Carlings collection, in these direct-to-consumer (D2C) sales on their website and the mobile app, customers select and pay for the garment(s) that they want to wear, send the DRESSX team a photo, and receive their finished product within a day or two. DRESSX, a female-led company founded in 2019 by Daria Shapovalova and Natalia Modenova—the authors of this book's Foreword—has since undergone multiple successful rounds of funding. By the end of 2021, DRESSX raised $3.3 million in seed funding[56] and in July 2022, it partnered with Meta to provide garments for avatars in the company's marketplace.[57] In early 2023, DRESSX topped their previous funding figures by raising $15 million in Series A funding from Greenfield, Slow Ventures, Warner Music, The Artemis Fund, and Red Dao, amongst others.[58]

DRESSX's marketplace has a wide variety of garments and accessories, ranging in price from \$0.00 (free) to as much as \$1,500, from major brands such as Balenciaga and adidas Originals, as well as independent brands like Placebo Digital Fashion House, Fatemeh Gholami, and Ilona Song. Scrolling through their listings, many of which include images of the garments alongside examples of real people wearing them, one may find themselves questioning whether they are, in fact, digital. Many digital garments have gotten to look so realistic, or rather, hyperreal, and their application to images and video are so convincing, that they blur the lines between reality and digitality. Likely due to prior instances of confusion and misunderstanding with consumers, most of DRESSX's garment listings have an important disclaimer in their description: "THIS IS A DIGITAL ITEM, IT ONLY EXISTS DIGITALLY AND WILL BE APPLIED TO YOUR PHOTO(s)." In addition to awe and even admiration for the skill of the designers who have created and fitted these garments on real people, one may also feel a sense of unease at how eerily hyperreal these garments may look.

Simultaneous Digital Fashion

Hyperreal digital fashion can also be experienced through AR and VR experiences, such as social media filters and virtual try-on technology. Social media filters apply garments and accessories, as well as beauty filters, to a user's face and body in real time, giving them the chance to save their look as a photo or video. Virtual try-on experiences employ the same methods, not just on hand-held mobile devices but on larger, body-length smart mirrors as well.

Journalist Tate Ryan-Mosley notes that the history of social media beauty filters is rooted in the advent of selfies in Japanese "kawaii" (cute) culture and *purikura* photo booths in the 1990s.[59] In the smartphone era, the Facetune app that debuted in 2013 quickly shot to the top of the list of paid apps because it was what one *Huffington Post* contributor called "Photoshop for your iPhone without the headache of Photoshop."[60] By 2019, the craze for natural-looking edits of peoples' faces was so ubiquitous that another, opposing trend had started. That year, pop-culture magazine *Dazed* declared that "futuristic beauty filters [were] taking over social media."[61] One of the designers that they featured was Johanna Jaskowska, of Iridescence fame, for creating "beauty3000," a filter that had by that point in time amassed over 200 million impressions.[62] The proverbial tide had turned once again by 2023, when Ryan-Mosley declared that "hyper-realistic beauty filters are here to stay," citing the "Bold Glamour" TikTok filter that had been used 16 million times in the span of a single month.[63]

Like social media filters, virtual try-on, which mimics the experience of physically trying on a garment, has become a mainstay feature of many a brand's toolbox. Ironically, one of the earliest virtual try-on software was not found at a store, but in the 1995 cult classic film *Clueless*, in which Cher Horowitz, the rich teenage protagonist, had bespoke digital wardrobe software that she used to pick out her daily outfits. In the film, Cher digitally dresses a 2D, flat representation of herself by overlaying images of the garments that she has in her closet. Steven Jordan, the film's production designer, recalls that

> ... the virtual closet was really new stuff in terms of computer animation. It was new and a very laborious process. But we were working with qualified people on the computer graphics side. We pulled it off. It was an enormous amount [sic] of developments. We worked on that for weeks and weeks and weeks.[64]

Although Cher's wardrobe inspired imitators, it was not until 2015 that her specific software was realized when Metail, the British virtual fit company, created a now-defunct, shoppable version called Cher Wears, which allowed users to try on and purchase *Clueless*-inspired apparel.[65]

Today's virtual try-on software is significantly more advanced than that of Cher's, tapping into our mobile and computers' photo and video features to bring us real-time simulations that can look rather convincing. Some major brands and companies that offer virtual try-on options in stores, on smart mirrors, or their websites include Sephora, Dior Beauty, Maybelline, Ed & Sarna eyewear, and Gap. In 2022, the big-box retailer Walmart debuted its own "Be Your Own Model" app,[66] effectively demonstrating that this type of simultaneous digital fashion has indeed become mainstream.

Figure 1.3 *A visitor tries on makeup digitally in a smart mirror-based virtual try-on experience during the "Kat Von D Inaugurates Studded Kiss Lipstick" event. Milan, Italy, April 4, 2017. Photo by Rosdiana Ciaravolo/Getty Images.*

Concluding, by Looking Forward

Across the various categories of digital fashion that exist today, hundreds of thousands, if not millions, of digital garments are produced each year; this is hyperconsumerism at its finest. Although there may not yet be a digital equivalent of a physical landfill, we must acknowledge that many of those garments will eventually necessitate a "home" or storage solution—be it temporary or permanent—that may bring up questions about sustainability and waste, much like physical fashion. Can we simply delete digital fashion files that are no longer needed? What is the environmental footprint created from the use and storage of so many digital files, and what can we do to prevent digital hoarding? For those items of digital fashion that will be deemed historically significant, digital archiving and museum solutions such as The Virtual Fashion Archive and The VR Fashion Museum are already available, but not widely in use. Suffice to say that such a quickly developing industry will need viable solutions in the very near future.

Notes

1   Jean Baudrillard, *Simulacra and Simulation*, trans. Sheila Faria Fraser, reprint (Ann Arbor: University of Michigan Press, 2023), 23.

2   Gilles Lipovetsky, *Hypermodern Times* (Cambridge: Polity Press, 2015).

3   Doron Swade, "Pre-electronic computing," in C. B. Jones and J. L. Lloyd (eds.), *Dependable and Historic Computing: Lecture Notes in Computer Science*, vol. 6875 (Berlin: Springer-Verlag, 2011), 58–83, DOI: 10.1007/978-3-642-24541-1_7.

4   James Essinger, *Jacquard's Web: How a Hand-Loom Led to the Birth of the Information Age* (Oxford: Oxford University Press, 2004), 36.

5   Essinger, *Jacquard's Web*, 17–18.

6   Essinger, *Jacquard's Web*, 35–6.

7   "The Engines," Computer History Museum, https://www.computerhistory.org/babbage/engines/.

8   Mindy Meissen, "Material Conditions: Fashion in the Bitstream," M.A. dissertation, Fashion Institute of Technology, May 2020, 39.

9   Meissen, "Material Conditions," 92–3.

10 Ivan Edward Sutherland, "Sketchpad, A Man-Machine Graphical Communications System," Ph.D. dissertation, Massachusetts Institute of Technology, January 1963, 130. Design World, http://images.designworldonline.com.s3.amazonaws.com/CADhistory/Sketchpad_A_Man-Machine_Graphical_Communication_System_Jan63.pdf.

11 Sutherland, "Sketchpad," 138.

12 Patricia Grice, *Digital Pattern Cutting For Fashion with Lectra Modaris®* (London: Bloomsbury, 2018), xv.

13 Nikki Blackburn, "Setting Clothes in Motion with Israel's Optitex," Israel21C, July 15, 2006, https://www.israel21c.org/setting-clothes-in-motion-with-israels-optitex.

14 Debbie McKeegan, "Exploring the development of CAD/CAM and the Future of Fashion Production with Tukatech," Federation of European Screen Printing Associations, April 11, 2022, https://www.fespa.com/en/news-media/features/exploring-the-development-of-cad-cam-and-the-future-of-fashion-production-with-tukatech.

15 Nicky Blackburn, "Designs on the future," Israel21C, August 17, 2003 (updates September 14, 2012), https://www.israel21c.org/designs-on-the-future/.

16 "Browzwear Strategic Restructure," January 2012, https://browzwear.com/browzwear-strategic-restructure-2/.

17 "Our Story," CLO, https://www.clovirtualfashion.com/story.

18 Rosalind Jana, "The Metaverse Could Radically Reshape Fashion," *Wired*, April 11, 2022, https://www.wired.com/story/extreme-fashion-metaverse/.

19 Meissen, "Material Conditions," 105–6.

20 Dana Thomas, *Deluxe: How Luxury Lost Its Luster* (New York: Penguin Press, 2007), 196.

21 The "Cyber" collection is also often referred to as the "Mad Max" collection, after the series of post-apocalyptic, dystopian-based movies of the same name. Laird Borrelli-Persson, "What Do Hairdryers and Cyberpunks and Have in Common? Jean Paul Gaultier's Fall 1995 Collection and His Camp Sensibility," *Vogue*, April 30, 2019, https://www.vogue.com/fashion-shows/fall-1995-ready-to-wear/jean-paul-gaultier?redirectURL=https%3A%2F%2Fwww.vogue.com%2Ffashion-shows%2Ffall-1995-ready-to-wear%2Fjean-paul-gaultier.

22 Amy M. Spindler, "Fashion's Future, in Computer Hues," *New York Times*, October 3, 1995, https://www.nytimes.com/1995/10/03/style/fashion-s-future-in-computer-hues.html.

23 Afroza Akter Rita and Shakinaz Mahamud, "Effectiveness of Technical Packages for the Apparel Production Process in the Global Apparel Industry," *IOSR Journal of Business and Management* 18, no. 9, Ver. II (September 2016): 47–51, DOI: 10.9790/487X-1809024751. Note: BGMEA is an acronym for Bangladesh Garment Manufacturers and Exporters Association, which founded the university in 2012; the school now has over 15,000 students. See https://buft.edu.bd/ for university statistics.

24 Jack Stanley, "Carlings launches Digital-Only Capsule Collection," *Hypebeast*, November 15, 2018, https://hypebeast.com/2018/11/carlings-digital-clothing-collection-details.

25 Rosie Perper, "NFT Platform Bitski Teams Up With PLEASURES for Digital Fashion Collaboration," *Hypebeast*, November 4, 2021, https://hypebeast.com/2021/11/nft-platform-bitski-pleasures-nft-fashion-collaboration.

26 Rosalind Jana, "WTF is Digital Fashion?," *i-D*, June 7, 2022, https://i-d.vice.com/en/article/pkgepg/digital-fashion.

27 Randy Ginsburg, "What Is Digital Fashion, And Why Is It Important?," Kiplinger, July 7, 2022, https://www.kiplinger.com/investing/cryptocurrency/604900/what-is-digital-fashion.

28 Lyst and The Fabricant, "The Digital Fashion Report," https://www.lyst.com/data/digital-fashion-report/.

29 "About Fabrix," Fabrix, https://fabrix.pmq.org.hk/en/#about.

30 Louisa Stein, "Playing Dress-Up: Digital Fashion and Gamic Extensions of Televisual Experience in Gossip Girl's Second Life," *Cinema Journal* 48, no. 3 (Spring 2009): 116–22 (117).

31 Stein, "Playing Dress-Up," 119.

32 Leanne Tonkin, "Conserving Electronic Textiles and Digital Fashion," *Text: For the Study of the History, Art and Design of Textiles* 49 (Fall 2022): 53–9 (53).

33 Sara Emilia Bernat and Doris Domoszlai-Lantner, "Digital fashion: Solutions and limitations for the LGBTQIA+ community," *Fashion, Style and Popular Culture*, September 13, 2022, DOI:10.1386/fspc_00146_1.

34 Abu Sadat Muhammad Sayem, "Digital fashion innovations for the real world and metaverse," *International Journal of Fashion Design, Technology and Education* 15, no. 2 (June 2, 2022): 139–41, DOI:10.1080/17543266.2022.2071139.

35 Italicization original to the authors' text. Judith Brachem and Lucas Stübbe, "Ways of Wearing," *Fashion Studies Journal*, August 15, 2022, https://www.fashionstudiesjournal.org/digital-engagement-a/2022/8/15/ways-of-wearing.

36 Doris Domoszlai-Lantner and Roei Derhi, oral interview (online), February 24, 2023.

37 Domoszlai-Lantner and Derhi, oral interview.

38 Jeremy N. Bailenson and James J. Blascovich, "Avatars," *Berkshire Encyclopedia of Human–Computer Interaction* (Great Barrington, MA: Berkshire Publishing, 2004), 64.

39 Richard Bartle, *Designing Virtual Worlds* (Sebastopol, CA: New Riders, 2003), 20–1.

40 Bartle, *Designing Virtual Worlds*, 24.

41 Trey Walker, "The Sims Overtakes Myst," Game Spot, May 17, 2006, https://www.gamespot.com/articles/the-sims-overtakes-myst/1100-2857556/.

42 "The Sims 3 Diesel Stuff Pack," Electronic Arts, https://www.ea.com/games/the-sims/the-sims-3-diesel-stuff, and "The Sims™ 4 Moschino Stuff Pack," Electronic Arts, https://www.ea.com/en/games/the-sims/the-sims-4/store/addons/the-sims-4-moschino-stuff-pack.

43 "About us," The Sims Resource, https://www.thesimsresource.com/about/index.

44 See Rose Bergdorf's @bergdorfverse profile on Instagram, https://www.instagram.com/bergdorfverse/?hl=en, as well as her Patreon fundraising page, https://www.patreon.com/bergdorfverse.

45 Jessica Howard, "The Sims 4's Newest Policy Update is Causing Tension And Panic Among Mod Users," Game Spot, August 3, 2022, https://www.gamespot.com/articles/the-sims-4s-newest-policy-update-is-causing-tension-and-panic-among-mod-users/1100-6506067/.

46 "Roblox Company Information," Roblox, https://en.help.roblox.com/hc/en-us/articles/203313370-Roblox-Company-Information.

47 Ari Levy, "While parents zoom, their kids are flocking to an app called Roblox to hang out and play 3D games," CNBC, April 8, 2020, https://www.cnbc.com/2020/04/08/roblox-is-seeing-a-surge-during-coronavirus-shelter-in-place.html.

48 "Wanna x Gucci," Wanna, https://wanna.fashion/gucci.

49 "The Gucci Garden Experience Lands on Roblox," Roblox, May 17, 2021, https://blog.
roblox.com/2021/05/gucci-garden-experience/.

50 Jake Silbert, "Gucci's Purses Are Worth More in Roblox Than IRL," *Highsnobiety*, May
2021, https://www.highsnobiety.com/p/gucci-virtual-purse-roblox-resale/.

51 Alexis Ohanian (@alexisohanian), Twitter post, May 24, 2021, https://twitter.com/
alexisohanian/status/1396869330877526021?ref_src=twsrc%5Etfw%7Ctwcamp%5Etw
eetembed%7Ctwterm%5E1396869330877526021%7Ctwgr%5E778b93e4ed205275f3cb
cf2414875b5720fe9cf7%7Ctwcon%5Es1_&ref_url=https%3A%2F%2Fwww.
highsnobiety.com%2Fp%2Fgucci-virtual-purse-roblox-resale%2F.

52 Andrew Webster, "Gucci built a persistent town inside of Roblox," *The Verge*, May 27,
2022, https://www.theverge.com/2022/5/27/23143404/gucci-town-roblox.

53 Jack Stanley, "Carlings launches Digital-Only Capsule Collection," *Hypebeast*,
November 15, 2018, https://hypebeast.com/2018/11/carlings-digital-clothing-
collection-details.

54 Robyn Mowatt, "The World's First-Ever Digital Dress Is Sold For $9,500," Hypebae, May
28, 2019, https://hypebae.com/2019/5/first-digital-blockchain-dress-sold-9500-usd-
fabricant-dapper-labs-johanna-jaskowska.

55 "Iridescence," The Fabricant, https://www.thefabricant.com/iridescence.

56 Illia Kabachynskyi, "DressX, a retail platform for digital clothes, raises an additional
$1.3M," AIN.Capital, September 27, 2021, https://ain.capital/2021/09/27/dressx-raises-
1-3-million/.

57 Maghan McDowell and Maliha Shoaib, "Meta's avatars just got a fashion upgrade with
Dress X," *Vogue Business*, July 19, 2022, https://www.voguebusiness.com/technology/
metas-avatars-just-got-a-fashion-upgrade-with-dressx.

58 Roxanne Robinson, "DressX raises 15 million USD in latest round of funding," Fashion
Network, March 14, 2023, https://ww.fashionnetwork.com/news/Dressx-raises-15-
million-usd-in-latest-round-of-funding,1496221.html.

59 Tate Ryan-Mosley, "Beauty Filters are changing the way young girls see themselves,"
MIT Technology Review, April 2, 2021, https://www.technologyreview.
com/2021/04/02/1021635/beauty-filters-young-girls-augmented-reality-social-
media/.

60 Hillel Fuld, "Facetune is an iOS Photo-Editing App That Can Truly Be Called Magical,"
Huffington Post, June 26, 2013, https://www.huffpost.com/entry/facetune-is-an-ios-
photoe_b_3501920.

61 Günseli Yalcinkaya, "Why Beauty3000 and other futuristic filters are taking over social
media," *Dazed*, February 4, 2019, https://www.dazeddigital.com/beauty/
article/43164/1/whybeauty3000-other-futuristic-filters-taking-over-social-media.

62 Yaclinkaya, "Why Beauty3000 and other futuristic filters are taking over social media."

63 Tate Ryan-Mosley, "Hyper-realistic beauty filters are here to stay," *MIT Technology Review*, March 13, 2023, https://www.technologyreview.com/2023/03/13/1069649/hyper-realistic-beauty-filters-bold-glamour/.

64 Maria Bobila, "Clueless Turns 25: An Oral History of Cher's Iconic Closet," *Nylon*, July 16, 2020, https://www.nylon.com/fashion/cher-closet-clueless-an-oral-history.

65 Rachel Arthur, "Cher's Virtual 'Clueless' Wardrobe Is Now A Reality, 20 Years Later," *Forbes*, July 17, 2015, https://www.forbes.com/sites/rachelarthur/2015/07/17/chers-virtual-clueless-wardrobe-is-now-a-reality-20-years-later/.

66 Denise Incandela, "Walmart Levels Up Virtual Try-On for Apparel With Be Your Own Model Experience," Walmart, September 15, 2022, https://corporate.walmart.com/newsroom/2022/09/15/walmart-levels-up-virtual-try-on-for-apparel-with-be-your-own-model-experience.

2

Existence, Aesthetics, and Meaning: A Philosophical Reflection

MICHAEL R. SPICHER

Introduction

A perennial question—What is the nature of reality?—carried philosophers through winding conversations and debates for the last few thousand years. In ancient Greece, Plato launched into this question with his famous allegory of the cave in his dialogue *The Republic*. He imagines people chained to a wall, and they believe that the shadows on the wall comprise reality. If released, they exit the cave and learn the truth about the world. For Plato, this allegory illustrates that the world in which we live exists as a shadow of ultimate reality; there are higher levels of reality. Even when discussing physical things, philosophers explore and make distinctions among the different things that exist, such as dogs, trees, or souls. Things that have different functions or abilities may instantiate a different kind or mode of existence. For instance, in his work *On the Soul*, Aristotle surmised three types of souls: nutritive, sensible, and rational. These souls corresponded to three broad categories of existence; namely plants, animals, and people. Beyond the physical objects and beings, philosophers also sought to uncover the foundation of reality, for which many asserted the existence of an immaterial being or reality, such as a god. Leaping forward to the present day, this debate rages on, stretching from some versions of realism to versions of antirealism, whether things—including digital objects, like fashion—are real in themselves or always interpreted through our language.

What is the goal of questioning the nature of reality? Since these debates have ensued for thousands of years, the goal is clearly not a consensus. Asking this question about the goal cuts to the heart of philosophical inquiry itself. While individual philosophers defend positions they believe are true or reasonable, the collective group of philosophers around the world fail every year to achieve consensus on anything. But consensus couldn't be the point. In working out their own positions, philosophers clarify concepts, question assumptions, and challenge alternate viewpoints. When done at its best, philosophy demonstrates a method to engage in the world without succumbing too easily to bad arguments or reasons for different beliefs. And this is why it continues to amass new ideas and ways of seeing the world.

Throughout the history of ideas, we've stumbled upon the vastness of the universe as it expands out into space. Our knowledge of the universe moves continuously beyond anything earlier scholars discovered; we've traveled both physically and through the invention of tools, like advanced microscopes and telescopes. Science and technology proceed in altering what we can know about the world and universe. But we've now also gone beyond that kind of spatial knowledge by creating another vastness in cyberspace. The billions (or trillions) of digital objects that hover somewhere in a server magnify—rather than settle—the boundaries of our questions about reality.

In trying to understand virtual things, I explore what it means for digital objects, especially digital fashion, to exist, since they cannot perform the regularly associated functions that they do in the physical world. Without these practical functions, digital fashion elevates the importance of meaning (or self-expression) and the aesthetic perspective of fashion. It's not that physical fashion downplays these aspects, but rather that physical fashion needs to consider functionality as part of the aesthetic and meaning. One day perhaps, it might serve unique digital purposes, but until then, digital fashion concerns itself primarily with the non-functional aspects of fashion. Finally, a recurring question about physical fashion involves whether it is an art in the same sense as painting or sculpture. Digital fashion may help resolve some of the issues that hinder physical fashion, for some people, from being conceived as an art. An interesting case study about digital objects provides an entry point to this discussion of the nature of digital fashion.

Case Study: Robbery of Digital Objects

In September 2007, two older boys in the Netherlands threatened a younger boy physically. They held him at knife point until he gave up his property. They weren't after money, a bicycle, or any other physical object. They demanded that he log into the massive multiplayer online role-playing game (MMORPG) *RuneScape*, and they forced him to drop two items—a magic amulet and an enchanted mask. Afterwards, one of the older boys logged into the same video game, and his character picked up those items.[1] A robbery occurs when one person threatens another with harm, unless they give up their property, such as money or a phone. Was a robbery committed in this case, since digital objects do not *really* exist? Imagine a hacker sneaking into your computer to delete a few dots on your old-school *Pac-Man* game. That might not make a huge difference to the integrity of the game, and the players do not earn or purchase those dots. In the *RuneScape* case, however, the Supreme Court of the Netherlands ruled that robbery—not just physical assault—had been committed. The digital items, they determined, met the requirement for stolen property, under the threat of violence.

The theft of the video game objects in The Netherlands raises an important question for digital fashion. In what sense does digital fashion exist? After all, people pay real money for digital garments, so they must carry value, which would make them susceptible to theft. As another kind of example, suppose you log into your bank account and notice that it lists your balance as zero, instead of whatever amount of money should be listed. Thoughts of identity theft, a stolen bank card, or other such nefarious possibilities would flood your mind. Now suppose you call the bank, and the banker explains that they don't regard the numbers in your account as being meaningful, since they are mere digital representations. Then, they confirm that all the money is still in your account in the vault. In this case, the digital representation ought to represent something in the real world, which makes this situation different from the video game example, which is purely digital. But as people continue to use less cash, the digital representations in bank accounts become more real, which of course provides an entryway into valuable digital assets. This distinction between the reality of a digital object and what it represents is at the heart of the metaphysical questions surrounding the existence of digital fashion.

Existence of Digital Fashion

Virtual objects contain enough importance and value for people to assault others in order to possess them. Not limited to crime alone, people also devote money and time to procure digital objects through legitimate means. Either people are woefully misguided or they have good reason to pursue and purchase these non-physical objects. Attempting to understand more deeply the aforementioned robbery, two philosophers, Nathan Wildman and Neil McDonnell, offer an analysis of the Supreme Court of the Netherlands' ruling about the nature of these digital objects, presenting a distinction between realism and irrealism. To explain these two positions, Wildman and McDonnell offer these definitions: "In particular, virtual realists claim that virtual objects are 'real'—that is, they genuinely exist—and virtual events genuinely occur. Meanwhile, virtual irrealists hold that virtual objects are not 'real' (i.e., they do not exist), and events that take place in virtual reality do not genuinely occur."[2]

Realism in relation to virtual objects allows for a relatively easy explanation. If true, then virtual objects exist in the same way that physical objects exist. Philosophers questioned the nature of reality before virtual objects entered our lives, and now they can apply those same ideas to virtual objects. While people cannot use virtual objects the same way they do physical objects, the reality of these objects is grounded in the bits and bytes encoded in a physical silicon chip, whether on a personal device or in a "cloud" storage facility. In other words, the chips and servers provide the connection to the real world for realists. This version of realism, however, seems little more than admitting that computers exist. Or it is similar to saying that people's thoughts are as real as physical objects because their immaterial thoughts are stored in their material brains. Yet we interact with virtual objects in experiential ways that we don't interact with thoughts, especially thoughts stored in other people's brains. So, realism demands that virtual and physical objects both really exist in the same (or a similar) way.

Now, irrealism presents some difficulties. Because we interact with virtual objects in meaningful ways, it seems contradictory to say that they don't really exist. It's worth noting that one could consistently adhere to realism about the physical world and irrealism about the virtual world. They do not depend on each other. Toward defending their irrealism, Wildman and McDonnell offer an example from the physical version of the game chess. Setting up for a game, chess involves one board and thirty-two figurines. Are the figurines absolutely necessary to play the game? Let us suppose that someone's imagination and memory were so astute that they could remember vividly and precisely where each piece would be throughout the duration of a game by only looking at a blank chessboard. Probably no one could do this. My assumption is that all people would lose track of their pieces and their opponent's pieces fairly quickly. The figurines enable people to track where their game pieces should be located at any point during game play. In other words, the figurines aid our imaginations as we play the game—they help us to experience playing the game. For Wildman and McDonnell, this explains why the amulet and mask are important, despite not being real. They are necessary to aid one's imagination in playing the video game.

While both realism and irrealism are metaphysical positions about the nature of objects, I suggest that an alternative approach to the question about digital objects, appealing to phenomenology, may prove more useful. Phenomenology is "the study of 'phenomena': appearances of things, or things as they appear in our experience, or the ways we experience things, thus the meanings things have in our experience. Phenomenology studies conscious experience as experienced from the subjective or first person point of view."[3] Stephan Käufer and Anthony Chemero add that "Phenomenology wants to explain the meaning of our experiences."[4] With digital objects, how people experience and interact with them becomes more important than most other facts about them, since they are intangible. In other words, how people perceive or experience digital objects is the salient aspect of our understanding of them. While phenomenology overlaps and influences other branches of philosophy, it distinguishes itself as a method of philosophy approaching conscious experience from the subjective or first-person point of view.

Phenomenology focuses on the intentionality of actions. Chad Engelland explains that "whenever we experience or think, we experience or think of things."[5] We could easily imagine meeting someone in a virtual space and having a conversation. Then, a few weeks later, we see that person in a physical location, and we might refer to the conversation that we had in the virtual location. Even though it was our avatars that appeared to be in close proximity— perhaps we were physically located on different continents—that conversation and the surrounding intentions were experienced as real and meaningful. "What seems natural and insignificant to the indifferent gamer is exactly the point where his or her body extends into the virtual and synchronizes with the avatar as a new part."[6] It's analogous to a person using a physical tool, like a hammer or a guitar, and forming a habit where the tool, in a sense, becomes an extension of their body. Thus, phenomenology seeks to circumvent (or bracket) the question about the precise nature of reality, in order to investigate our conscious experience of people, places, and things.

Without the ability to use all of our senses in a virtual space to perceive virtual objects, we might worry that we will become fully immersed in a mere simulacrum. Perhaps the metaverse is human beings re-entering Plato's cave, albeit in a more sophisticated way. The digital objects mimic the shadows on the cavern wall, and we might mistake these images for reality. Regardless, some people may want a more solid notion of the nature of digital objects than our experience of them. But this is a good starting point; it may take more immersive experiences than we have yet attained to develop a fuller understanding or theory about virtual spaces and phenomena. For now, phenomenology offers a framework for that to be disclosed. People, for the time being, do not seem to think about the metaverse and digital fashion as ends in themselves. So, suffice it to say that if digital objects are to remain tools to ultimately help us in the physical world, then we might have less to be concerned about anyway.

Regardless of the nature of digital objects, people experience those objects in some sense, even if they are currently limited to the senses of seeing and hearing. Whether people or objects in virtual spaces are real matters less than the intentionality that motivates real people in those spaces. Someone selected a particular combination of digital garments, including shoes, jewelry, hairstyle, and other accessories. Someone intentionally controls the actions of their digital self, interacting with other digital selves and that environment. How we experience digital spaces matters more than the exact metaphysical standing of the space and the objects within it.

I offer this brief explanation from metaphysics and phenomenology as a framework with which to approach discussions about digital objects. When it comes to fashion, it matters less whether digital garments *really* exist or not. Clearly, something is there for us to experience, whether as a *real* garment or a tool for our imagination. The thing that everyone agrees about is that digital garments cannot provide certain practical functions that physical garments can. Digital fashion cannot keep you warm, cannot protect you from rain or snow, and cannot shield you from the sun's rays. Yet people devote a lot of hours and money to pursue the development of digital garments, including accessories and other adornments. There must be a purpose for this creation, consumption, and appreciation. We could offer the partial answer that it is fun or entertaining, but then this might be easier to dismiss as a fad. I think there are at least two more possibilities that are more robust: meaning and aesthetics.

Meaning of Digital Fashion

Clothing means something. Our clothes serve our bodies to highlight, diminish, or enhance natural traits and meaning. And we also want to express personal meanings. At different points in the history of fashion, garments (and, for example, their color) indicated a person's class or status (often by law). Specific norms have changed, but clothing and adornments can still mean that someone is married, works in a particular profession, or belongs to a subculture. Even when people try to pretend their clothing is neutral, this still conveys some meaning. Take, for example, the term "normcore," meaning that a person wears clothing that is supposed to be unassuming. Fashion is a building block for meaning, in different ways, even if the meaning is unwitting. In physical spaces, however, we might occasionally (or, for some people, frequently) prioritize function or comfort over meaning or aesthetics, but virtual spaces, without possessing practical functions, elevate meaning.

With the higher prominence of meaning, it becomes crucial to understand in what ways do clothing, fashion, or other adornments mean. Attempting to discern this issue, Roland Barthes wrote *The Fashion System*, where he studied two publications—*Elle* and *Jardin des Modes*—for the one-year cycle of June 1958 to June 1959. Informed by his early commitment to structuralism, Barthes approached fashion as the wearer encoding a message for the viewer, who then decodes that message. For accepted symbols within a culture, such as a police uniform, this theory seems to work. But meaning in people's clothing and adornment presents a more nuanced picture than structuralism allowed, which is why Barthes eventually abandoned it.

Philosopher Marilynn Johnson, in her book *Adorning Bodies: Meaning, Evolution, and Beauty in Humans and Animals*, revives an interest in theories of bodily adornment. Drawing from philosopher of language H. P. Grice, Johnson explains the distinction between natural and non-natural meaning, which helps set the stage for meaning in fashion.[7] Natural meaning involves things that occur without intentionality, such as a person's white hair indicates that they are older than thirty. Non-natural meaning requires intentionality. Someone wears the uniform of a firefighter either to indicate their profession or as a costume, but it isn't accidental, unless the wearer is not informed (or misinformed) about the meaning.

People also wear clothing with subjective or personal meaning. These kinds of meaning require a bit more understanding. I may not realize that someone wears a red shirt to indicate that they love tomatoes. This example, silly as it is, shows that the rationale behind some clothing choices sneaks into situations with other people staying unaware of any symbolism or meaning.

We convey meaning or express aspects of ourselves through our clothing, even subconsciously. But clothing options and the physical world limit what we can wear through costs, materials, and availability. We might believe that a garment that costs $5,000 would be the perfect addition to our self-expression, but the cost might prohibit our purchase. Some clothing options, especially in terms of sizing, might not fit someone in a way that makes them comfortable.

The cut may be off, or the sizing might fall just outside their preferences. Digital fashion allows people to wear the clothing they want, albeit digitally. The primary limitation will be someone's own imagination; other important limitations include ethical and cultural considerations.

Beyond the fit that hinders people in physical fashion, digital fashion allows wearers to construct garments or accessories out of impossible materials. For example, shoe company Buffalo London collaborated with the Fabricant and made shoes that are on fire.[8] The flames burn on the digital feet without, of course, consuming the feet. Without the constraints of practical concerns, like money, space, and function, people can more thoughtfully consider what they want to wear in virtual worlds, and, more to the point, precisely how they want to express themselves or present their identity. To be fair, money still presents some concerns because someone needs to own or access a computer or other device, and digital fashion also comes in a range of prices, like physical fashion. But many designers and advocates believe that the costs are able to be kept much lower, for the most part, than the physical counterparts. The costs of digital fashion should at least be less of a constraint.

Meaning and expression have long been an aspect of physical fashion, but this role heightens with digital fashion. The nature of digital fashion strips away materiality, availability, and functionality concerns to leave meaning as the crux of its ontological status. In other words, digital fashion serves as a new means for a person to express their identity or present their narrative. But paired with meaning is the other imperative for digital fashion, namely aesthetics.

Aesthetics of Digital Fashion

Aesthetics drives a lot of our decisions. Daily decisions about what we wear or how we decorate our homes consume a lot of resources and time, but they provide an immediate aesthetic payoff. Beyond our daily life, we spend time, money, and energy traveling around our countries and the world to experience natural and human-made environments and objects that we believe will provide a kind of aesthetic experience. A more specific example: Harvard

Business School professor Gerald Zaltman claims that 95% of our retail purchase decisions are made because of how a product—subconsciously—makes us feel, which relates to its appearance (i.e., its aesthetics), as opposed to any facts about the product.[9] This claim, even if mostly true, will have big implications for virtual worlds and fashion, where functionality isn't a major factor.

We care about how we appear before others. To use an example from sports: it was demonstrated that basketball players can increase their free-throw percentage by throwing the ball underhand, or what some call "granny-style." You'll never see NBA players shoot this way, as some have said that they'd rather shoot zero percent than look stupid.[10] How we appear to others is very important, and it continues to become exceedingly more important in virtual contexts, whether flat photos on social media or eventually three-dimensional renderings in metaverse spaces.

Whatever we wear, our clothing appears, often intentionally, a certain way to ourselves and others, which hearkens back to the discussion about phenomenology. The aesthetics of physical clothing involves the look, smell, sound, and feel of the garment. By contrast, digital fashion, for the moment, mostly involves sight. While music, often electronic, usually accompanies animations of digital fashion, any sound the digital garment should make is often drowned out. But adding sound qualities probably isn't too difficult or far off. Smell and touch presumably enter the field when someone invents sensors that manipulate feelings on hands, and molecules that cause certain smells in a face covering of some kind. Taste might be part of future digital experiences, though not likely necessary for clothing. Even if people are one day able to use all their senses in virtual spaces, digital clothing will still exist only as perceived (just with more senses than sight), not as garments that supply the practical purposes of protection from cold, rain, or snow.

The term "aesthetics" was coined in the eighteenth century by Alexander Baumgarten as he wanted to distinguish between the higher faculties of science and reason and the lower faculties of sense experience and feelings. He likely intended this distinction to be about better and worse faculties for understanding the world, which presumably isn't a contentious interpretation. However, I think a better way to understand the distinction between higher and lower faculties is to consider more specific versus more common ways of seeing the world. For example, when thinking about climbing a mountain we often focus on the height, but another way to think about it is that the top gets narrower compared to the broad base. Unlike the specific understanding of a small number of people trained in specialized disciplinary knowledge, the aesthetic is experienced by everyone.

Aesthetics is the branch of philosophy that focuses on beauty and art. But it is so much more than this limited perspective. Aesthetic experience is a core motivation for human action, and it will carry over into virtual spaces. So, aesthetics is common to all people in a way that certain kinds of specific knowledge, like theoretical physics, is not. As human beings, we actively pursue aesthetic experiences in our lives. This desire will not change, since we don't (or shouldn't) abandon our humanity in the virtual world. But virtual worlds may help expand our understanding and habits concerning aesthetics. With fashion, we adopt ways to imitate those things we like, and we find ways to differentiate ourselves from others. This unique, aesthetic blending of imitation and differentiation enables us to craft particular narratives or identities.

In terms of our lifelike digital representations of our physical selves, we get to experiment with our looks in ways that are not always feasible in the physical world. Digital fashion that exists only in a digital space provides some of these benefits, but some benefits derive from the digital experience and impact the physical world. If you want to experiment widely with your clothing choices, the limits of time, energy, and money, not to mention waste, hinder your ability to experiment as much as possible. Philosopher Immanuel Kant, in his *Critique of Judgement*, claimed that an experience of beauty requires the free play of the imagination and understanding. Digital experiences enhance our imaginations' ability to be as free as possible without the limitations imposed by finance, materiality, and society.

Digital Fashion as Art

A long-standing debate that divides people concerns whether fashion is a fine art, like painting and sculpture. While designers appear to perform a similar function in respect to their garments as artists do with respect to their work, the objects themselves yield some differences. People wear fashion. Regardless of carefulness, wearing garments wears them out eventually. With controlled environments, paintings and sculptures persist for much longer. They are not immune from wear, however, as light impacts certain kinds of paint or pigment. For fashion, not only do the physical aspects of garments wear out, but people consider fashion as a whole to be a fleeting enterprise, since new styles and designs replace older ones in a continuous progression. But in the art world, there remain certain pieces that exist as classics or exemplars of great art, even after the art world moved onto something else. The final difference involves appreciation: art by famous artists increases in value over time, especially after they die and can no longer create, while fashion by famous designers does not increase in value to the same extent. A garment worn by a celebrity sells for more money than a comparable garment without that connection, but this involves the fact that a celebrity wore it, rather than the garment gaining value by itself. Digital fashion overcomes these difficulties of physical fashion.

Digital fashion will not wear out. As technology advances, the digital fashion of today could potentially become more vibrant in the future. We can only speculate whether digital fashion will gain value years from now, but this problem presents a difficulty for digital art as well. If digital art is indeed counted as art, then digital fashion would more easily be subsumed as art, since it relates to digital art. In other words, whatever happens to the value of digital art remains possible for digital fashion, as they use similar technologies. In this section, I expand on the key ideas of this debate in order to suggest that digital fashion has the potential to become a fine art, especially as it relates to digital art. I discuss three reasons—though there are likely more—why people have resisted thinking of fashion as an art: cost, longevity, and functionality. Then, I show that digital fashion might be a means of overcoming these concerns.

On November 15, 2017, *Salvator Mundi*, a painting by Leonardo da Vinci, sold for $450 million.[11] Works of art, especially by dead artists, continue to increase in monetary value. Some painters, like Vincent Van Gogh, struggled to earn a living and survive when they were alive, and today his paintings sell for millions of dollars as well. The same cannot be said about most items of fashion. For a garment to sell at a high price, it usually possesses additional value from a celebrity who wore it or some other cultural significance beyond the garment itself. For instance, Charlie Chaplin's bowler hat and cane sold for $62,500 in 2012.[12] Despite being associated with Chaplin, the cost of these items didn't even crack a million, which is rare for garments, while artworks of similar ilk will often fetch well over a million dollars. Without Chaplin's association, the cost would have plummeted. Of course, a painting realized to be a forgery would also plummet without the association of the celebrated artist. But it doesn't matter so much who owned a painting—a valued artist's work will still increase in value. So, the garment by itself did not increase to that auction cost. It's clear that, for whatever reason, fashion does not increase in monetary value at the same rate as works of art.

Art possesses a longevity that fashion does not. This statement contains two meanings. The first is that what counts as good fashion changes rapidly, so most clothing gets left behind eventually. This meaning of longevity seems to be easily dismissed. There are many examples of ephemeral art, such as land-based art that washes away, or performance art that cannot be truly replicated. Plus, the early twentieth century shows multiple art movements rapidly changing and overlapping. These kinds of art do not appreciate and they don't last, but they are still classified as art. The second meaning relating to longevity, which may be more useful, is that the items of fashion wear out in a literal sense, especially if they are worn as intended. The da Vinci painting, mentioned above, that sold for $450 million was painted around the year 1500, just over 500 years ago. Throughout the world, individuals and museums own other paintings by da Vinci, Michelangelo, Van Gogh, and others. These paintings have survived for centuries. Generally speaking, fashion does not survive as long in pristine condition. This is one reason that hinders the monetary value of fashion reaching as high as most art, and therefore, some people do not consider fashion to be art.

In *The Picture of Dorian Gray*, Oscar Wilde proclaimed that all art is useless. This recent idea strengthens the difference between art and fashion. Earlier art had more specific functions, such as to preserve family members' images or teach a religious lesson. As more people became literate and photography became more prominent, art became free to explore and move in different directions. Art no longer cared as much about function. On the other hand, people design fashion for bodies; it is inherently functional. A painting hangs on a wall, but fashion is worn by a person. Models even wear avant garde garments on a runway, even if these garments are not practical for daily use.

While physical fashion presents some difficulty in being considered art, digital fashion does not present the same difficulties. And it may even count as art. When it comes to cost, non-fungible tokens (NFTs)—which prevent digital art from being endlessly copied because the coding verifies the original—have developed too recently to know whether their value will increase in the same way that traditional artworks have increased. Even though some NFTs sell for lots of money, that could still be attributed only to the hype of their newness. Time will tell. But digital fashion uses the same technology, so if the value increases (or isn't a concern) for digital art, then it should be likewise for digital fashion.

Digital fashion also resolves the longevity concern. As noted, physical fashion deteriorates the more it is worn, even with the greatest care. But fashion left in glass cases ceases to have its primary purpose; the enclosure relegates it to historical interest. Technology will continue to evolve, and people will continue to use digital tools. Computers, including laptops, desktops, phones, and tablets may be replaced by something unforeseen, but a total removal of digital technology is nowhere in sight. In other words, as long as people use digital technology, digital fashion, along with digital art, will also continue. Digital technology may improve to such a degree that the digital fashion of today will eventually look simplistic, though the digital fashion itself has not decayed. It might merely look older compared to newer garments.

The function of digital fashion marks a significant difference in the debate about whether fashion can be art. Digital fashion does not bear the same functionality as physical fashion—it cannot protect someone from rain, cold, wind, or heat. Moreover, aesthetics of imitation and differentiation, along with meaning, become the direct functions of digital fashion. Therefore, as digital fashion helps someone express themselves by presenting their narrative, it moves even closer to art, insofar as art's function revolves around some notion of expression. Since digital fashion does not have the same kind of functionality as physical fashion, then it overcomes this limitation of physical fashion as well. This is not to say that digital fashion is useless—after all, it expresses a person's narrative and identity—but that it does not have parallel functions with physical clothing. Digital fashion offers a new way forward in the debate about whether fashion can be art.

Conclusion

Digital fashion exists—that much is a fact. But the nature of this existence eludes our traditional categories. As the world progresses toward the metaverse, people realize the potential to change a lot about how we live and interact, particularly as we interact with digital objects. Virtual worlds and objects will affect our laws, our commerce, our government, our education. But one thing that will stay the same is our desire for meaning and aesthetics. The specifics will, of course, change, but our desires will continue. We need to enhance our resolve to focus on what makes us human, rather than being too enthralled with what we can do in the metaverse. Flying around cyberspace won't be worth the time, money, and effort, if we lose our humanity.

It's important to remember that there is no formula for applying meaning and aesthetics to our fashion. But they are durable concepts. While technology changes rapidly, human motivation is surprisingly constant. We want friendships, knowledge, aesthetic experience, meaningfulness, and more. It's not enough for technology to merely perform a function, even doing it well. The future of the internet—Web3 and the metaverse—are immersive experiences. Without fulfilling the basic human motivations, like meaning and aesthetics, they risk being empty. By keeping core human values an integral aspect of these developments, we ensure that the future moves in directions befitting our dignity.

Notes

1   Nathan Wildman and Neil McDonald, "The Puzzle of Virtual Theft," *Analysis* 80, no. 3 (July 2020): 493–9.

2   Wildman and McDonald, "The Puzzle of Virtual Theft," 494.

3 David Woodruff Smith, "Phenomenology," in Edward N. Zalta (ed.), *The Stanford Encyclopedia of Philosophy*, Summer 2018 edn, https://plato.stanford.edu/archives/sum2018/entries/phenomenology/.

4 Stephan Käufer and Anthony Chemero, *Phenomenology: An Introduction*, 2nd edn (Cambridge: Polity Press, 2021), 38.

5 Chad Engelland, *Phenomenology* (Cambridge, MA: MIT Press, 2020), 37.

6 Tobias Holischka, "Heidegger's *Building Dwelling Thinking* in Terms of *Minecraft*," in Erik Champion (ed.), *The Phenomenology of Real and Virtual Places* (New York: Routledge, 2019), 168.

7 Marilynn Johnson, *Adorning Bodies: Meaning, Evolution, and Beauty in Humans and Animals* (London: Bloomsbury Academic, 2022), 25–6.

8 Jennifer Hahn, "Buffalo London sets platform trainers ablaze for first digital-only product release," *Dezeen*, January 28, 2021, https://www.dezeen.com/2021/01/28/buffalo-london-the-fabricant-classic-burningfor/.

9 Manda Mahoney, "The Subconscious Mind of the Consumer (And How to Reach It)," *Working Knowledge*, Harvard Business School, January 13, 2003, https://hbswk.hbs.edu/item/the-subconscious-mind-of-the-consumer-and-how-to-reach-it.

10 Colton Wesley, "Underhand Free Throws Work, so Why Don't Players Shoot Them?" *Fansided*, Detroit Jock City, https://detroitjockcity.com/2017/05/31/underhanded-free-throws-work-dont-players-shoot/.

11 Christie's, "Leonardo's *Salvator Mundi* Makes Auction History," Christies.com, November 15, 2017, https://www.christies.com/features/Leonardo-and-Post-War-results-New-York-8729-3.aspx.

12 Andrea Burzynski, "Charlie Chaplin's bowler hat and cane fetch over $60,000 at auction," *Reuters*, November 19, 2012, https://www.reuters.com/article/us-charliechaplin-auction/charlie-chaplins-bowler-hat-and-cane-fetch-over-60000-at-auction-idUKBRE8AH0K020121119.

3

Spooling and Neuroaesthetics: How Technology Helps Fashion Progress

VIRGINIA ROLLING

Introduction

With the advent of 3D printed apparel, smart textiles, digitally printed garments, and virtual clothing, digital fashion has evolved significantly from its origins stemming back to the spool. The term "spool" seems to have originated in the textile field to describe a textile tool made of clay, stone, and wooden cylindrical spools (or spindles) during the Neolithic and Bronze Ages.[1] However, spools eventually emerged to become more than merely thread carriers. Spools found their place in both the musical and computer science fields.[2] With their usage in these intersecting fields, spools have been considered the carriers of binary code (digital) data.[3] Binary code data—created using zeros and ones—is used to operate computers, looms, three-dimensional printers, textile digital printers, and more. In particular, the term spool is associated with the computer science acronym for the computing process describing the input and output of data, known as Simultaneous Peripheral Operation On-/Off-Line (S.P.O.O.L.).[4]

Interestingly, binary data used to operate computers in the creation of digital textiles and virtual clothing is the same as that employed by the Jacquard loom that was used centuries earlier to make fabric. Initially, the Jacquard loom functioned with punch-card technology that stored binary data in the form of punch-card paper to instruct the machinery in its operation. However, today the Jacquard loom is aided by a computer rather than by punch cards to perform its processes more efficiently. Thus, the computer took the place of punch cards through its ability to process binary data in a function known as spooling.

The Jacquard Loom

One of the most influential textile machines to be invented during the Industrial Revolution was the Jacquard loom. Commonly referred to as the precursor to the computer, the Jacquard loom was invented in 1801 (patented in 1804) for the purpose of creating complex weavings by using punch-card data. Although its final success and name are attributed to Joseph Marie Jacquard, the invention itself had many contributors along the way.

Among those influential to the Jacquard loom was Basile Bouchon, a Lyon textile worker. As the son of an organ-maker, Bouchon was familiar with the practice of punching holes into paper for the layout of data to be transferred to the metal cylinders of musical automata.[5] This musical data happened to be binary code and is considered the first direct application of binary-code information.[6] Bouchon enjoyed unique and notable success in finding a new application for binary information from its original use in musical data to weaving codes for looms in 1725. Without his knowledge of creating musical codes, he could not have applied his understanding of these codes to the realm of textiles. It is with this insight that his clever textile invention allowed for the weaving of patterns from binary code.

Three years later, Jean Falcon is commonly known to have converted the perforated roll of paper that Bouchon worked with into a chain of punched cardboard cards to change programs more quickly. From this idea, Jacques Vaucanson, a talented watchmaker and musician, created the first automated (self-operating mechanical) loom that would use these cards as pattern guides or programs for various weave structures in 1745.

The Computer

The computer is now a modified descendant of the Jacquard loom's punch-card technology. This creates a fascinating historical loop, as the modern-day computer is not only a product of the loom but a facilitator of it. Initially, the first computers needed the loom's punch-card technology to run, but has since taken over the function of punch cards in a process known as S.P.O.O.L. By processing binary code information in this way, the computer is utilized by what initially created it, the Jacquard loom. Therefore, fashion has always had an impact on technology and vice versa.

Charles Babbage, known as the modern father of computing, worked with Ada Lovelace on the Difference Machine and Analytical Engine in the early nineteenth century.[7] The Difference Machine was intended to automatically calculate mathematical tables, but was only partially complete over a decade later, when Babbage conceived of the idea for the Analytical Engine in 1834. This second machine was intended to use Jacquard punched cards to control an automatic calculator that, as Lovelace wrote, "weaves algebraic patterns just as the Jacquard loom weaves flowers and leaves."[8] However, this all changed after Babbage's ideas taken from the loom were put into use by others to create the mechanical computer.

Some influential contributors to the modern-day computer include Georg Scheutz and George Barnard Grant, who both created a working model of Babbage's Difference Machines. However, it was Herman Hollerith that moved punch-card technology into the field of computer science. By doing this, Hollerith created data storage for computers and is commonly known to have patented punch cards for the 1890 Census Bureau that would eventually be used by IBM. One of the world's largest computer companies, IBM (International Business Machines) was founded by Herman Hollerith in the late nineteenth century. Over time, this company experienced dramatic changes in information technology from computer chips to PCs.

As new developments in computer technology occurred, various other fields were quickly impacted. In particular, the field of textiles became the recipient of its own technological by-product, the computer. The computer, the device which superseded punch-card technology, has allowed the Jacquard loom to complete extraordinarily complex digital weavings. Therefore, the computer and the loom work together to create binary-encoded textiles. In addition, current digital fashions such as wearable technology have emerged due to the computer science field becoming a by-product of Jacquard loom technology. A tangible example of this is the interactive dress, the Marchesa IBM Watson Cognitive Dress, worn by Karolina Kurkova at the 2016 Metropolitan Museum of Art (Met) Gala entitled *Fashion in an Age of Technology*.[9]

Wearables as a Subset of Digital Fashion

As the fascinating history of binary code evolves from punch-card data into present day binary (digital) computer data, digital fashion could be called "spooling on steroids." Digital fashion is not merely fashion that exists in the virtually engaging world of the metaverse in the form of NFTs, for example, but also belongs in the physical realm that allows the wearer to engage in the world of binary code through wearables. Therefore, wearables that are technology-enabled (i.e., wearable technology) are a subset of digital fashion. For instance, wearable technology bridges the gap between the virtual world of binary code and the tangible existence of binary code as encoded messaging emitted from digital music played to the sequencing of LED lights. Musical codes and LED lights are digital sensory cues that emit binary code. The virtual realities of binary code can be actualized and perceived in the physical realm through varying pitched musical tones that are sequenced to programmed colored lights. Thus, wearable technology connects the historical roots of textile spools with computer science S.P.O.O.L.s, similar to how the physicality of the loom led to the existence of the computer's metaverse and looped back again to program the loom that created it. The computer would not have existed without the Jacquard loom, and arguably, the metaverse would not be as impactful without the existence of wearables to actualize binary code in order to interact with a virtual realm. It is one thing to simply play a video game, but another to engage in it as a living reality, which is in essence what wearable technology does by making virtual interfaces part of everyday life.

This merging of technology with fashion has become of particular interest over recent years. For instance, fashion has become even more advanced whether examining Iris Van Herpen's digitally printed runway collections using 3D printing, laser-cut garments by the recently deceased Kyoto Prize winner Issey Miyake, or Zac Posen's Cinderella fiber-optic gown designed for Claire Danes featured at the Met Gala.[10] Garments that feature digital fashion at an extraordinary level include the interactive *Spider Dress* designed by Anouk Wipprecht that blends robotics with fashion using digital sensors reacting to proximity movement.[11]

Furthermore, designers have created garments such as *The Hood, MiMu Musical Gloves*, and the *Synesthetic Dress* that have all merged the antecedents of binary code through the use of musical, textile, and computer science technologies. For instance, *The Hood* uses lit-touch sensors in a wearable technology jacket to act as a musical instrument in accessing Bluetooth technology to sound like a guitar. *The Hood* has been described as a wearable electronic instrument that combines design, computer science, engineering, fashion, cultural diversity, and musical composition through a collaboration by Italian musical artist Rho, designer Delton Moore, engineer Scott Gilliland, and wearable computing specialist Clint Zeagler.[12] Similarly, *MiMu Musical Gloves* are also considered a wearable musical instrument using computer chips that create musical sounds, but from mere hand gestures.[13] These musical data gloves using motion sensors were designed in collaboration with Grammy Award-winning electronic artist Imogen Heap and a team of contributors.[14] Each glove gesture is designed to produce a unique sound. For instance, there are eight flex sensors for bending fingers and nine hand postures which can produce different sounds such as drum beats.[15]

Another example of a musical garment is the *Synesthetic Dress* which mimics the phenomenon known as synesthesia, where a wearer (or beholder) of the garment can experience seeing colors corresponding to sound and vice versa. This silk painted kimono garment with musical LED felted belt created through a collaboration between designer Virginia Rolling and engineer Jim Schnupp utilized Wi-Fi technology to control a portable Raspberry Pi computer with speakers attached inside the LED belt. The music for the *Synesthetic Dress* was digitally modified in UJAM online software programmed to correspond to the flexible tape LED-colored lights programmed in Microsoft Paint software. Thus, the belt's digital song frequencies were matched to the digitally programmed colored light prism waves (e.g., the LED color green corresponded to the musical note C in the song, the LED color blue to the musical note D, the LED color purple to the musical note E, the LED color dark purple to musical note F, the LED color red to musical note G, etc.).

Other examples of wearable digital fashions that operate in response to sound are the *Sound Shirt*, which allows deaf wearers the experience of sensing music through vibrations, and the *Professor on Fire Shawl*, which pulsates light in response to sounds such as applause. The *Sound Shirt* by Junge Symphoniker Hamburg converts sounds from eight different musical stage instruments into data sent wirelessly through the shirt's sixteen vibrating micro actuators, relating the exact musical intensity to the wearer.[16] In particular, the shirt allows the wearer to feel the music by different orchestra instruments being experienced on different areas of the shirt. For instance, bass instruments (e.g., cello) activate actuators located in the base of the shirt, so deeper sounds can be felt as vibration in the lower area of the shirt and lighter notes from the violin are experienced on the upper body located around the shirt neck.[17] This shirt was named one of *Time* magazine's Best Inventions of 2020.[18] On a similar note, the *Professor on Fire Shawl*, designed by Clint Zeagler, Jessica Pater, and Ceara Byrne and worn by Elizabeth Mynatt as an Association for Computing Machinery Fellow, also responds to sounds by acting as a personal spotlight that pulsates light during applause.[19]

In each of these instances, Basile Bouchon's contribution of converting binary code originally from a musical application to a textile application (e.g., the Jacquard loom) is taken a step further by reincorporating musical sound into these digital fashion applications. The blending of binary-spool data from its musical origins in textiles and computer science is climactic, as wearable technology incorporates music into digital fashions in view of the musical origins of spooling history. For instance, *The Hood*, *MiMu Musical Gloves*, and

Synesthetic Dress all have in common a perfect loop of reincorporating music back into the actual textiles to be experienced auditorily. Inventors such as Bouchon, Jacquard, Babbage, and Hollerith are but a few of the people who contributed to the current acceleration of digital binary data into digital fashions such as musical wearable technologies.

Neuroaesthetics of Wearables

Due to the increasing adoption of digital fashions such as wearable technology by society, emerging neuroaesthetic research has ensued to gain a greater understanding of how these unique hybrid digital fashions that merge computer science with textiles are perceived. Neuroaesthetics is a fascinating field dedicated to understanding the physiological responses to aesthetic experiences (e.g., viewing wearable technology).[20] As such, neuroaesthetics research utilizes various technologies (e.g., eye-tracking glasses that record eye movements, electrodermal activity wristbands that capture various neurological responses such as heart rate through skin sensors, etc.) to capture automatic physiological responses to digital fashions.[21] Therefore, we are in a unique age considering that neuroaesthetic tracking and data collection aids (e.g., eye-tracking glasses, skin sensor wristbands) are the wearable technology used to assist in our present understanding of digital fashions due to their ability to collect physiological data.

For instance, research conducted on the *Synesthetic Dress* musical garment displayed in the Museum of Design Atlanta (MODA) used physiological measures (e.g., eye-tracking glasses and skin sensors), observational data, and interview data to triangulate results for a qualitative study. During this study, visitors to MODA were given the opportunity to view this garment with no digital sensory cues (i.e., neither digital music nor LED lights), a single digital sensory cue (i.e., either digital music or LED lights), or both digital sensory cues (i.e., both digital music along with LED lights). While visitors viewed the garment, their total viewing time, observational responses (e.g., facial responses, approach-avoidance response, etc.), eye movements, and fixations on the garment were recorded using eye-tracking glasses, and electrodermal activity (EDA) responses such as micro-perspiration using skin sensor wrist bands were recorded. After viewers had finished viewing the garment at their own pace, they were invited to answer a series of interview questions adapted from Shimamura's I-SKE model questions for the museum to determine the viewer's aesthetic experience of this digital fashion garment.[22]

Results from the MODA study suggest that wearable technology's multisensory digital cues provide an enhanced aesthetic experience.[23] Therefore, it is suggested that digital fashion incorporating various sensory cues such as music and lights enhance the aesthetic experiences for beholders. As such, digital fashion designers should consider utilizing multiple digital sensory cues (e.g., music with LED lights) to stimulate viewers. For instance, rather than merely using LED lights such as Hussein Chalayan's *Video Dress* operating with 15,600 LED lights or *PIXI Interactive*'s 600 LED lights, digital fashions using LED lights may be best enjoyed with the addition of digital music for the viewer's auditory pleasure as well.[24]

This study also highlighted that digital fashions that use no technological cues are perceived as fashion, whereas musical cues in a wearable technology garment shift the perception of the garment to be viewed as art.[25] Thus, the addition of digital musical sensory cues being perceived as art as opposed to fashion may be linked with stronger associations to the musical arts such as orchestra music, rather than simply fashion. Furthermore, LED light cues in the *Synesthetic Dress* shift the wearable technology garment to be perceived as a costume even in the presence of additional musical cues.[26] As such, LED lights appear to be a very dominant cue strongly associated with the theatrical performing arts. These findings will assist digital fashion designers in their decisions about which digital cues to align with the digital fashion garments' intended end-use.

Of particular note is that the MODA study is considered unique in that it utilized wearable technology (i.e., skin sensors and eye-tracking glasses) to assess wearable technology (i.e., a multisensory wearable technology garment). Therefore, wearers of eye-tracking and skin sensor wearable technology had their neuroaesthetic data collected to better understand how they responded to beholding wearable technology. As a result, the beholder of wearable technology (e.g., viewing the *Synesthetic Dress*) became at the same time the wearer of wearable technology (e.g., using eye-tracking glasses and skin sensors) in order to physiologically assess wearable technology in the unique digital age of fashion.

The Aesthetic Triad and Future Research

The *Synesthetic Dress* is a recent example of neuroaesthetic research conducted to assess the viewer's responses to wearable technology.[27] This research used a modified version (the SKE-I model) of the original I-SKE model developed by Arthur Shimamura, who was a University of California Berkeley's psychology professor and founding member of the Cognitive Neuroscience Society, which assessed the artist's intention (I) and beholder's sensory (S), knowledge (K), and emotion (E) response to viewing a wearable technology garment as an artwork.[28] Shimamura's I-SKE model essentially examined aspects that the theorists Oshin Vartanian and Anjan Chatterjee describe as the "aesthetic triad," which is the aesthetic experience emerging from three interacting systems in the brain: sensory (motor), knowledge (meaning), and emotion (valuation).[29] These three distinct aspects, the SKE or aesthetic triad, of the viewer's responses to an aesthetic object such as wearable technology are extremely important to analyze for future neuroaesthetic research.

As Anjan Chatterjee points out—drawing on his expertise in neurology, psychology, and architecture as a professor at the University of Pennsylvania and founder of the Penn Center for Neuroaesthetics—not only is the aesthetic experience multifaceted, involving three systems (i.e., sensorimotor, reward, and cognitive), but these three systems are interconnected to work in sequence.[30] For instance, a viewer's sensory (S) system first obtains aesthetic information through the process of gazing or beholding an aesthetic object.[31] Then the brain's reward system connected to emotion (E) or valuation can activate the experience of pleasure or happiness in the brain in order to continue to seek out more pleasant aesthetic experiences.[32] Finally, the third process is knowledge (K), or meaning-making, which is based on context (e.g., personal history, cultural norms, time as well as place in which someone lives, etc.).[33] As such, theorists Vartanian and Chatterjee would sequence this experience as SEK rather than Shimamura's SKE, which has the same basic components for brain-system processing yet a different sequencing order for processing each. Also, the *Synesthetic Dress* research that used the SKE-I model (not necessarily focused on the sequence of processing each system, but rather examining the different components of each system of S, K, and E) further defined the artist's intention as the "aesthetic experience" that is provided to the viewer through various wearable technology sensory cues.[34] This definition in the modified model is helpful in analyzing whether the artist's intention of providing an aesthetic experience has been experienced by the viewer.

As a result of the *Synesthetic Dress* research, a grounded theory model was developed for use in future research.[35] This model expounds upon the modified SKE-I model to also include viewers' preferences for high or low Optimal Stimulation Levels (OSL) to gauge an individual's preferred stimulation levels.[36] This affords a more accurate measure of whether and to what extent the aesthetic triad is being heightened to individuals' preferred optimal levels so as not to be over- or under-stimulating.

Furthermore, to adjust terminology for future neuroaesthetics research, it is suggested that future researchers adopt the terminology "experiencers" for individuals who are processing varied aesthetic experiences, since not all aesthetic experiences are merely visually-based. Therefore, language such as "viewers" or even Shimamura's "beholders" seems to limit the type of sensory input being processed to just a visual aesthetic experience by not allowing room for auditory, olfactory, or other sensory input.

Moreover, it is suggested that future research be conducted to gauge the neuroaesthetic experiential differences between wearable technology and NFTs. Currently, there is a limited understanding of how our brains process such vastly different expressions of digital fashion and what that means for the future of fashion.

Conclusion

Digital fashion has its origins in the conception of a simple wooden textile tool that evolved into binary code used in musical punch cards, Jacquard looms, and eventually the computer. The musical and computer science influences intertwined into textiles through spooling over the centuries has emerged in the present-day digital fashions of wearable technology. Currently, wearable technology may well be considered the epitome of digital fashion, as these smart textiles directly incorporate the antecedents of spools with both musical and computer science binary digital codes.

As interest in wearable technology has persisted, so has the present understanding of the viewer's neuroaesthetic responses to wearable technology. Therefore, the results of neuroaesthetic research conducted on wearable technology that uses both musical and LED light sensory cues were determined to enhance the viewer's aesthetic responses, which is interesting to note considering the strong historical association of spools within the fields of textiles, music, and computer science. Furthermore, wearable technology has advanced to the point of being used to assess itself through physiological measures (e.g., eye-tracking glasses and skin sensors). The present age of digital textiles completes the full circle from the digital past of spooling through to the future age of wearable technology. However, there is scope for more exploration in the realm of neuroaesthetics research, not only for wearable technology but also the various forms of fashion including digital.

Notes

1　Lorenz Rahmstorf, "An introduction to the investigation of archaeological textile tools," in Eva Andersson Strand and Marie-Louise Nosch (eds.), *Tools, Textiles and Contexts. Investigating Textile Production in the Aegean and Eastern Mediterranean Bronze Age*, Ancient Textiles Series 21 (Oxford: Oxbow Books, 2015), 1–24.

2　Virginia Rolling, "Spoolooops," MFA thesis, Savannah College of Art and Design, Savannah, 2010.

3　Rolling, "Spooloops."

4　"Spool," in Mary Rose Bonk (ed.), *Acronyms, Initialisms & Abbreviations Dictionary*, 26th edn (Farmington Hills, MI: Gale Group, 1999).

5　David Suisman, "Sound, Knowledge, and the 'Immanence of Human Failure': Rethinking Musical Mechanization through the Phonograph, the Player-Piano, and the Piano," *Social Text* 28, no. 1 (2010): 13–34.

6 Albert N. Link, *Economics of Technological Change I* (Philadelphia: Harwood Academic Publishers, 2002), 67.

7 Hans Blohm, *Pebbles to Computers: The Thread* (Toronto: Oxford University Press, 1986), 88–9.

8 Bruce Collier and James MacLachlan, *Charles Babbage and the Engines of Perfection* (Oxford: Oxford University Press, 2000), 68.

9 Cara Kelly, "Marchesa, Zac Posen and Claire Danes light up the Met Gala red carpet," *USA Today*, May 2, 2016, https://www.usatoday.com/story/life/entertainthis/2016/05/02/claire-danes-wore-light-up-cinderella-dress-met-gala/83858594/.

10 Kelly, "Marchesa, Zac Posen and Claire Danes light up the Met Gala red carpet."

11 Kelley Dickens, "Fashion and Tech Join Forces to Create a Dress that Signals When People Get Too Close," *NPR*, August 5, 2021, https://www.npr.org/2021/08/05/1025090658/inspire-social-distancing-proximity-dress-merges-computers-couture.

12 Clint Zeagler, "Rho and the Hood," *Clint Zeagler*, December 7, 2015, https://www.clintzeagler.com/2015/12/07/rho-and-the-hood/.

13 MiMu, "Music Through Movement," *mimugloves.com*, https://mimugloves.com/.

14 CNN Business, "Imogen Heap's Sci-Fi Gloves Make Anyone a Musician," 2015, https://www.cnn.com/2015/01/12/technology/imogen-heap-mimu-music-gloves-blk/index.html.

15 MiMu, "MiMu Gloves Overview," *mimugloves.com*, https://mimugloves.com/documentation/mimu-gloves-overview/.

16 Sound Shirt, "Enabling Deaf People to Feel Classical Music," https://sound-shirt.jimdofree.com/english-1.

17 House of Hearing, "The Sound Shirt: A New Innovation that Helps People Hear," https://www.houseofhearing.co.uk/news/sound-shirt-new-innovation-helps-people-hear.

18 *Time*, "The Best Inventions of 2020", November 19, 2020, https://time.com/collection/best-inventions-2020/5911419/cutecircuit-soundshirt/.

19 Clint Zeagler, "I'm here for the applause," *clintzeagler.com*, https://www.clintzeagler.com/2016/06/24/im-here-for-the-applause/.

20 Anjan Chatterjee and Oshin Vartanian, "Neuroaesthetics," *Trends in Cognitive Sciences* 18, no. 7 (2014): 370–5.

21 Virginia Rolling, "Aesthetic Experience of a Synesthetic Dress," Ph.D. dissertation, Auburn University, 2018.

22 Arthur Shimamura, *Experiencing Art: In the Brain of the Beholder* (New York: Oxford University Press, 2015), 264.

23 Virginia Rolling and Karla Teel, "Beholding: the neuroaesthetic experience of a synesthetic dress," *International Journal of Fashion Design, Technology and Education* 15, no. 1 (2022): 98–108.

24 Andrew Bolton, *Manus x Machina: Fashion in an Age of Technology* (New York: Metropolitan Museum of Art, 2016); Z. Cochran, S. McCall, K. Kenna, K., and S. Cao, "PIXI interactive dress from Georgia Tech," 2015, https://www.youtube.com/watch?v=EHhRitHHVoo.

25 Virginia Rolling and K. P. Teel, "Perceptions of an Electronic Dress as Fashion, Art, and Costume," *Dress* 47, no. 2 (2021): 167–79.

26 Rolling and Teel, "Perceptions of an Electronic Dress."

27 Rolling, "Aesthetic Experience of a Synesthetic Dress."

28 Shimamura, *Experiencing Art*.

29 Oshin Vartanian and Anjan Chatterjee, "The Aesthetic Triad," in Anjan Chatterjee and Eileen R. Cardillo (eds.), *Brain, Beauty, and Art: Essays Bringing Neuroaesthetics Into Focus* (Oxford: Oxford University Press, 2021), 27.

30 Susan Magsamen and Ivy Ross, "Hitting the aesthetic triad while gazing at art," Literary Hub, 2023, https://lithub.com/hitting-the-the-aesthetic-triad-while-gazing-at-art/

31 Magsamen and Ross, "Hitting the aesthetic triad while gazing at art."

32 Magsamen and Ross, "Hitting the aesthetic triad while gazing at art."

33 Magsamen and Ross, "Hitting the aesthetic triad while gazing at art."

34 Rolling, "Aesthetic Experience of a Synesthetic Dress."

35 Rolling, "Aesthetic Experience of a Synesthetic Dress."

36 Rolling, "Aesthetic Experience of a Synesthetic Dress"; P. S. Raju, "Optimum stimulation level: Its relationship to personality, demographics, and exploratory behavior," *Journal of Consumer Research* 7, no. 3 (1980): 272–82.

Julie Zerbo Interviewed by
Doris Domoszlai-Lantner

Many of the major issues surrounding fashion can be distilled or addressed through the lens of the law, whether it be through case law that is established through the court system, or through the act of passing legislation. In this interview, Julie Zerbo, fashion law and business expert, and founder of media and information platform The Fashion Law, *discusses the legal foundations upon which digital fashion is being built and may continue to be built in the future. Zerbo points to several major cases under litigation at the time of the interview (December 2022), such as* Hermès v. Mason Rothschild, *to underscore her major assertion that many of the legal foundations that are already in place around IRL fashion are, and should be, the same for digital fashion.*

Doris Domoszlai-Lantner   In the field of law, what is "digital fashion"? How do you define it through a legal lens?

Julie Zerbo   There is currently no set definition for the term "digital fashion" in law. However, the way that we can, and will probably define it will likely depend on individual instances and events, as we generally so often approach law on a case-by-case basis. I think generally we can define digital fashion as virtual and/or 3D garments, apparel, and accessories that are designed for a medium that is different to the "real," or the physically-tangible world. So, these refer to goods that are designed with digital avatars in mind, but that are not necessarily removed from the "real" world, because some digital fashion exists in the form of filters that people can superimpose on their bodies and use in photo form; that is not, I would argue, totally removed from considerations of humans and the real world. Also, when we are talking about digital fashion from a design perspective, while the attributes and characteristics can be very different from "real world" designs, to some extent, we are still talking about designs that are very much rooted in the "real world" and that involve the reformulation of real-world clothing for a different media, with that medium being the metaverse or gaming.

If we are approaching that question as trademark lawyers and seeking out trademark registrations that cover the use of a trademark in the virtual world, for instance, what we have seen is that trademark offices want more specificity in terms of how we are defining these things. So, in addition to trademark offices requiring that a trademark application-filing party list the goods and/or services that the mark is being used on, they might want more specificity about the garments themselves. For example, are we talking about shirts, pants, or footwear? And how exactly are those garments and accessories being used in the digital world? Are these virtual garments being used as, or somehow tied to, NFTs? Are these virtual garments being offered up in a virtual retail capacity? There are all of these specificities that trademark offices are calling for, and to a large extent, that is because the use of trademarks in the virtual world is developing in real time and the law is developing alongside that use to some extent. So, I think that if we were to think about this as lawyers, we would want to be as specific in our definitions as possible, to the extent that it is possible.

Doris Domoszlai-Lantner   Is there a certain definition for the word "garment" in the law, and would that definition change when it comes to digital garments?

Julie Zerbo   Usually, courts will look at a dictionary definition. To my knowledge, there isn't a universal legal definition for the term "garment," and that is in part because we have relatively few laws that apply specifically to garments. For example, we have the Flammable Fabrics Act, which in theory applies to garments by virtue of the fact that garments are made of fabrics, but we don't have the court telling us precisely that this is what the word "garment" means. That leaves courts with room for interpretation, which is important in law because things like virtual fashion take shape and the law has to adapt to it and have room to encompass and integrate new innovations, including technical ones, like those at the heart of digital fashion. And a critical part of that, I think, is not having set-in-stone definitions for what things like "garment" mean. It's actually helpful for digital fashion to not have a "shoe-in-the-box" definition of a physical garment because it allows existing laws to potentially apply to novel technologies for rights' holders. It is probably helpful that the law is potentially expansive enough to encompass new developments.

Doris Domoszlai-Lantner　　Based on your explanation above, in the eyes of the law, would the definition of "digital fashion" change if it were part of, or tied to, an NFT?

Julie Zerbo　　No, because an NFT essentially consists of two parts—the underlying record (the transaction record that exists), which is separate from the asset itself that is tied to that transaction. So I would argue that the fashion itself is not that different if we're talking about a virtual handbag that is tied to an NFT versus a virtual handbag that is not tied to an NFT that just lives exclusively in the *Roblox* ecosystem, for example. So no, I would not say that the underlying asset in those situations is necessarily different, save for the technicalities of one potentially being tied to an Ethereum transaction—blockchain transaction—whereas *Roblox*, the gaming platform, is not blockchain-based.

Doris Domoszlai-Lantner　　Does that mean, that all the court cases and verdicts that apply to IRL fashion and the fashion industry be applied to digital fashion and the field of digital fashion as well?

Julie Zerbo　　I think that a lot of the laws that we currently have that apply to IRL fashion could also apply to digital fashion, either directly or indirectly. I'm thinking of trademarks, and the Lanham Act, which is the federal law that governs trademark law in the United States. It is applicable to digital fashion in the same way that it applies to trademark-bearing physical products, or the trademarks that appear on physical products. I'm talking about this primarily from an IP [intellectual property] perspective, because that's where my interest and my experience lies when it comes to virtual fashion and metadata. I don't think that we have any reasons to believe that trademark law, for instance, applies any differently in the metaverse or Web3 than in the real world. For example, Hermès filed a lawsuit against Mason Rothschild [see note 1] for offering up what he calls MetaBirkins—NFTs tied to digital images of various digitally created bags that look like the famous Birkin bags—and they specifically filed for trademark infringement. Part of what was claimed was that the infringement was Rothschild's use of the Birkin design and mark in connection with its name. Hermès has many trademark registrations in the United States and elsewhere around the world for the Birkin name for use on physical bags, physical retail services, etcetera, but they don't have a specific registration for Birkin for use in any of the quintessential "metaverse classes" of US trademark law, so Class 9 or Class 35, so basically, Hermès doesn't yet have a metaverse presence in the eyes of the law.

In the United States, the way to amass trademark rights is to use your trademark on certain types of goods and services. Just because I'm using "The Fashion Law" on digital media does not mean that I have trademark rights in "The Fashion Law" for use on lamps. But, obviously, there are exceptions, and there's more wriggle room when it comes to really famous marks because of their recognizability and potential for confusion with counterfeits.

Hermès filed their lawsuit in the Fall of 2021. After reviewing it, in refusing to toss out Hermès' case, the court has essentially interpreted Hermès' rights to the Birkin mark in the real world as extending to the virtual world. I think that's a really good example of a court indicating that trademark law applies in the metaverse in Web3, in much the same way as it does in real life. The court also said, in that case, that there is a chance that Mason Rothschild's NFTs are infringing Hermès' trademark, so that also implies that Hermès does have trademark rights in the virtual world, without legislators needing to change legislation; I would say that that's a good example of other laws being applicable in the virtual world, and I don't think that this is 100% removed from things that we've already seen; you know, brands across the board have rights, or had rights, while operating in a purely bricks-and-mortar capacity, and then kept those same rights when they started ecommerce and transacting businesses during the Web2 boom. This is really a continuation of that transfer of rights from one era to the next.

So, has the law shifted to some extent to accommodate for the changes that Web2 has brought? Certainly, and we've also seen additional laws put in place. The Digital Millennium Copyright Act, for instance, focuses on copyright infringement in the Web2 world. Does it drastically alter the landscape of copyright law? No, but I suspect that we will see some additional interpretations of our existing IRL laws to remedy issues with URL, in other words, virtually. But I would argue that our IP laws, to a large extent, are applicable in Web3.

Doris Domoszlai-Lantner   Is there a field of law that's tied specifically to digital issues; digital communications, maybe? Or is that not the case?

Julie Zerbo   Maybe, I think. It's hard for me to say because my specialty is intellectual property law, and so that encompasses cases that go back before we had digital technologies through today. So, it really is steeped in digital elements, but I don't think there is a field of law that looks specifically at digital technologies, or digital communications. But I tend to look at it as a facet of other types of law, whether that be IP, advertising, or finance, or something else.

In October 2021, Nike filed some of the first heavily publicized trademark applications for virtual footwear, and that prompted a huge number of companies to file their trademark applications for their existing real-world marks to be used in the metaverse. So I've been tracking the trademark applications that fashion, luxury, and sportswear brands have been filing for digital fashion in the United States since October 2021, and from that I've been able to garner which are the most well-represented classes of goods and services that most brands are filing applications for. Whereas we see a lot of brands filing for marks for tangible, physical clothing and footwear under Class 25, the primary classes that we see brands filing applications for their names and logos in a digital capacity, in the metaverse, are Classes, 9, 35, and 41. Class 9 refers to downloadable virtual goods, Class 35 is for retail store services featuring virtual goods, and Class 41 is entertainment services, namely, providing online, non-downloadable, virtual goods for use in virtual environments. There are also additional ones that have been less common, like Class 16 for digital collectibles, and Class 42 that includes the use of a mark in connection with cryptocurrencies.

Doris Domoszlai-Lantner   So digital fashion can technically fall into any of those depending on the way that the case is structured?

Julie Zerbo　Yeah, absolutely. I mean, in some of the cases that we're seeing with NFTs, for instance, regulators are arguing about whether or not these NFTs—which could be tied to anything from an image of a Bored Ape to one of a Birkin bag—are securities that need to be disclosed and regulated. I would argue that there are many potential pathways to consider when we're talking about digital fashion, so it's not just an IP issue. It is potentially an issue that involves the Securities and Exchange Acts and other fields of law, like advertising law.

Doris Domoszlai-Lantner　What legislation, if any, has been passed in the United States that applies specifically to digital fashion?

Julie Zerbo　Nothing to my knowledge, and frankly, that's not surprising to me, because if we think about it, there's not that much legislation that specifically targets physical fashion in the United States when it comes right down to it. You know, it's just not one of those things that is high up on the list of priorities for legislators.

　　When I was in law school, I was working for a lobbyist who was lobbying on behalf of a piece of legislation that would amend the Copyright Act to provide specific protection for fashion, and it just never passed. And there were revisions, but I don't get the sense that fashion is high up on the list of priorities. And I suspect that same notion is true, when it comes to the virtual world, when companies like FTX exist, and billions of dollars are in the mix. I don't foresee any specific legislation for digital fashion anytime soon, either. That's not to say that it won't be impacted by other legislation, but it's just not viewed as important enough of a thing to regulate, or legislate, compared to major money grabs, like Bored Ape Yacht Club NFTs.

Doris Domoszlai-Lantner　What legislation, if any, has been passed globally that applies specifically to digital fashion?

Julie Zerbo　I think practitioners in this space are looking to the United States and looking to cases that have been filed in the United States for guidance. I think the EU bloc has been among the more forward-thinking and forward-moving when it comes to thinking about IP and digital fashion. Countries in Asia, like China and Singapore, have had cases as well. There was one in Singapore, where the court said that NFTs, and the assets associated with those NFTs, can be treated by courts in the same way as physical property, and that legal remedies can be created for causes of action associated with those virtual goods in the same way as for physical goods.

A lot of these cases are kind of stepping stones, or building blocks towards some kind of understanding of what we're dealing with right now, and some of those involve really seemingly rudimentary questions, such as what is an NFT, and where does its value come from? What are we dealing in? And those questions are at the heart of a lot of these early lawsuits, and so while we might not have legislation, we are getting case law. Judges are making decisions that could be binding, and could set a precedent for future cases. Some of the big questions that we are asking right now are: does the use of someone's trademark in the virtual world, without their authorization, amount to infringement? And if so, what damages, or what remedies can we award?

Doris Domoszlai-Lantner   What cases are you following or watching that are either specifically about digital fashion or applications for the field of digital fashion?

Julie Zerbo   The *Hermès v. Mason Rothschild* is a big one. And that one is particularly interesting because it's asking, though not explicitly, how will existing real-world trademark rights apply to virtual fashion? It's not asking how they will apply specifically to NFTs, but more so how will brands, like Hermès, with very strong, real-world rights, translate or parlay those into the virtual world? And so that case is being closely watched, because it's expected to have implications for brands across industries, as well as for assets that are tied to NFTs, and ones that aren't.

Probably also there's the *Nike v. StockX* case, which Nike filed against StockX [the online fashion marketplace and reseller] for selling NFTs that are tied to physical sneakers. StockX has claimed that it should be shielded from liability because the NFT is really just acting like a receipt, or a claim ticket, for these physical goods that it can legally sell. This case is important because it is asking questions about what NFTs are, what person/people they serve, and what value they have; do they have value separately from the things, the assets, that they're tied to?

The other one that I'm closely watching is *Yuga Labs v. Ryder Ripps* [see note 2]. Like the *Hermès v. Mason Rothschild* case, Yuga Labs is also about NFTs. Yuga Labs, the creator of the popular Bored Ape Yacht Club NFTs, sued Ryder Ripps for copying their Bored Apes and in this case, the digital assets are essentially the same because they are not creating new Bored Apes. But they were creating distinct, new NFT codes, for the same assets, so I just think it's a technicality for which Ryder Ripps may be shielded from trademark infringement claims. The court seems stuck on the fact that he didn't create new assets per se—he just created new NFTs. So that's another case that will tell us just how courts are viewing and defining the NFT versus the underlying digital asset.

Doris Domoszlai-Lantner   Are there any digital fashion initiatives that you foresee having major legal consequences, positive or negative?

Julie Zerbo   When I think about the virtual world in the metaverse over the past year, and about Web3, I see that the interest is really fractionalized. There are people that are interested in NFTs, and that is a pretty small, pretty distinct group of people. There's much greater room for interest and adoption, I would argue, when it comes to virtual fashion that's not tied to NFTs, that is available on gaming platforms like *Roblox*. Given the sheer number of people that are using those platforms—millions, and tens of millions of people are using *Roblox* and *The Sims*—there's more room for potential legal conflict. On *The Sims*, third parties can create and sell virtual goods, called "custom" content, that may very well be infringing on existing trademarks, which to me opens up a massive can of worms that can create future legal conflict.

Doris Domoszlai-Lantner   It sounds like third-party vendors and their activity on gaming platforms are a major risk factor for potential legal trouble then, correct?

Julie Zerbo   I think so, yes, because companies like Roblox and Fortnite have engaged in legal collaborations and partnerships with brands, whether it be Gucci and Nike with Roblox, or Fortnite with Balenciaga. As soon as they start involving third parties that can make and sell whatever they want, it opens up the door for legal trouble. It's like Amazon allowing tens of thousands of third-party sellers to use their platform without enough oversight; in the end you're going to have a platform inundated with counterfeit goods.

And that also then raises questions about what the role of the platform owner is in policing these instances of infringement. Which frankly brings me back to something that I feel pretty strongly about when it comes to legal issues in Web3, with NFTs, and with virtual fashion, which is that the issues that we're seeing companies suing and fighting over are not divorced from what we're seeing in the real world. To a large extent companies are suing over the exact same things that they're suing over in the real world. They're suing over unauthorized uses of their trademarks. They're suing because they want to be able to control the mediums, and the ways in which their marks and their brand is used.

Doris Domoszlai-Lantner   What are the most surprising or biggest misunderstandings when it comes to law and digital fashion?

Julie Zerbo   You know, many people approach Web3, metaverse, and virtual fashion like it is some "Wild West," and that anything goes and you can kind of operate however you want because we don't know what's going on yet. There is some truth to that; however, I think that just looking at some of the laws that we talked about, there are already structures and guidelines in place, there are parameters. There are things, policy-wise and in terms of the black letter law [see note 3] that exist. And so it's not the "Wild West." You can't just take a famous trademark, like how many custom content creators are doing in *The Sims*, and make virtual goods using those marks. Just because we're in a different medium does not mean that the law does not apply. From what I've seen so far, the attitude towards the metaverse and virtual fashion has been to view it as a totally new realm, with people asking "What do we do?" and I find that to be a bit perplexing and a little bit of a cop-out. Unfortunately, I don't foresee that this phase of questioning and learning is going to be over anytime soon, given how slowly case law and legislation tend to progress. I do, however, think that there's merit to addressing the fact that we have a lot of questions and not remotely enough answers.

Editor's Notes

1 In March 2023, after this interview was conducted, the court reached a decision in the *Hermès v. Mason Rothschild* case. The jury in the New York federal court found Mason Rothschild (whose real name is Sonny Estival) liable for trademark infringement, brand dilution, and cybersquatting, awarding Hermès a total of $133,000 in damages. Mason Rothschild vowed to appeal the decision, and continued his operation, causing Hermès to file for a permanent injunction to bar him from promoting and selling his NFTs, which they won in June 2023. See "Hermès vs. Mason Rothschild: A Timeline of Developments in a Case Over Trademarks, NFTs," *The Fashion Law*, June 23, 2023, https://www.thefashionlaw.com/hermes-v-rothschild-a-timeline-of-developments-in-a-case/.

2 Ryder Ripps is an American conceptual artist who created RR/BAYC (Ryder Ripps /Bored Ape Yacht Club) in 2022 as an exercise in appropriation art. Making minor changes, if any, to the characters in the original BAYC, Ripps "re-minted" and sold them as RR/BAYC, which he asserts "recontextualized—illuminating truths about their origins and meanings as well as the nature of Web3—the power of NFTs to change meaning, establish provenance and evade censorship." His actions are a direct result of his research into the origins and meanings of the original BAYC. Through a combination of rather compelling visual and textual evidence that he has published on his website, www.gordongoner.com, Ripps makes the case that the BAYC is a racist project of the alt-right, featuring Nazi imagery, including the simianization (representation of a foreigner or minority as an ape) of Black people, people of color, and Jewish people, and of direct references to Adolf Hitler and Nazi organs. Interestingly enough, Ripps also claims that the Yuga Labs v. Ryder Ripps lawsuit should be

dismissed because he successfully refuted, in court, a Digital
Millennium Copyright Act (DMCA) notice in 2021 from Larva Labs,
the creator of the CryptoPunks line of NFTs, on the basis of his
argument that due to the unique nature of Blockchain, one cannot
copy an NFT. See "Bored Ape Yacht Club is Racist and Contains Nazi
Dog Whistles." https://gordongoner.com/. "RR/BAYC." https://rrbayc.
com/.

3   Black letter laws are established, generally well-known laws that are no
longer subject to undue scrutiny.

Part Two

Practices and Applications of Digital Fashion

4

Balmain x Barbie: A Fashion NFT Case Study

PETRA EGRI

Introduction

The collaboration between the luxury fashion brand Balmain and the toy brand Mattel is a striking example of the creativity and technological evolution of the fashion industry. Three exclusive NFT Barbies, dressed in Balmain couture, were up for bidding in an auction held on the MintNFT platform from January 11th to 14th, 2022. This auction raised fundamental questions of aesthetics and theory of image that were previously unknown.

Fashion and the Barbie universe have been mutually inspired since the doll's creation in the 1950s. NFT Barbie is a new step in the complex history of Barbie dolls, and the NFT fashion object (in a sense, an art object) operates in a particular epistemological manner. It is an image, a spectacle, that isn't necessarily based on an "original" art object or physical dress; nothing physical has to be reproduced in the digital image. The digital image is the spectacle and it is original; it exists just like a painting or dress presented at a physical fashion show.

The novelty of NFT existence can be understood by following Walter Benjamin's idea of aura and reproduction. In his famous essay "The Work of Art in the Age of Mechanical Reproduction," Benjamin suggests that in the age of reproducibility, the aura, the magic of the artwork, dissolves:

It might be stated as a general formula that the technology of reproduction detaches the reproduced object from the sphere of tradition. By replicating the work many times over, it substitutes a mass existence for a unique existence. And in permitting the reproduction to reach the recipient in his or her situation, it actualizes that which is reproduced.[1]

The reproduction-like image is the absolute original, so it must have some aura, even if it's a kind of perverse aura. So, the NFT is not a copy of a fashion spectacle but a new form of existence, through blockchain technology and the unique mode of ownership, and it creates an exclusive aura. The case study of the Balmain Barbie demonstrates the radical newness of the NFT object/ process. It erases the classical Marxist "use-value"[2] character of fashion objects, and it creates an impossible commodity based entirely on exchange value. It is an extra "spectacle" (in Guy Debord's sense), a kind of postmodern "super spectacle" that doubles the basic spectacle object. In our world, the increasingly influential metaverse that includes the NFT images indicates a new postmodern spectacle. "It is not a supplement to the real world, an additional decoration. It is the heart of the unrealism of the real society,"[3] in which the "fragmented views of reality regroup themselves into a new unity as a separate pseudo-world that can only be looked at."[4] It is unreality on the level where no material reality can be found in its background. And its modern/postmodern nature suggests an existence where "an evident degradation of being into having"[5] took place.

This chapter explores how the relationship between the famous American Barbie doll and fashion is changing in light of the Balmain–Mattel collaboration. I examine how people's relationship with fashion is being transformed by access to things like the Balmain clothes as NFTs.

Balmain x Barbie in the Digital World

It seems that the fashion house Balmain (and the luxury fashion industry itself in general), precisely because of people's vanity and desire for possession (which has always driven the fashion industry and pushed the consumption of objects to the top), did not doubt the profitability of the NFT business when it collaborated with Mattel to create a Barbie collection that could be bought as NFTs. The few real ready-to-wear garments released separately as part of the collaboration did not have the glamour and visual appeal in the real world that the three collections offered as NFTs did:

> Barbie fashion is getting a digital makeover with NFTs designed exclusively by French luxury brand Balmain. We're thrilled to introduce Barbie to the digital art world via NFTs, and these authentic pieces of collectible, digital fashion will be available by auction right here. All you have to do is bid! We're giving your closet a luxury digital upgrade. Our NFT auction features three unique Barbie and Ken avatars wearing exclusive pieces from the Balmain x Barbie collection. The highest bidders will win both the avatar and a physical, one-of-a-kind Barbie-scaled version of the outfit their avatar is wearing.[6]

From January 11th to 14th, 2022, the digital outfits Balmain x Barbie NFT1, Balmain x Barbie NFT2, and Balmain x Barbie NFT3—three different NFT Barbie styles—were up for bidding on the MintNFT.com auction site. Launching the special collection, a discussion was organized in the online space before the bidding, with Mattel's CEO and creative director of Balmain, Oliver Rousteing, discussing the inspiration behind the collaboration. Both the online discussion and the auction were subject to registration, limited to 5,000 registrants in the digital space. For both collaborating brands—luxury fashion house Balmain Paris and Mattel—this was the first digital series to be produced. The heads of both companies said the launch of NFTs was a historic moment for both the new Web3 technology and the fashion and toy industries. According to the Balmain brand representative, the future of NFTs will be a vital tool for fashion brands to drive strong customer engagement, as Txampi Diz notes: "I believe it is going to change the fashion industry completely, and it will have the same impact as when social media first started or when the internet first launched."[7]

The risk of losing materiality is a problem for both fashion and the traditional arts. Physical garments are objects whose materiality is by nature necessary and indispensable, since clothing's functional purpose is to cover the body and protect it from the forces of nature. At present, the digital suit cannot be worn by its wearer at IRL social events, nor can the mere projection of the material protect the body. Despite owning something, its "wearer" remains literally naked in the real world. The elimination of the materiality of matter thus has severe consequences in real social life. Moreover, when one chooses to buy the Balmain x Barbie NFT dress, one is also supporting the fashion house as well as the technological development of the fashion industry.

The Toy Universe Meets Luxury Fashion

From the point of fashion history, Mattel's first Barbie doll was unveiled to the public on March 9, 1959, at the American International Toy Fair in New York. The doll was designed by Ruth Handler, who named the dress-up doll "Barbie" after her daughter. Charlotte Johanson, a fashion designer at Mattel, designed Barbie's first dress.[8] In her comprehensive essay, Beauregard Houston-Montgomery notes that the development of the so-called "designer Barbies" was a surprisingly belated move on Mattel's part, despite the company's generally quick reaction to various fashion trends.[9] He explains that Americans were already fans of name brands in the 1970s. Still, it was not until 1984 that an Oscar de la Renta clothing collection for Barbie appeared seemingly out of nowhere.[10] According to fashion historians, Oscar de la Renta was one of the first designers to dress the legendary Barbie character in luxury fashion, almost twenty years after the debut of the famous and popular children's toy. Since then, of course, not only have the styles of Barbie's miniature toy clothes been inspired by contemporary fashion, but contemporary fashion has also thematized—sometimes even critiqued—the idealized world surrounding Barbie. Therefore, it seems that (luxury) fashion and the Barbie universe inspired and used each other from very early to build a brand image. Her "ideal body image" has been a boon for the fashion industry, and in 2022, the toy industry was set to be a significant beneficiary of the Balmain x Barbie NFT collection.

Juliette Peers' book chapter, "Not Only a Pretty Face: Towards the New Millennium with the Designer Doll," also points out that throughout history there has been a lively professional debate about whether Barbie *dictates* fashion or *follows* fashion.[11] Peers presents the Barbie universe as an arena in which key ideas and trends around art and haute couture are now accessible to the general public. In this sense, it is through Barbie's idealized body that (high) fashion, which for a long time was the privilege of only a few, could be "democratized" or, more precisely, made widely known. According to Peers, the widespread enthusiasm for haute couture and, at the same time, the assimilation of haute couture into the everyday female experience, created a de facto unity between French style and the booming American toy trade.[12] Mario Tosa also suggests that the reactive quality of Mattel's Barbie fashions makes the doll an unusually effective platform for communicating about fashion, processing knowledge hitherto closed to the general public.[13] Couture can thus be made meaningful through Barbie's body, which will have serious consequences for people's body ideals and norms. Since the late 1990s, Mattel's interest has shifted from Barbie's original function of "dressability" to the idealized representation of the body, leading to a change in the Barbie doll format, which also marked the end of the twentieth century, when the problem of the constructed, perfected, artificially "enhanced," modified, and prosthetic body began to peak.[14] Barbie was then already an example of the latest conceptions of the body, according to which the body (image) is not a fixed thing, but rather the (final) product of gradual modifications, and thus subject to a discursive, cultural reconstruction.[15] Thus, Mattel's ongoing transformation of Barbie's body (and its function) is nothing more than a direct expression of the trend to which many adults will be subjecting their bodies in the future, ranging from sport to plastic surgery. As Mary F. Rogers puts it in her book *Barbie Culture*:

> Culturally, Barbie is aligned with contemporary bodies shaped by consumer markets, fantastic desires, and new technologies of the flesh. She symbolizes how today's bodies defy boundaries once deemed constants of nature. Barbie is thus an icon of an emergent, consumerist "somatics"—a technology of the body driven by the idea that our bodies can be whatever we like if we devote enough money and attention to them. This development makes the body an aerobic instrument, a surgical object, a dietary experiment, a fleshy clay capable of endless remolding.[16]

With *Superstar Barbie*, a false norm was created that Juliette Peers says has remained relevant ever since. In her study, she vividly describes how, as the years went by, this once seemingly healthy, athletic-looking doll began to wear increasingly strange, exaggerated, and unnatural make-up. It is this embodied and distorted body image that many criticize. Mattel, as a manufacturer, was of course forced to respond to these criticisms in the interests of marketability and to present an intermediate position in which Barbie remains who she is known to be, while still adapting a little to the criticisms leveled at her. This is why we will see the emergence of Barbies with different physical characteristics and of different races.[17]

Barbie enters the world of digital art dressed in Balmain. The NFT1 avatar that was up for bid wears a striped sweater dress with a cut-out shoulder and holds a pink maxi bag with the Balmain monogram and the Balmain x Barbie logo. The NFT2 avatar shows a puffy dress with maxi bow detail in pink silk satin. While NFT3 is a Ken avatar in a white cotton T-shirt with pink trim and a vest blazer, a long-collar jacket paired with loose pleated trousers (all in pink satin crepe), and a logo baseball cap to complete the digital set. Barbie maker Mattel has since collaborated with Gucci on a Hot Wheels NFT, but the brand's CEO says Barbie x Balmain could be a more profound and more fruitful partnership for the luxury fashion brand, one that could also boost the global toy company's future NFT plans. The Balmain x Barbie collaboration is "incredibly meaningful and powerful as we effectively roll out our NFT strategy across Mattel. It's part of our business and staying relevant,"[18] said Mattel President and Chief Operating Officer, Richard Dickson. Undoubtedly, the digital transformation has affected computer games, so big brands like Mattel must compete with online video games. Indeed, this was particularly true in the Covid-19 period, when the virtual world of video games was almost the only recreational and free-time option for a generation. The use of the digital universe was a counterpoint to otherwise limited or banned physical social events.

There is also no doubt that NFT partnerships are redefining the meaning of brand ownership for customers, as it "symbolizes a purchase into the company's ethos,"[19] and the amazing thing is that they are not just buying an NFT. They are saying, "I want to be part of this brand on the blockchain."[20] In this sense, buying an NFT is also an important symbol of brand loyalty and commitment.

Over the decades, Mattel has also (re)used references from the fashion industry and has presented its designers as characters from the Barbie universe in its product range. Their Karl Lagerfeld Barbie, which launched in 2014, was almost immediately snapped up by collectors and fans and is being offered for sale on eBay for as much as $7,275;[21] in this sense the Barbie figure as an iconic object becomes a collectible object of value. The famous Barbie doll, besides being a muse and decorative object for countless fashion brands, has also attracted strong criticism from some designers, notably by Maison Martin Margiela and Tim Walker. As Juliette Peers notes, the link between the Barbie brand and the consumption of fashion products was thus particularly close.[22] As in the case of the Balmain x Barbie NFT collection, the aesthetics of the clothes[23] also echo the Balmain logo and the Barbie brand name, even though counterfeiting in the world of digital fashion is currently a problem that seems impossible to solve with intent. In addition, the great advantage of NFTs is that, because of digital rights management, the artist's profitability does not automatically cease once the original work has been sold. A digital copy can be resold any number of times, and the artist always receives a commission on sales, so if someone buys a work of art and resells it, the artists benefit from that too.

Digital Barbie and Luxury Fashion on her Digital Body

Whether the plastic Barbie's clothes can function in real life is questionable (Juliette Peers' example is a layer of tulle under an office uniform), they can act as a provocative gesture to unpack new ways of thinking about clothes.[24] A little later in her book, Peers adds that "possibly future fashion historians will cherish both ends of the Barbie market—the named designer tie-ins and the pink box Barbies—as more accurate documentations of dress in the early-twenty-first century."[25] Fashion historian Valerie Steele, in her foreword to David Levinthal's book on Barbie (titled after Barbie's full name in a fictional world: *Barbara Millicent Roberts*), suggests that the way modern Barbies function as toys tends to undermine the documentary overview of the fashion style.[26] Barbie's digital version, created in collaboration with the house of Balmain, becomes, as an NFT, a collectible artifact. In the digital space, the 3D graphics that are possible with the use of modern technology would not be imaginable in real physical space. In real life, however, the toy Barbie has always been a collectible artifact (in the case of a limited number of special editions). Linked to the world of NFTs, whose very essence is the experience of "collecting" and possession, Barbie is a collectible artifact that represents and embodies other collectible (art) objects worn on its person.

In the metaverse, Barbie's digital body is already a collector of digital luxury fashion, but Barbie's body and the clothes she wears cannot be exhibited as an object in real life—we know that in specific eras, dolls were a significant decoration of the interiors of homes for adult people—and since her digital body exists only in a simulated space, it cannot be a factual basis for comparison for people. The avatar, however, holds the promise of a plastic body and a body image shaped by technology. It is a ghost that, in Derrida's terms, *returns*, and "one cannot control its comings and goings because it begins by coming back"[27] as a new (digital) ghost of capitalism that no longer assigns either materiality or tangibility to the amount spent on commodities. The nature of the commodity fetish in the Marxian sense persists but is radically transformed. The exchange value remains. Still, the use value, the materiality, and the reality of the thing sold disappear and become ghostly: the digital clothes bought cannot be worn by people in the physical world. The question is, of course, how this will change as technology develops and the possibilities of the digital universe expand. In any case, the production of NFTs is currently quite polluting. The data produced on the blockchain and then distributed on digital platforms uses large amounts of electricity, which in turn produces a lot of emissions. In an era when we think and debate about the environmental impact of fast fashion, it is essential to remember that fashion produced digitally and maintained in digital space has an ecological footprint, even if, in the real world, we don't have an exorbitant amount of clothes hanging in our wardrobes that we once bought but don't use.

The advantage of the digital Balmain Barbie is that it can create 3D works of art that would be impractical and unwearable in real life. Thus, Mattel's opening to the NFT market is likely to be a milestone in the same way that Oscar de La Renta was asked to design the first luxury dress for Barbie. In January 2022, the fashion press gave a favorable reception[28] to the new digital collection. Bids for the Balmain x Barbie auction were around $2,000. As *Highsnobiety*'s Tora Northman wryly puts it, "Sorry, kids—Balmain's version of the iconic toy isn't playing around."[29] This gesture transforms the famous children's toy into a collectible art treasure.

On January 10, 2022, the three partners—Mattel, Balmain, and MintNFT—held a project presentation to the public before the auction of the digital collection, which was later published on their YouTube channel.[30] It makes it clear that Mattel and Balmain started the project in the wake of the Covid-19 outbreak: "We were thinking about how we could bring fashion closer to people who currently can't leave their homes, in the wake of Covid-19,"[31] notes Shelby Powell, a marketing representative for Balmain. The conversation also reveals that collaboration was foreshadowed early on when, at the onset of the pandemic in 2020, a digital version of the famous Barbie herself sat as a "guest of honor" behind a digital display at a fashion show in which real models walked a physical runway, but whose audience was solely online.[32] The particular fashion show took place so that while the models were live in the showroom, the audience's digital bodies appeared on screens and were projected onto them. The small monitors were positioned in the same way and the same place as if the guests were "sitting" (everyone in their usual place) at a show with a physical presence.

This project presentation was also necessary because the joint Balmain–Mattel advertisement was likely to attract the attention of many. Still, in January 2022, knowledge of the metaverse and its mechanisms was less widespread than it is now. In addition, the collaboration debuted in the post-Covid-19 era, when most people in the world were no longer forced into quarantine, so physical fashion was once again in the spotlight. In response, Balmain launched a wearable, physical capsule collection version of fifty pieces on January 14, 2022, after the NFT auction ended.[33] Still, there has yet to be a record of Mattel releasing a Balmain Barbie specifically. Balmain's kind of "dual marketing" is not new among luxury brands, as fashion houses such as Prada, Gucci, or Louis Vuitton have already adopted a similar strategy of simultaneously launching an NFT collection (sold in the digital space) and real wearable pieces. At

Balmain, in addition to the usual luxury bags, there were T-shirts with logos, baseball caps, and evening suits completed by Swarovski stones. According to *Vogue*, prices for the physical pieces started at $295 and ranged up to $42,494. One of the vital fashion innovations and theoretical debates of the post-pandemic era will unfold around digital fashion.

The products of the Balmain x Mattel relationship, the objects of my case study, go beyond the realm of digital fashion. Here, the digital is presented through the medium of NFT, and therefore a complex, far-reaching direction in fashion theory is taking shape. This significant experiment, Barbie's recreation on the NFT interface, presents a radically new visual representation and creation. Its radical characteristic is the absence of materiality, the material (blockchain-based) existence of the spectacle, and a new form of buying and owning fashion objects. The NFT creates a unique aura of the image object, an example of the birth of a postmodern spectacle.

Notes

1   Walter Benjamin, "The Work of Art in the Age of Mechanical Reproduction," in *Selected Writings 1935–38, vol. 3*, ed. Howard Eiland (Cambridge, MA: Belknap Press of Harvard University, 2006), 104.

2   Karl Marx, *Contribution to the Critique of Political Economy* (Moscow: Progress Publishers, 1977).

3   Guy Debord, *The Society of the Spectacle*, trans. Ken Knabb (London: Rebel Press, 1994), 7.

4   Debord, *The Society of the Spectacle*, 7–8.

5   Debord, *The Society of the Spectacle*, 10–11.

6   For a description of the collaboration and to purchase NFT Barbie x Balmain avatars, see https://nft.mattelcreations.com.

7   Tanya Klich, "How Balmain and Barbie are Defining the Future of NFTs for Fashion, Tech, and Toys," *Forbes*, January 12, 2022, https://www.forbes.com/sites/tanyaklich/2022/01/12/balmain-barbie-and-the-future-of-nfts-for-fashion-tech-and-toys/.

8   Juliette Peers, *The Fashion Doll: From Bébé Jameau to Barbie* (Oxford: Berg, 2004), 172.

9   Beauregard Houston-Montgomery, *Designer Fashion Dolls* (Grantsville, MD: Hobby House Press, 1999), 86.

10 Houston-Montgomery, *Designer Fashion Dolls*, 86.

11 Peers, *The Fashion Doll*, 175.

12 Peers, *The Fashion Doll*, 186.

13 Mario Tosa, *Barbie: Four Decades of Fashion, Fantasy and Fun* (New York: Abrams, 1998).

14 Peers, *The Fashion Doll*, 185.

15 Peers, *The Fashion Doll*, 185.

16 Mary F. Rogers, *Barbie Culture* (London: Sage Publications, 1999), 112.

17 For a critique of its main tendencies, see Jeannie Banks Thomas, *Naked Barbies, Warrior Joes and Other Forms of Visible Gender* (Urbana: University of Illinois Press, 2003).

18 Klich, "How Balmain and Barbie are Defining the Future."

19 Klich, "How Balmain and Barbie are Defining the Future."

20 Klich, "How Balmain and Barbie are Defining the Future."

21 Klich, "How Balmain and Barbie are Defining the Future."

22 Peers, *The Fashion Doll*, 181.

23 The visuality of the clothes designed by Oliver Rousting also reflects the historicity of the clothes that appeared on Barbie in different eras.

24 Peers, *The Fashion Doll*, 180.

25 Peers, *The Fashion Doll*, 189.

26 Valerie Steele, preface to *Barbara Millicent Roberts: An Original*, by David Levinthal (New York: Pantheon Books, 1998), 8.

27 Jacques Derrida, *Specters of Marx, The State of the Debt, the Work of Mourning and the New International*, trans. Peggy Kamuf (New York: Routledge, 1994), 11.

28 Sarah Spellings, "Now You Can Dress Like a Barbie in Balmain," *Vogue*, January 5, 2022, https://www.vogue.com/article/barbie-balmain-collaboration.

29 Tora Northman, "Balmain, Barbie & the Blockchain," *Highsnobiety*, https://www.highsnobiety.com/p/balmain-barbie-collection-nft/.

30 "Project Showcase: MintNFT—Barbie x Balmain," January 10, 2022, https://www.youtube.com/watch?v=ELhuUaZFcpw.

31 "Project Showcase: MintNFT—Barbie x Balmain."

32 Sarah Maisey, "Catwalks to computer screens: Has the pandemic brought about the end of the traditional fashion show?" *National News*, https://www.thenationalnews.com/lifestyle/catwalks-to-computer-screens-has-the-pandemic-brought-about-the-end-of-the-traditional-fashion-show-1.1008542.

33 "Balmain x Barbie," Balmain, https://us.balmain.com/en/experience/balmain-x-barbie.

5

Street to Digital: The Evolution of Sneaker Culture

MINDY MEISSEN

Introduction: The History of Sneaker Culture

The story of sneakers comes from culture born of cities and of *en plein air*—events and activities that play out in the open street, from city basketball courts to hip-hop concerts, break dancing exposés, sprayed lines of painted-on graffiti, and skate decks hitting wheels against city curbs and handrails. It is creative, made for impromptu moments yet meticulously practiced; it is a calling born of neighborhood community, amateur and professionalized sport, and celebrity. The formative period in which sneaker culture went online—and when sneaker design and production became increasingly informed by computing and digital tools—marks an especially nascent time, in which grassroots enthusiasm, creativity, and commerce exploded into a $72.7 billion industry[1] with an estimated $10 billion secondary market derived from resale.[2] Current "digital" aspects of sneaker culture—drops, botting, online communities, software design tools, NFTs—would not exist today without emergent online sneaker communities of the 1990s–2000s.

Today, sneaker culture still resonates around familiar origin points: the 1970s convergence of hip-hop, NYC streetball, and athlete endorsements ushered in a golden era of commercialization that fueled enthusiasm for sneaker collecting, especially around neighborhoods in New York City. As Bobbito Garcia, self-described sneaker-addict, historian, filmmaker, and radio host described it:

> [T]he mid 70s saw the burgeoning evolution of hip-hop culture, and the look changed from being rugged to being fly. Cats were rocking knit polyester mock necks with pleated and stitched AJs [dress pants], and the attending sneaker style became clean. "Fresh out the box" was the preferred look.[3]

Media spread the mystique. Before sneaker communities connected to like-minded fans by typing, uploading images, and clicking "send," internet sneaker culture had precedent in mixtapes, streetball VHS recordings, the WKCR college radio show known as *89tec9*, TV spots, and marketing posters. Basketball shoes were about to reach a peak popularity never before witnessed with the release of Michael Jordan's signature Air Jordan I in 1986. In 1985, Nike's Air Force 1 was rereleased (after its original release in 1982 to little fanfare) in three Baltimore shops—Charley Rudo Sports, Cinderella Shoes and Downtown Locker Room—which sold out of 3,000 pairs within days.[4] Harold Rudo, owner of Charley Rudo, recalled, "We had people coming from New York, Washington, D.C. They were coming from all over Pennsylvania. They knew we had 'em, and they'd all come running to Baltimore to buy them from us."[5]

In basketball, nowhere connected style and sneakers as pointedly as New York City, where at the beginning of the sport's adoption in 1910, seventy-five out of ninety-two of the city's public schools had outdoor basketball hoops.[6] The popularity of pickup games during the 1970s took place across hundreds of outdoor basketball courts throughout the city. Bobbito Garcia expressed the difference between 1986–7 and now: "[I]t was such an unheralded time. You maybe had a new model come out once a year and a different color here and there . . . Only the best players got the free colors . . . If you wanted green and chocolate brown you had to be on the team that had those colors."[7]

Streetball legends of the Rucker Park Tournament in Harlem, NYC loom large in the history of basketball, hip-hop, style, and sneakers. Renowned streetball player Richard "Pee Wee" Kirkland wrote of the culture of playground basketball, "All the best moves of tomorrow are being invented today by some unknown kid in Philly, Chicago, Atlanta or you name it. Razzle and dazzle, creation and devastation—these are what the street brings to the game."[8] And so it was with sartorial choices players brought to the courts. Sonny Vaccaro, who worked with Nike from 1973 spotting and recruiting young basketball talent, supplied players with free Nike shoes and gear, associating the brand with the best players.[9]

In the early 1990s, on a pitch assignment based on Phil Knight's directive that Nike was losing relevance on the streets of New York, Weiden + Kennedy creative director John C. Jay quickly assembled a "SWAT team" that scoured the streets of NYC, reaching out to basketball communities to find a way to tell their stories, making connections to streetballers with cultural fidelity and authenticity. In November 1993, Dave Perez, a director hired by Weiden + Kennedy met Bobbito Garcia at Garcia's apartment for a research interview:

> I was breaking it down to them: talking about the Nike Blazer's sole, which pairs were made in Taiwan, and I had the Nike Franchises right there to show them ... "This kid knows his shit. He knows more info, than, like, a 'PLM ' stands for product line manager."[10]

A recording of Garcia[11] speaking in the initial interview went into Nike's "City Attack" campaign—a campaign that spoke to NYC ball players through TV spots featuring voiceovers from people in the streetball community, borough-specific billboards, and NYC subway posters. Jay described the term "City Attack" as:

> ...our term of endearment for being relentless on authenticity, for getting deep in local culture, to never be superficial in our expression of the social history, to find ways to support the neighborhood and to inspire the next generation while paying respect for those who paved the way. If a lot of advertising is self-reverential, City Attack would always be about earning the respect of the audience. Authenticity was the cost of entry.[12]

Jeff Staple, founder of streetwear brand STAPLE, told Jay that during his student days at NYU he was "floored" by the campaign and would descend into the NYC subways at 3 am to steal the campaign posters.[13]

Figure 5.1 *Michael Jordan in action.* Credit: Focus on Sport/Getty Images

Through this local network of creative talent and ballplayers, Nike once again won a reputation on NYC streets. By the early to mid-90s, streetball-specific shoes were released by adidas and Reebok.[14] With the Air Jordan and the success of its campaigns featuring Michael Jordan and Spike Lee, Nike was poised to continue dominating basketball shoe sales. This was the time that sneaker culture was ready to come online.

For sneaker enthusiasts in the mid- to late 1990s, early websites and forums initially accessed via dial-up internet connections opened a world of sneaker culture online. From 1992 to 1994, America Online was reported to have grown from less than 180,000 users to over one million.[15] Companies such as Compuserve, Prodigy, America Online, and Microsoft offered low-cost and free options for internet access, with AOL offering free diskettes, and Microsoft Network included with every copy of Windows 95. As Kevin Driscoll notes in *The Modem World*, "Gradually, all of these platforms became on-ramps to the internet and the World Wide Web."[16]

With a personal computer, by the late '90s people could log on to a myriad of sites such as Jumpman St./Retrokid, Kazu's Faborte Nike + (Japan),

Shoetrends.com, Sneaker Nation, Swooshtown, The Place To Be Online, Vintage USA, Vintage Kicks, and others. The blog DeFY New York, run by Scott Frederick, chronicles many of these early sites alongside historical screenshots.[17] Sites were run by passionate fans looking to share their collections or buy, swap, and sell rare pairs. With basic HTML styling peppered with default blue HTML links, images, banner ads, page counters, and webrings, the sites had all the sparsely styled charm of the early web.

Prior to online sneaker culture, access to sneakers was limited—knowledge about which styles were dropping where was akin to specialized access shared through informal networks of friends, family, and connections. British DJ and sneaker collector Kish Kash remembers getting a pair of Reeboks "around 1982 on my first family trip to Winnipeg ... Sometimes I had access to the Nike catalog because friends worked at [a] sporting goods store ... Later on I scored a pair of Reebok Phase 2 runners on the early because of this relationship."[18] Sneakers scored in some far destination and when brought home gave the wearer an element of prestige: "I was in the States again when the Jordan IVs dropped in black ... When I brought them back, I wore them to London. I remember the feeling of people staring at me, turning their heads sideways and asking questions—where did you get those? What are those?"[19]

Salehe Bembury, a sneaker designer well-known for his work on Yeezy and (more recently) New Balance and Crocs, remembered growing up and having to know the local map to gain access to certain sneakers. Although a generation removed from Bobbito, he still remembers a kind of clandestine culture: "There were underground spots. Back when I was a kid, the appeal to being a part of the whole sneaker culture was that it had this secret society feel to it."[20] Fans often speak with reverence of times when sneakers were less known; when the territory was yet to be more fully mapped. "Right below 96th Sprint Sports. With the mom and pop stores, those were the secret spots because you could always get some kind of hookup, like getting things early, or maybe getting a couple more pairs than you needed ... You really had to do your research to find them, which was what made them cool."[21]

This sneaker underground was the paradigm under which the culture first came online in the mid- to late 1990s. In 1995, the size of the US athletic-shoe market was $6.5 billion, according to the *Wall Street Journal*.[22] After a decade of growth fueled by the popularity of basketball shoes, the industry's growth flattened in 1997–8 and continued to struggle until the second half of 2003.[23] With the success of limited releases, retro re-releases, and Nike's foray into skateboarding around the turn of the millennium, the industry rebounded, spurring unprecedented growth in sneaker sales. Yet advanced knowledge of rarefied pairs retained an element of scarcity even into the mid-2000s. Sneakers had to be sought out, catalogs closely scrutinized, relationships built, in order to gain access to sought-after pairs.

In 1996, the site Nike Park, founded by then-teenager Eric Brothers, gained popularity amongst sneaker fans logging on to the World Wide Web. Nike Park's homepage featured several subpages including "Shoe Reviews" sourced from reviewers identified by their email addresses; a list of "ALL Nike Factory Outlets and Nike Town Locations"; "The Brains of Nike"—a list of the company's corporate addresses; "Nike Footwear and Apparel Cleaning System"; "Nike-AIR Cushioning System"; "Nike Summarized Student Research Packet"; a "Nike PaRk Guestbook"; and of course, a disclaimer in the footer that:

I DON' T WORK FOR NIKE
Do not copy ANY Images without permission or else.[24]

After listing site updates, the shoe models Brothers owned at the time—"Air Adjust Force (black & white), the Nike Zoom Flights, the Air Pro Flight Max, and the Air Grill"—and Brothers' UIN Number for ICQ (943536), a link to the "Nike Park Picture Archive" beckoned from below images of the Nike swoosh logo and a "JUST DO IT" graphic. In July 1997, the Nike Park archive featured forty-eight links. Most navigated to images of sneaker models, while others included links to an image of "Phil Knight," "A swoosh and a mouth," and one link leading to plain text that detailed a "Way to clean Nike Shoes."[25] By April 1999, the Nike Park Picture Archive had grown to over 500 images, including scans from the Eastbay catalog *SLAM* and Japanese magazine *Boon*.[26] The image credits, listed as "courtesy of . . ." also serve as a rolodex to other sneaker sites of the time: Al Bundy Society, Footaction, Nike Domain, Nike Playaz Online, Shoetrends, and more.

The legacy of Nike Park endured through the site's message board. The board was live as early as October 1997, utilizing a system from InsideTheWeb[27] that granted basic HTML threading and allowed for posting and replying to messages. Much of the conversations on Nike Park revolved around sharing rare pairs. A post from April 29, 1999 linked to a Japanese site displaying photos of a rare Air Jordan XI Lo sales sample, complete with an image of the shoe's sewn-in tag on the inside tongue, marked "Made in Taiwan ... Sales Sample F96."[28] The same site had photos of the 1985 Nike Dunk High Michigan, a sneaker made in Michigan University's bright yellow and navy blue. In 2023, the Michigan Dunk is listed on eBay and Grailed for anywhere between US$1,000 and US $8,000.[29] Some Nike Park posts discussed whether specific stores had certain styles; what styles were available in North America vs. Europe; while others shared product details—for instance, debating whether Nike's "tensile air" or "Zoom air" technology was in the Air Jordan XI;[30] others requested particular shoe models to buy. Some needed to sell, such as user Phillie:

> I have a pair of purple flightposites that I must sell because I need money for my prom which is on May 26th. They are deadstock, new in box in size 11. These sneakers are going to be worth a lot of money in the near future because they did not make many of these sneakers and the zipper part is different then [sic] any other flightposite.[31]

Others would post to schedule an online chat elsewhere: "chat at hypesite or phils if it isnt workin. now or at 9est ..."[32]

These early network dynamics—forming communities, trading online, creating visual representations of sneakers—remain central to sneaker culture today. Buying and selling via early online hubs laid the foundation for today's

QR Code 1 *Nike Park homepage, July 7, 1997, accessed via the Wayback Machine.*

QR Code 2 *The 1985 Nike Dunk High Michigan. May 1, 1999, accessed via the Wayback Machine.*

networked dynamics, in which sneakers are traded across commercial resale platforms and informal connections on forums, social media, and email. Several Nike Park posts linked directly to eBay listings. Founded in 1995 in San Jose, CA by Iranian-American entrepreneur Pierre Omidyar, eBay was seminal in the history of online sneaker culture. The site became a premiere hub for online trading in all manner of hyped collectibles, including vintage watches, trading cards, and, of course, Beanie Babies. In a 1999 article for *Wired*, William Gibson wrote of his experience collecting vintage watches on eBay, calling the site "a swap meet in cyberspace."[33] He wrote that the boomer generation participated in an "ongoing democratization of connoisseurship, in which curatorial privilege is available at every level of society."[34] Gibson saw eBay as an uber-conduit of his generation's penchant for collecting: "the main driving force in the tidying of the world's attic, the drying up of random, 'innocent' sources of rarities, is information technology. We are mapping literally everything, from the human genome to Jaeger two-register chronographs, and our search engines grind increasingly fine."[35]

In 1999, sneakers lacked their own category on eBay, although several listings (with active bids) for styles such as the Nike Air Max and Air Jordan were nested beneath "Miscellaneous > Sporting Goods > Basketball." By 2003–6, sneaker sellers had their own eBay stores: SHOEBACCA, which advertised "the best shoes in the galaxy,"[36] promising "SLAM DUNK SHOES AT LAY-UP PRICES";[37] and Sneaker Shack, specializing in "adidas Originals and other hard to find or rare adidas gear."[38] By around 2006, eBay had introduced "User Guides" written by members, and several appeared for sneakers including "How to buy Air Jordan shoes on eBay!," "The Guide to Buying Authentic Air Jordans," and "Top Selling Basketball Shoes—2005 Best Selling Shoes."[39] Although the number of sneakers for sale was small

QR Code 3 *A rare Air Jordan XI Lo sales sample, accessed via the Wayback Machine.*

by today's standards, sneaker resale appears to have been with eBay from the beginning. The search term "nike" under category "Men's Shoes" yielded 18,047 results in 2006.[40] Today the same search returns over 1.4 million results. William Gibson, chronicling his participation in eBay's collector culture, offered the enigmatic observation, "There's a sense of taking part in an evolving system, here. I suspect that eBay is evolving in much the way the Net did."[41]

The Nike Park message board lacked formal moderation and was increasingly plagued by trolling, profanity, and offensive comments. By 2000, Brothers was moving on, and Nike Park shut down on August 30, 2000. In a farewell letter that professed "as you can tell, now-a-days, information is scarce," Brothers thanked those who had helped steer the site and whom he'd befriended over the years, "Signing off for the final time as the Nike Park webmaster for over 4 years, Eric Brothers."[42]

Many of Nike Park's brethren had already moved over to a new forum called NikeTalk, founded by Nelson Cabral as an alternative to Nike Park in 1999. NikeTalk became the central internet gathering hub for sneaker and streetwear fans of all types—with an internet connection and a profile, one could join a kind of reality hive that elevated sneakers to new heights of connoisseurship and allure. Will Hardison (NT user mclilbit), who joined NikeTalk as a teenager from his bedroom in Indianapolis, told a story of flipping his first pair of sneakers at fifteen years old on the *Sneaker History* podcast:

> One evening I'm in a chat room called Hype Site.
>
> Chat ran by . . . this dude was in there just talking about all these samples that he owned and all these player exclusives . . . I was like, "this guy's crazy.

Like, there's no way he has this stuff." I'm talking like Tim Duncan player
samples, you know. Jordan samples, like, look-see colorways … no one's
ever even heard of all this stuff.[43]

Yet indeed this dude did have the stuff. And in this case, the stuff was a pair of
rare Air Jordan Retro V white and silver samples, procured because Andy
Chang (who had the samples) rented a basement room from one of the
directors of Nike basketball, who reportedly would bring home "duffel bags"
full of samples. After negotiating to borrow funds from his dad, Hardison
bought the rare AJ Vs for $250 and almost immediately secured a buyer,
Hiroshi, who agreed to buy the pair for $750 + $30 shipping to Japan. The
transaction was proffered through a complicated sequence of sending money
orders, photographing the shoes on disposable camera, bike riding to and from
CVS to develop and scan the photos to 3.5-inch floppy disk, and uploading
them from a Gateway PC at dial-up speeds (Hardison estimates the upload
took around six hours).[44] A new supplier secured, Hardison went on to procure
more rare samples from Chang for around $100, selling around "90%" of them
to Hiroshi for $1,200–$1,500 each.

It is, perhaps, a Sisyphean task to characterize the depth of influence
NikeTalk has had on sneaker and streetwear culture. In the same vein as early
BBS (bulletin board system) pioneers, NikeTalk had a passionate, engaged user
base that was highly educated on the nuances of sneakers, resale, and collecting.
A new wave of connoisseurship was established on the NT boards, one that
had real access to samples, player exclusives, rare pairs, and that traded in
specific terminology, acronyms, shorthands, and a shared language of sneaker
culture. Acronyms such as PE (player exclusive), NDC (Niketown.com), OBO
(or best offer), WTB (want to buy), WDYWT (what did you wear today), and
ekin (Nike employees responsible for storytelling, educating, and spreading
awareness of the brand, products, and technology)[45] were fired off all over the
boards.[46] By late 2002, the site had 18,417 users;[47] however, Bobby Hundreds
estimates that "there couldn't be more than a few thousand of us in the world
who were truly dedicated NikeTalk users."[48] In 2012, *Complex* posted "The 30
Most Influential Niketalk Members of All Time,"[49] which, of course, garnered
twenty-seven pages of discussion on NikeTalk.[50] The post ended on a final

word from user b20 eg8: "Am I the only one that's happy that NT was actually given some credit for something? I constantly see us looked over and not mentioned even though everyone knows where **** comes from first . . . I'm proud to be a part of this board, even more so since it hasn't soled out like everyone else."[51] Scores of sneaker designers, product managers, stock associates, entrepreneurs, boutique founders, and countless others frequented the pages of NikeTalk, making connections, and, for many, getting their start in the industry.

NikeTalk was a direct line to underground and grey market resale. NTers such as jerseyjoe and air ewayz ran independent businesses that didn't carry traditional stock, instead selling one-offs or specific models received through connections to stores and/or well-placed individuals. In 2002, air ewayz, a.k.a. sixteen-year-old Eric Eways, was the subject of a *Wall Street Journal* article that profiled sneakerpimp.com, Eways's resale business with co-founder Joe Guerrero. The two had reportedly sold over 1,500 pairs the previous year, and, through relationships that spanned Canarsie, Brooklyn, Toronto, Hong Kong, London, and Paris, were able to quietly secure access to rare Nike models. Sneakerpimp.com had recently acquired 100 pairs of the Nike "Supreme Dunks," which in 2023 were listed at Sotheby's for US$5,200 and as high as US$11,249 on StockX.[52] NTers were concerned over the mainstream attention, particularly with Nike's potential ability to curb the resale market by imposing quantity restrictions for customer purchases or exerting pressure on store owners and account managers. NTer jerseyjoe posted a warning on August 22, 2002, and over 100 posts of thoughtful conversation ensued.[53] Despite any perceived concern from the industry, flipping, swapping, and grey market trade continued. Derek Curry, founder of Sneaker Politics in Lafayette, LA, recalled purchasing the entire stock of a mistaken shipment of Halloween patent Air Force 1s during his time working the stockroom at Finish Line: "[I] convinced the manager to sell me all pairs and I was trying to hustle them on NikeTalk, where this guy hits me up and he's like, 'Dude how did you get these? I want them so bad. I work at a sneaker store in Boston and we're not getting those. Is there anything I can do? Trade you, buy them, whatever.'"[54] When the two set up a call, the person on the line was Deon Point, founder of Concepts in Cambridge, MA.

Figure 5.2 *NikeTalk, October 3, 2008, accessed via the WayBack Machine.*

NikeTalk brought communities together, and the enthusiasm wouldn't hold within the bounds of the forum's message boards alone. In the early 2000s, one site maintained a singular presence for its voice, independent reviews, and inside access, exploring the confluence of sneaker performance, design, and production—so much so that, nearly twenty years after its closing, fans still reminisce about the site, sharing archived pages online. The site was *Kicksology*—parked at kicksology.net—founded by Ernest Kim in 2000. Kim recalls that the site was "purely just a passion project. Just something I did for fun."[55] And, he adds, "partly just as an excuse to buy more shoes, because I did have this inexplicable fascination with sneakers, particularly basketball shoes."[56] Kim adopted the moniker Professor K and wrote, designed, and photographed sneakers for the site, eventually bringing on guest contributors—one of whom was Alex Wang, a.k.a. RetroKid, known for his sites JumpanSt./retrokid.com and NikeTalk presence. Kicksology's sneaker photos, shot at dynamic angles, their silhouettes breaking the image frame, were photographed in Kim's bathroom (where lighting was best) using foam core, and afterwards required laborious Photoshop to mask out the background: "[T]hese little cameras were not very good, and I didn't have any kind of photo studio, but I just tried as much as I could to really ... 'honor' is sort of a big word, but to honor the products, and help people see them the way I saw them."[57] Kicksology gained a loyal following. Eventually a PR rep from adidas connected Kim to the company's designers, and Kim began receiving shoes to review. Designers from Nike reached out directly to Kim, and he recalled being invited to the North American Auto Show by D'Wayne Edwards, then head of design for Air Jordan.

Kicksology's interviews were in-depth and offered an inside look into the creation of sneakers, touching upon craft, creativity, and engineering. The interviews revealed sneakers as both revered objects and as a spectrum of collaborative achievement involving problem-solving, design, and collaboration. Prof. K's 2003 interview on the making of Nike's Air Ultraposite included in-depth commentary from Jeff Johnson, then Product Creation Director of Nike Basketball, and Aaron Cooper, Creative Director for Nike Basketball. The interview unveiled the decisions that went into developing the Ultraposite: technology, prototyping, and, ultimately, manufacturing at scale. Details included innovations in materials with Daewoo Synthetic leathers, size grading using 3D modeling, and the process of making molds—the first of which was solid steel, weighed over 100 lbs, and cost "three quarters of a million dollars."[58] In addition to publishing over 150 reviews, Kim interviewed Wilson Smith, now legendary Nike designer known for his work on countless sneakers; Natalie Calandrian, adidas footwear designer; and more. Kim remained an active NikeTalk user while running *Kicksology*:

> We were all learning as a community, and that was what was so great about it. There was no way that any one person could amass that much knowledge on their own. So to have this place where you can share these stories and get these insights was fantastic, and then that would absolutely inform things I would write in *Kicksology* ... to be able to get access to some of the history that I wouldn't have known myself because of folks who were immersed in the culture longer than I was.[59]

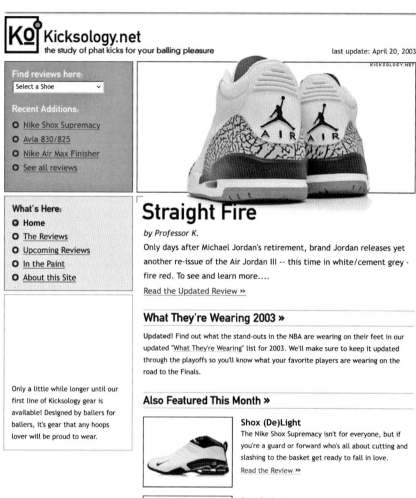

Straight Fire

by Professor K.

Only days after Michael Jordan's retirement, brand Jordan releases yet another re-issue of the Air Jordan III -- this time in white/cement grey - fire red. To see and learn more....

Read the Updated Review »

What They're Wearing 2003 »

Updated! Find out what the stand-outs in the NBA are wearing on their feet in our updated "What They're Wearing" list for 2003. We'll make sure to keep it updated through the playoffs so you'll know what your favorite players are wearing on the road to the Finals.

Also Featured This Month »

Shox (De)Light
The Nike Shox Supremacy isn't for everyone, but if you're a guard or forward who's all about cutting and slashing to the basket get ready to fall in love.
Read the Review »

Revelations
Though the Avia 830 is an old-school shoe, it provides performance that bests much of its more expensive new-school competition.
Read the Review »

Rhapsody in Blue
For those who've been waiting for the colorway of the Air Jordan XVIII that MJ has worn for much of this season, your wait is over. To learn more...
Read the Updated Review »

Kicksology.net
the study of phat kicks for your balling pleasure

last update: April 20, 2003

KICKSOLOGY.NET

Find reviews here:
Select a Shoe

Recent Additions:
- Nike Shox Supremacy
- Avia 830/825
- Nike Air Max Finisher
- See all reviews

What's Here:
- Home
- The Reviews
- Upcoming Reviews
- In the Paint
- About this Site

Only a little while longer until our first line of Kicksology gear is available! Designed by ballers for ballers, it's gear that any hoops lover will be proud to wear.

Figure 5.3 Kicksology, *April 20, 2003, accessed via the Wayback Machine.*

On September 12, 2004, *Kicksology* shut down with a farewell Q&A between Prof. K and "Imaginary Person," explaining:

> It's simple dawg—I'm tired. I've been running Kicksology.net on the side for four years now and it's taken a lot out of me ... I want to be able to read books and listen to music again. But, most of all, I want to be able to hang with my wife again ... I don't like the looks she's been giving the checkout guy at Safeway."[60]

When the site closed, it was receiving 750,000 visitors per month.[61] Kim began working at *Sole Collector*, and after three to four years writing in-depth coverage moved on to Nike as a product manager. *Kicksology* endures in its fans, and although Kim says it feels "like a former life," he remembers those days fondly:

> I think that's something you saw in the early days of sneaker culture, too, where the intent of the makers came through in the product. Like Jordans, you felt that there was something there that was beyond. And that's, I think, what attracted a lot of people to those products—that they were better than they needed to be ... And there was a spirit of something there ... the fingerprints of the makers that came through.[62]

In his farewell note, Prof. K made a call to readers, writing, "I wholeheartedly encourage fans of Ko to start similar sites of their own. The reason I started Kicksology.net was to help ballers find the right shoe for their needs and their game, and there's definitely still a need for that ... it's always a good thing to have a multiplicity of voices."[63] By the passing of Y2K, formalized commercial sneaker media appeared alongside fansites, including crookedtongues.com (2000), a site/print magazine; Instylshoes.com (1999), the online home of *Sole Collector* that would launch ISS, a rival forum to NikeTalk in 2005; and the magazine *Sneaker Freaker* (2002). At the same time, specialty sneaker boutiques were opening globally, including Alife (1999) and Nort (2001) in NYC; atmos (2000) in Tokyo; Footpatrol (2002) and Opium (2001) in Paris; Sneakersnstuff in Stockholm (1999); Solebox in Berlin (2002); and Undefeated (2001) in Los Angeles.

Yu-Ming Wu, founder of *Sneaker News* (2006) and SneakerCon (2009), described his reason for founding *Freshness Mag* in 2003: "My hunger for news

So we were inspired a lot by what was happening on the Air Jordan XVIII game shoe, and Michael's influence about clean-ness and simplicity.

figure 3. Smith explains the function of the removable midfoot strap on a finished version of the Jumpman Team FBI. On the screen behind him are production sketches of the shoe in a few of its released colorways.

Prof. K: You had mentioned that the design for the FBI came really fast...
Wilson: Yes it did, it did come really fast.

[Tate Kuerbis walks over]

Wilson to Tate [holding the FBI and pointing to the midfoot strap]: You did the early concept to the XVIII and then this was the midfoot strap that really made sense in terms of support. It just kind of came together like that.
Prof. K to Tate: He's giving you all the credit...
Tate: You have to take some credit Wilson!
Wilson: [Laughs] I know, I take credit, I did work on it.

[Tate Kuerbis gets pulled away]

Wilson: I like it a lot without the strap...it's real clean. To me, the dream is that you put the strap on to play...so that it performs. I think visually the strap is a lot cooler on the court, but then if you're just walking around you can take the strap off.

Prof. K: You had mentioned to me previously that you were in the

Figure 5.4 *Nike designer Wilson Smith,* Kicksology, *accessed via the Wayback Machine, July 11, 2003.*

figure 6a - f. The photos above show the Nike Air Ultraflight as it progressed from Cooper's initial 3d "sketch" to the final product available at retail (note the "green destiny" influence in Cooper's final sketch, second from the top). The amazing thing about it all is that the Ultraposite is not just a thing to look at, but a product that bends and flexes and that you can use and abuse out on a basketball court. And, best of all, the shoe backs up its stunning looks with equally stunning performance. It's truly a piece of performance art.

Figure 5.5 Kicksology, *accessed via the Wayback Machine, October 9, 2003.*

and information and the culture was insatiable, and as I just kind of dug around the web, I didn't see anything moving at the right speed. I wanted something that was updated daily, you know? … no one was really covering it on that daily level except NikeTalk."[64] At that time, sneaker sites relied on tips from local boutiques, friends employed at sneaker shops, and tips that came through NikeTalk or other connections. In the early 2000s, personal web pages and sites with frequent updates became known as weblogs, then blogs, and published outside the traditional purview of broadcast and print media. Sneaker blogs began posting photos and information that emphasized timeliness and breaking news—including international store directories, images of limited and rare sneakers, and more. This first step in making information widely available via the speed and access of the internet would remain central to "digital" aspects of sneaker culture. And the industry was in—it was reported in *WSJ* and on the boards of NT that Nike employees routinely read the site.[65] In the early days of *Hypebeast*, founder Kevin Ma recalled that "Eight months in, we had about 10,000 users per day. I became so passionate about building and improving that I left my full time job at a bank to focus on *Hypebeast*. There were difficulties at every turn—server crashes, trying to stay awake through late nights of work."[66]

Community Access

In the mid- to late 1990s, geography determined which sneakers were available in respective global markets. While enthusiasts were just beginning to link up online, international travel was part of collecting if one wanted to "be there" to access rare sneakers, streetwear, or collectibles. Bobby Kim wrote that "you were working airfare into your clothing budget."[67] Entrepreneurs founding bricks-and-mortar retail stores were open to grey market trade, connecting lines of dialogue and one-off trade between the United States, Europe, and Asia, most notably Hong Kong and Japan. European stores Patta and Sneakersnstuff started in truly grassroots fashion—without official wholesale accounts—instead flying to global sneaker destination cities to pick up inventory, often on the grey market; at other times taking advantage of price disparities between different locales. Sneakersnstuff co-founder Erik Fagerlind recalled that "in Singapore ... you could buy Air Jordans for like a third of our price."[68] In 1996–7, Fagerlind and co-founder Peter Jansson spent two weeks in NYC "to pick up shoes that we knew didn't exist here in Europe ... At that time there weren't many pure sneaker stores. It was a lot of mom-and-pop shops. There were a lot of Foot Lockers, obviously. But we went to Fulton St.; we went to 125th St ... Those trips were how we built stock to open."[69] This unofficial trade, like Bobbito Garcia's earlier depiction of sneakers as a secret society, required knowing the map—neighborhoods, stores, local dealers.

Sneakersnstuff was one of the first Nike accounts to sell online according to Treis Hill, who joined downtown NYC store Alife in 2005. Hill affirms that some level of unofficial trade was implicitly permitted in the early days of specialty sneaker retail:

> The sales people didn't care; they knew we did the swaps. Patta couldn't sell Jordans; we didn't need Air Maxes. Retail was different. They didn't care as long as we didn't sell it online. We were killing it back then and we didn't care. Sneakersnstuff Sweden got one of the first online stores. They could ship. Now they have like nine stores.[70]

Sneakersnstuff also took private requests through its email account sneakerdetectives@sneakersnstuff.com. Fagerlind recalls, "People connected with us, looking for specific shoes. People emailed from all over the world asking for stuff from Japan and US and Hong Kong ..."[71]

Collecting Craze

In the early 2000s, journalists became fascinated with sneaker collecting—Nike had ascended the ranks to become a large American corporation, and the competition between Nike, adidas, Reebok, and smaller players AND1, Converse, LA Gear, and British Knights was releasing new technology and styles, and signing talented athletes with a fury, leading headlines to call the competition the "sneaker wars."[72] Bobbito Garcia's article "Confessions of a

Sneaker Addict," published in *The Source* in 1991, is often cited as the seminal article that opened popular audiences to the inner world of sneaker obsession. In 1999, the release of the Nike "Killer Bee" Dunk High—a collaboration between Junya Watanabe and the Wu-Tang Clan that featured the Dunk in contrasting bright yellow and black—brought increased attention to collaboration.[73] The late Sandy Bodecker, former Nike VP of Special Projects and head of Nike SB, reflected that "There were a number of independent but loosely connected movements happening, and the time was ripe for things to come out from the deep underground to broader acceptance."[74]

In April 2005, Ian Callender, then twenty-three and "sneaker collector since 1999," was featured in the *Washington Post* article "Sole of the Sneakerhead." Callender's sneaker obsession was all-consuming, lucrative, and drew in efforts from his girlfriend and parents, including enlisting his girlfriend to stand in a queue to acquire a pair of adidas Roc-a-fella shell toes (she did, for $159+tax). The reporter writes humorously of how sneakers-as-financial-assets had become situational to Callender's life:

> "I think about how crazy it is sometimes. I think, man, I just sold a pair of shoes to buy another pair."
>
> [The article response:] No, crazy is selling your sneaker collection to fix your parents' car after you wrecked it. Which is what Callender did a couple of years ago.
>
> . . .
>
> "I am still really mad about that," he says. As most kids would be after crashing their parents' car.
>
> "I was heartbroken because a lot of them were Holy Grails," he says.
>
> Holy Grails?
>
> "That is the shoe you would do anything for."[75]

In somewhat defensible logic, sneaker enthusiasts characterize their obsession as concordant with any other form of collecting. William Gibson wrote of watch collecting on eBay that "The idea of the Collectible is everywhere today, and sometimes strikes me as some desperate instinctive reconfiguring of the postindustrial flow, some basic mammalian response to the bewildering flood of sheer stuff we produce."[76] The term "gear acquisition syndrome," or GAS, is the tendency to purchase more equipment than justified by usage and/or price,[77] and typically refers to spheres of hobbyists who purchase large amounts of photography equipment or musical instruments for no explicable reason other than obsession. Indeed, a Google Ngram Viewer search for "gear acquisition" shows a growth trajectory that begins around 1945 and rises sharply in the ensuing decades[78]—giving some credence to Gibson's idea that collecting bears partial affinity with "boomer demographics and a cult of nostalgia." Sneakerhead Todd Krevanchi, sometimes listed as a NikeTalk co-founder, wrote that sneakers are like any other fanatic item: Hummell figurines, luxury handbags, Beanie Babies, baseball cards, Longaberger Baskets, souvenir spoons, or magnets. "People who are collectors of ALL of the above items, as well as other things have questioned my hobby … How is my propensity for buying footwear less appropriate? … [A]ll of those other collectible items . . . have similar online communities, I could never look at one of those people and feel that their passion is substandard."[79]

Fraser Cooke, Nike Brand Energy Director, said of Japanese collectors, "Young people are very expressive in how they dress. They like to archive things and know what's behind a thing, whether denim or redwing boots or cars or Nikes. I think you can find, like, a lunatic here who is an obsessive collector of anything."[80] Sneaker collaborations with retailers, publishers, athletes, and celebrities drew cultural references onto the stable form of sneaker models. Referring to Tokyo specifically, Cooke said that perhaps sneakers took off in part due to "Japan's island mentality of taking things from outside, bringing them in, curating, archiving, and being very detail-oriented."[81] Bodecker observed that after over a decade failing to break into skateboarding, Nike SB finally connected the sneaker as "a canvas for creative storytelling. We were able to make things more personal and more deeply connected, first to the skate community and then to the broader collector community."[82] Subtle design flourishes, collaborations, imaginative style names, and cult status all fueled the unrelenting demand for the rare, exclusive, and peculiar. Sneaker styles drew on the outside world, from the subtle—the Air Force 1 chlorophyll, the Air Jordan cement—to the overt—adidas x Arizona Green Tea, Reebok's Allen Iverson Question, encrusted with 246/25.5 carats of diamonds with a retail price of $65,000 in the Eastbay catalog.[83]

Hypebeast's collaboration with the adidas UltraBOOST was said to have looked "hacked," inspired by fans who'd already been cutting the cages off their BOOST sneakers.

Key to the mystique in distributing pairs was select wholesale accounts reserved for prestigious stores. Nike's Tier Zero accounts grant special access to some of the most limited product runs. The term "Tier 0" has widespread usage in technology industries, often referring to the most important or highest-performing levels of data storage or architecture.

Amsterdam-founded Patta was an early Tier Zero account. Edson Sabajo and Guillame Schmidt recalled that, "There was this new thing called Tier Zero. We said if we're going to do this, we want to do the parallel shopping. They said okay."[84] Nike's Quickstrike (a wider release, boutique-only sneakers) and Hyperstrike (an extremely rare release, only to friends and/or family) offer other levels of releases,[85] the latter still making their way into resale and collector markets.[86]

For shoes that had to be purchased in-store, long queues formed outside boutiques in anticipation of in-demand releases. The famed 2005 "Sneaker Riot" covered in the *New York Post* featured queue chaos outside the drop of the STAPLE x Nike Dunk Pro Low SB "NYC Pigeon," a collaboration with Jeff Staples' namesake brand. Many coveted releases went straight to online resale via eBay, NikeTalk, or direct transactions via email or chat.

With the number of releases ever-increasing, drop culture—and therefore reselling—became a more routinized form of buying. By design, demand for limited releases outweighs supply. The exclusivity brought higher resale prices on the secondary market, and brands increased the number of releases to facilitate more drops. In 2019, there were at least eighty versions of the Air Jordan I released and eighteen drops of the Air Jordan IV.[87]

> Products once worshipped and impossible to obtain is [sic] just a PayPal click (and customs charges) away . . . Accessibility kills desire. What would have been ripped out of a magazine and memorized for life, or identified from an album cover for a cult lifespan of sorts is now page 2 within the morning and page 4 the following day, then a targeted Google search away in longtail limbo.[88]

Sneakers Mapped

[T]he cut-rate treasures, the "scores" of legend, are long gone.
The market has been rationalized."

WILLIAM GIBSON, *WIRED*, 1999

Around 2012, Josh Luber had an idea while working at IBM: "My obsession with sneakers and obsession with data were growing at the same time."[89] In 2013 Luber founded Campless, a blog that analyzed price data from eBay sneaker sales, creating a price discovery database for the sneaker resale market. Campless gained popularity and in early 2016 transformed into online resale platform StockX.[90]

The arrival of Flight Club, StockX, GOAT, and other commercial resale platforms magnified the intensity of flipping sneakers for profit. Sneakers became a kind of blunt financial instrument, known to anyone with internet access as a secondary markup waiting to be gamed. With price discovery available to nearly everyone and resale prices averaging 200–300% or more—including a pair of Nike Dunk SB Low Paris with an ROI of 149,385%[91]—groups of sneaker speculators hit the market, some forming "cook groups" to strategize and coordinate nabbing the latest releases. Justin Snowden, a sneakerhead interviewed while shopping at Undefeated in Los Angeles, spoke to the availability of shopping for sneakers online:

> Everything is within a click. If I know the store in Madrid or whatnot, I'm able to find what I need. If other people don't know about it, I love it, because then I'm able to get them without them selling out. Everybody knows a site like sneakersnstuff—great selection. But so many people know about it that it almost guarantees you won't be able to get a pair even if it's on their website.[92]

QR Code 4 *"Yea … Imagine … ☺" Reddit post by u/Funny_Compote_3682, reposted by u/Repsneakers, March 1, 2023.*

Thus arrived the paradigm of "taking an L," or, being more likely *not* to have access to a sneaker than being able to purchase it. The confluence of financial fallout, supply chain disruptions, and increased time at home during the Covid-19 pandemic brought increased attention to sneaker speculation, fueled by ascendant enthusiasm for cryptocurrency. The "swoosh curve"—a line chart illustrating the dip and then exponential increase of a sneaker's value after its initial release that (coincidentally) follows the form of Nike's swoosh logo[93]—was proselytized amongst overlapping crypto and sneaker enthusiast communities as a sign of ever-increasing value for both types of assets. The swoosh curve was also shared online through the HODL meme, in reference to user GameKyuubi's post on the Bitcoin Talk Forums on December 18, 2013.[94] In 2017, a meme created by user tryingtodoart was posted to Reddit pairing the value curve of BTC overlaid on the Nike logo with the phrase "Just HODL it."[95]

Online sneaker releases are ever in conflict with bots. Bot activity was not new, having been implemented for decades on eBay and Ticketmaster, with eBay sniping software inserting automatic, winning high bids at the last possible time fraction before auction-end. William Gibson remembered his own frustration bidding against bots for vintage watches on eBay:

> The idea of this software ran entirely counter to the peculiar psychology of bidding at auction. The software-driven sniper isn't really bidding; he's shopping. Skimming an existing situation . . . I sent eBay a message to the effect that allowing autobid software detracted from the eBay experience. That it spoiled the chemistry of the thing, which in my view was a large part of what they offered as a venue."[96]

Search terms "shoe bots," "nike shoe bot," "sneaker bot," and "sneaker bots" are all represented in Google Trends in 2004 (the earliest date tracked), many reaching their peak popularity in 2004.[97]

Former Shopify CTO Jean-Michel Lemieux points to adidas's Yeezy releases from 2015 to 2017 as the point at which sneaker e-commerce changed for the platform. Lemieux recalls that "the platform really was exploding. I was at my kid's sporting events over the weekend, and my phone was going off all the time . . . Servers were overheating and I was like, what the hell? We're only selling 3,000 pairs. Why, [are] there 5 million people on the site, you know? So I think we got pulled into this by necessity of protecting our servers."[98] The company employed a number of fairly standard procedures to protect servers from being overrun by human and bot activity, including load balancing, shedding traffic, and placing certain Shopify stores in "pods" to isolate traffic volume from the wider Shopify server system. Lemieux discussed other defense methods such as CAPTCHAs, biometrics (such as Apple Pay with Touch/Face ID), raffles, and games used to prove a customer's humanity.[99] Additionally, the company holds at least one patent for "Systems and Methods for Bot Mitigation."[100] Several initiatives have been put in place to curb automated purchasing of sneakers, including Nike's SNKRS app, with marginal success. As of 2023, the secondary market has cooled, with repercussions for bot companies. Jake, host of the Sockjig podcast told Lemieux that "Botting is a bit down because the market is not backing it up . . . a lot of prices are going down . . . Some have closed up shop."[101]

Born Digital

"Hmmm, should I buy a picture of a shoe, or the shoe, tough decisions"[102] wrote Reddit user FireDemon216 replying to the thread "NFT's on StockX . . . also I know my phone is about to die lol," on January 19, 2022. The thread's 267 comments are overwhelmingly negative, citing high prices and calling the product "meaningless," likening it to a "ponzi scheme."[103] The surge in cryptocurrency, Web3, and sneaker speculation reached a fever pitch during the Covid-19 pandemic, but as the crypto bubble burst in 2022 and the global economy experienced record levels of inflation, the resale market cooled. Cryptockickers, a San Francisco-based company that signed NBA player Wilson Chandler in 2021, has gone quiet, with no posted updates to Twitter since August 2022.[104] Nike purchased virtual collectibles company RTFKT in 2021, and after dropping a physical sneaker at Art Basel Miami in December 2022, faced backlash based on pricing, lack of communication, and misleading information about exclusivity/availability.[105] Bobbito Garcia and Scottie Pippen dropped NFT sneakers in 2021 and 2022, respectively.

Regardless of where the hype cycle stands on NFTs, physical sneakers have been undergoing digital creation for decades. Sneaker designers and engineers have worked with sketches and communication tools such as fax machines, working across paper, prototyping, software, and interfacing directly with machines. Wilson Smith related to *Kicksology* in 2003 that he had recently moved from hand-sketching to computer-sketching for the Nike FBI:

> [I]n the past I've done things old-school, I've always sketched and rendered by hand. It was really great on this product to start with early computer drawings of the Air Jordan XVIII and work from there. We also got a much quicker read on the way the project was going to look by putting the new shoe on a player [by compositing a digital sketch onto a digital photograph] and doing studies like that."[106]

Perhaps Flyknit[107] and Primeknit offer examples of sneakers that are truly "born digital." Both are created using advanced knitting machines that must be programmed first to produce a pattern.[108] These artifacts exist first as software—which is itself material (based on physical computers reading and writing to a storage medium)—before being realized in woven thread, composite soles, and various adhesives. Adidas 4D and Nike React used generative data to create 3D-simulated forms in software before being produced. Sneaker components are created using digital-first tools, in which algorithmic functions "write" the parameters for what the shoe will look and feel like based on data input from sneaker designers and engineers. Ultimately, the sneaker is a prototype or production model born of software, a program "crafting" from data parameters before the sneaker is created in shoe form. Rather than a sketch or a tech pack file, the shoe is stored in data structures that define its existence in software first.

For the adidas Futurecraft 4D (2017), then Global Creative Director Paul Gaudio spoke to the digital process of creating the sole's structure, produced in collaboration with 3D printing company Carbon. Gaudio stated that they needed a "latticework, a three-dimensional structure that could support a foot and deform and flex as needed. So you start by deciding what you want that structure to look like, and you create structure based on data input; say, the nature of a runner's foot or their stride."[109] According to adidas, the software drew upon "17 years of athlete data and 5 million lattice variations."[110] The digital parameters were then 3D-printed using a Carbon-developed technique called Digital Light Synthesis, which involves directing light and oxygen at resin to turn liquid into solid form.[111]

The Nike Epic React (2018) used generative design to convert data into structural patterns, then instructing the software system "on what outcomes it should produce."[112] Bret Schoolmeester, a senior global footwear director, told *Wired*, "All the texture you see on the shoe is done computationally. We started with what we call an envelope, which is just a generic form, and then we add all the texture you see there through generative design."[113]

In April 2023, Nike presented an exhibition and workshop at the Milan Design Week, exploring sustainable practices and featuring three projects born of the company's ISPA (Improvise Scavenge Protect React) group.[114] The ISPA Universal, a molded shoe made of Bio-EVA foam developed from sugarcane, was created using AI-generated designs that combined data from four shoe models: Nike Solarsoft HTM (2010), Air Max 270 (2018), Air Zoom Pegasus 37 (2020), and Air Zoom Type (2020).[115] Five years after the Epic React, Nike design VP Darryl Matthews spoke of striving for balance between automation and elements of the hand with ISPA Universal: "When you're designing a shoe digitally it's an amazing tool . . . But what happens then is you have an element of disconnect; the understanding of shape and form is a different dialogue than you normally have if you do it by hand."[116] To balance the disparity, the exhibition invited designers to create clay sneakers out of 3D-printed molds that were produced at Nike headquarters. "We're basically working backwards from the digital form by connecting all the points for people to make them by hand, manipulating it themselves and have a better understanding of why they are doing what they're doing. That's designing with emotion."[117]

Archiving

As one generation moves on from collecting, they channel their memories, nostalgia, and experiences into its own kind of archive. Kevin Driscoll says of BBS communities, that "amateur activities played a critical role in shaping social computing practices and platforms of the 1980s and 1990s,"[118] asserting that "the typical middle-class American amateurs worked out of their homes using the 'free' time and money left over from their commitments to work and family."[119] The work of the early online sneaker community was, like the BBS pioneers, "either self-archived or, more often, lost to time."[120] In a 2012 post to Nike Talk, NTers fondly remember the Kicksology site, sharing their downloads of the site's entire HTML and linked files so that others could relive the experience of the site. In addition to being preserved by the Internet Archive's Wayback Machine, the site's fans kept original pages of *Kicksology* intact, trading memories and files after it shut down.

Sneaker luminaries such as Bobbito Garcia, Russ Bengston (formerly of *SLAM* and *Complex*), Nick Engvall (formerly of *Complex*) and the *Sneaker History* podcast, OG Nters, and many more are sharing stories that show younger sneakerheads what came before. Others, such as Jordan Geller of Shoezeum, are actively preserving rare sneakers for wider appreciation. Eric Brothers's *Nike Park* site, accessed via the Wayback Machine, offers not only a time capsule of the late 1990s but includes image scans useful to the sneaker historian.[121] And sneaker collectors remain ever at large, preserving artifacts, maintaining histories, and creating new ones.

But what of the shoes themselves? Conservator Giorgio Riello asks:

> Are we going, in the future, to have few examples of the most common type of footwear, either because they fall into pieces or because museums refuse to collect them? . . . [A]ll of these were goods—items of apparel—artifacts that were never intended to last. Or last long. So their struggle to survive seems to be part of a mass consumeristic genetic code embedded in them.[122]

The original adidas Superstar is left to such a fate:

> The original sole and toe of the Superstar was made from rubber injected with polyurethane. That meant the rubber was softer and non-marking, but

QR Code 5 *Differences. Comparing pairs of the Air Jordan 3. Reddit post by u/dirtyjordanjones, March 3, 2023.*

clay fillers, calcium carbonate and magnesium carbonate meant that it would yellow in UV light, harden and crumble over time. Not so good for collectors, as anyone who has had a treasured pair dissolve on their feet or in the box can attest. Subsequently, a purer non-marking rubber was introduced to the Superstar shell in the early 90s.[123]

Riello is sanguine when facing time's ultimate destruction of our stuff:

> Material preservation and conservation are investment plans. The care for the future. I come from a country, Italy, that owns about a quarter of the world's artistic heritage. And you hear stories of fresco ceilings losing bits, or entire houses in Pompei falling down. [I'm] not always amazed that it does not happen more often just because of the sheer inability of preserving a continually expanding material past. So in conclusion, I would not worry too much.[124]

Investment in the future requires sound evaluation of our extraction from the planet's ecosystems—and the cycles of consumption that promote it. To "preserve" today and in the future will mean, perhaps, something else entirely.

Amidst the mass consumption, commoditization, and historicizing of sneakers, some are betting on the virtualization of sneaker culture to bring about a new era of enthusiasm and collecting after the crypto crash and decline in sneaker resale values. Only time will tell. Virtual sneakers may be another experiment, a new frontier, or merely a bump in the road in sneaker culture. As Rafer Alston, one of a select number of NYC streetball players to have made it to the League said of the streetball scene, so it goes with sneakers: "It's just another thing to fall in love with. That's how I look at it. Just another thing to fall in love with."[125]

Notes

1   P. Smith, "Global sneakers market revenue from 2014 to 2027," *Statista*, February 14, 2023, https://www.statista.com/forecasts/1017918/sneakers-market-value-forecast-worldwide.

2   Piper Sandler, "StockX Snapshot: Trade is a Global Game," Innovator Spotlight: StockX, February 2021, https://stockx.com/about/sx-market-insights/stockx-snapshot-trade-is-a-global-game/.

3 Bobbito Garcia, *Where'd You Get Those? Tenth Anniversary Edition* (New York: Testify Books, 2013), 16.

4 Tanika White, "Thanks to Baltimore, Air Force 1 still flying," *Baltimore Sun*, January 25, 2007, https://www.baltimoresun.com/news/bs-xpm-2007-01-25-0701250054-s.

5 White, "Thanks to Baltimore, Air Force 1 still flying."

6 Elizabeth Semmelhack, *Out of the Box: The Rise of Sneaker Culture* (New York: Rizzoli Electa, 2015), 96.

7 Simon Wood, *The Ultimate Sneaker Book* (Cologne: Taschen, 2018), 441.

8 John C. Jay, John Huet, and Jimmy Smith, *Soul of the Game* (New York: Workman Publishing, 1997), 1.

9 Ian Stonebrook, "How Nike Sold Streetball," *Boardroom*, August 12, 2021, https://boardroom.tv/sportswear-streetball-and1/.

10 Rodrigo Corral, Alex French, and Howie Kahn, *Sneakers* (New York: Razorbill, 2017), 100.

11 From 1993 to 1998, Bobbito Garcia collaborated with Nike on numerous projects, working on around forty commercials, writing scripts, announcing basketball tournaments, and being the voice of the company's 800 number, where callers could vote on the top five streetballers of all time and find information on local tournaments. Corral, French, and Kahn, *Sneakers*, 100–1.

12 John C. Jay, "What makes a Legend most?" *John C Jay*, Tumblr, Nov 9, 2016, https://johncjay.tumblr.com/post/132880391468/what-makes-a-legend-most;

13 Staple uploaded the NYC City Attack TV spots to YouTube, a playlist of which is available at https://www.youtube.com/playlist?list=PLrVSqVA8W5dQvwDsu-0k2UHIoySd308hZ; Jeff Staple, "For John C Jay There Is No Such Thing as an Excuse," May 19, 2019 in *Business of HYPE* produced by Hypebeast Radio, podcast audio, 63:10, https://hypebeast.com/2019/5/john-c-jay-wieden-kennedy-fast-retailing-interview-business-of-hype-jeffstaple-episode-41.

14 Russ Bengston, "The Complete History of Streetball Sneakers," *Complex*, May 21, 2013, https://www.complex.com/sneakers/2013/05/the-complete-history-of-streetball-sneakers.

15 Kevin Driscoll, *The Modem World: A Prehistory of Social Media* (New Haven, CT: Yale University Press, 2022), ch. 6.

16 Driscoll, *The Modem World*, ch. 6.

17 Wood, *Ultimate Sneaker Book*, 442.

18 Corral, French, and Kahn, *Sneakers*, 236

19 Corral, French, and Kahn, *Sneakers*, 236.

20 Corral, French, and Kahn, *Sneakers*, 6.

21 Corral, French, and Kahn, *Sneakers*, 6.

22 Joseph Pereira, "Sneaker Attacks: In Reebok–Nike War, Big Woolworth Chain Is a Major Battlefield—Among Reebok's Problems, It Needs Better Relations With Foot Locker Stores—A Tiff Over Exclusive Shoes," *Wall Street Journal*, September 22, 1995.

23 Maureen Tkacik, "Foothold: As Extreme Goes Mass, Nike Nips At Skate-Shoe Icon— Swoosh Sneaks Up on Vans, Backing Its Rivals to Woo Hipster Youth Market—On the Bumper: Don't Do It," *Wall Street Journal*, April 22, 2002; Stephanie Kang, "Foot Locker Profit Jumps 25%, Boosted by Influx of Nike Shoes," *Wall Street Journal*, March 3, 2004.

24 Eric Brothers, *Nike Park*, nikepark.simplenet.com, July 7, 1997, accessed via the Wayback Machine, https://web.archive.org/web/19970707025224/http://nikepark. simplenet.com:80/.

25 Brothers, *Nike Park*, Nike Park picture archive, July 7, 1997, accessed via the Wayback Machine, https://web.archive.org/web/19970707025414/http://nikepark.simplenet. com/nikepic.html.

26 Brothers, *Nike Park*, April 29, 1999, accessed via the Wayback Machine, https://web. archive.org/web/19990429041027/http://www.nikepark.simplenet.com/picture.html.

27 According to users on Reddit, the service shut down in 2000. Fun_Wonder_4114, "Does anyone remember the InsideTheWeb internet forums from 90s and late 2000s? . . .," *Reddit*, August 10, 2021, https://www.reddit.com/r/nostalgia/comments/p211od/ does_anyone_remember_the_insidetheweb_internet/.

28 Accessed via the Wayback Machine, December 6, 1998, https://web.archive.org/ web/19981206090200/http://www.246.ne.jp/%7Emax95/trea.html.

29 Accessed via the Wayback Machine, May 1, 1999, https://web.archive.org/ web/19990501044311/http://www.246.ne.jp/%7Emax95/dunk.html; eBay listing, "Nike Dunk High Michigan for Sale," March 14, 2023, https://www.ebay.com/b/Nike-Dunk-High-1985-Michigan/15709/bn_7119078971; Grailed listing, March 14, 2023, https:// www.grailed.com/listings/42000822-nike-x-vintage-nike-dunk-og-1985-michigan-made-in-korea.

30 Fonkee, Nike Park message boards, April 28, 1999, https://web.archive.org/ web/19990429112641/http://www.insidetheweb.com/mbs.cgi/mb332260.

31 Phillie, Nike Park message boards, May 19, 2000, https://web.archive.org/ web/20000520043604/http://www.insidetheweb.com:80/mbs.cgi/mb332260&sa=D&so urce=docs&ust=1678770936285196&usg=AOvVaw1yfNtqQfO0PkIGTPBhOVvj.

32 Nike Park message boards, April 28, 1999, https://web.archive.org/ web/19990429112641/http://www.insidetheweb.com/mbs.cgi/mb332260.

33 William Gibson, "My Obsession," *Wired*, January 1, 1999, https://www.wired. com/1999/01/ebay/.

34 Gibson, "My Obsession."

35 Gibson, "My Obsession."

36 SHOEBACCA, eBay, accessed via the Wayback Machine, https://web.archive.org/web/20060427025037/http://stores.ebay.com/SHOEBACCA.

37 SHOEBACCA, eBay, accessed via the Wayback Machine, https://web.archive.org/web/20030609193542/http://www.stores.ebay.com/shoebacca.

38 Sneaker Shack, eBay, accessed via the Wayback Machine, https://web.archive.org/web/20060613054143/http://stores.ebay.com/Sneaker-Shack.

39 eBay, accessed via the Wayback Machine, https://web.archive.org/web/20060613034213/http://reviews.ebay.com/The-Guide-to-Buying-Authentic-Air-Jordan-Shoes_W0QQugidZ10000000000871412?ssPageName=BUYGD:CAT:-1:LISTINGS:3; https://web.archive.org/web/20060613025601/http://reviews.ebay.com/How-to-buy-Air-Jordan-shoes-on-ebay_W0QQugidZ10000000000835113?ssPageName=BUYGD:CAT:-1:LISTINGS:1; https://web.archive.org/web/20060613050508/http://reviews.ebay.com/Top-Selling-Basketball-Shoes-2005-Best-Selling-Shoes_W0QQugidZ10000000000102956?ssPageName=BUYGD:CAT:-1:LISTINGS:4.

40 eBay search for "nike," accessed via the Wayback Machine, April 11, 2006, https://web.archive.org/web/20060414132050/http://clothing.search.ebay.com/nike_Mens-Shoes_W0QQfromZR4QQfsooZ2QQfsopZ2QQsacatZ63850QQssPageNameZWLRS.

41 eBay search for "nike."

42 eBay search for "nike."

43 Nick Engvall, "Is It Time For a NikeTalk Reunion? Getting Nostalgic Talking Sneakers and Epic Stories With Will Hardison," *Sneaker History Podcast*, February 14, 2022, https://sneakerhistory.com/podcasts/is-it-time-for-a-niketalk-reunion-getting-nostalgic-talking-sneakers-and-epic-stories-with-will-hardison/.

44 Engvall, "Is It Time For a NikeTalk Reunion?"

45 timelessflight, "Can someone school me on EKIN please . . .," *NikeTalk*, April 10, 2008, https://niketalk.com/threads/can-someone-school-me-on-ekin-please.63569/; "10 Things You Didn't Know About Nike's EKIN Program," *Complex*, April 13, 2013, https://www.complex.com/sneakers/2013/04/10-things-you-didnt-know-about-nikes-ekin-program.

46 dirtylicious, "Commonly used abbreviations (NT & web) . . . list em here . . ." *NikeTalk*, April 5, 2006, https://niketalk.com/threads/commonly-used-abbreviations-nt-web-list-em-here.388/.

47 Maureen Tkacik, "Fancy Footwork: How Young Dealers o f Rare Sneakers Challenge Nike—Using the Web, Mr. Eways, 16, Subverts a Giant's Control of Its Marketing Strategy—Air Jordans for $700 a Pair," *Wall Street Journal*, August 20, 2002.

48 Hundreds, *This Is Not A T-shirt*, 112. Hundreds goes on to cite notable members including celebrity jeweler Ben Baller, John Mayer, Anti Social Social Club's Neek, and the rapper Wale.

49 "The 30 Most Influential Niketalk Members of All Time," *Complex*, October 25, 2012, https://www.complex.com/sneakers/2012/10/the-30-most-influential-niketalk-members-of-all-time.

50 jonastheprince, "The 30 Most Influential Niketalk Members of All Time by Complex Magazine," *NikeTalk*, October, 25, 2012, https://niketalk.com/threads/the-30-most-influential-niketalk-members-of-all-time-by-complex-magazine.511756/page-27.

51 b20 eg8, *NikeTalk*, December 8, 2012, https://niketalk.com/threads/the-30-most-influential-niketalk-members-of-all-time-by-complex-magazine.511756/page-27.

52 Maureen Tkacik, "Fancy Footwork," *Wall Street Journal*, August 20, 2002; Sotheby's, https://www.sothebys.com/en/buy/_nike-dunk-sb-low-supreme-black-cement-9-fd68; StockX, https://stockx.com/nike-dunk-sb-low-supreme-ny-black-cement-2002.

53 jerseyjoe, "Comments on SneakerPimp.com Wall Street Journal article," *NikeTalk*, August 22, 2002, https://niketalk.com/threads/comments-on-sneakerpimp-com-wall-street-journal-article.461/.

54 Corral, French, and Kahn, *Sneakers*, 201.

55 Ernest Kim, in discussion with the author, January 2023.

56 Ernest Kim, in discussion with the author.

57 Ernest Kim, in discussion with the author.

58 Ernest Kim, "1on1: Making the Ultraposite," *Kicksology*, August 31, 2003, accessed via the Wayback Machine, https://web.archive.org/web/20031009060557/http://kicksology.net/inthepaint/oneonone/qa_nike_ultraposite.html.

59 Ernest Kim, in discussion with the author.

60 Ernest Kim, "It's been a hell of a ride . . ." *Kicksology*, September 12, 2004, https://web.archive.org/web/20040912021120/http://www.kicksology.net/index_prof.html.

61 Kim, "It's been a hell of a ride . . ."

62 Ernest Kim, in discussion with the author.

63 Kim, "It's been a hell of a ride . . ."

64 Corral, French, and Kahn, *Sneakers*, 18.

65 Tkacik, "Fancy Footwork"; jerseyjoe, "Comments on SneakerPimp.com Wall Street Journal article," *NikeTalk*, August 22, 2022, https://niketalk.com/threads/comments-on-sneakerpimp-com-wall-street-journal-article.461/.

66 Corral, French, and Kahn, *Sneakers*, 77.

67 Bobby Kim (aka Bobby Hundreds), *This Is Not a T-Shirt* (New York: MCD, 2019), 86.

68 Corral, French, and Kahn, *Sneakers*, 189.

69 Corral, French, and Kahn, *Sneakers*, 189.

70 Jeff Staple "Alife's Rob Cristofaro and Treis Hill on Being an Originator of Hype," October 21, 2019, in *Business of HYPE*, produced by *Hypebeast* Radio, podcast audio, 45:00, https://hypebeast.com/2019/10/alife-rob-cristafaro-treis-hill-interview-business-of-hype-jeffstaple-episode-58.

71 Corral, French, and Kahn, *Sneakers*, 189.

72 Stephanie Kang and Geoffrey A. Fowler, "A Big Shot in China; To fight Nike, a Beijing sneaker giant aims to turn NBA journeyman Damon Jones into a star," *Wall Street Journal*, June 24, 2006.

73 Wood, *Ultimate Sneaker Book*, 21.

74 Wood, *Ultimate Sneaker Book*, 120.

75 Stephen A. Crockett Jr., "Sole of the Sneakerhead," *Washington Post*, April 21, 2005, https://www.washingtonpost.com/archive/lifestyle/2005/04/21/sole-of-the-sneakerhead/0a89baba-9183-4d67-9612-eef5501853a2/.

76 Gibson, "My Obsession."

77 "Gear acquisition syndrome," *Wiktionary*, https://en.wiktionary.org/wiki/gear_acquisition_syndrome.

78 Interestingly, a case-sensitive search for "Gear Acquisition" yields few results before 2000, and an exponential spike from the year 2000 to 2019. "gear acquisition," Google Books NGram Viewer, https://books.google.com/ngrams/graph?content=gear+acquisition&year_start=1800&year_end=2019&corpus=en-2019&smoothing=3#.

79 Todd Krevanchi, "Outside Looking In: Your Hobby Is Not Better Than Mine," *Kicks on Fire*, December 28, 2015, https://www.kicksonfire.com/outside-looking-in-your-hobby-is-not-better-than-mine/.

80 Corral, French, and Kahn, *Sneakers*, 243.

81 Corral, French, and Kahn, *Sneakers*, 242.

82 Corral, French, and Kahn, *Sneakers*, 243.

83 Sneaker Freaker, "The Most OutrAgeous, Over-The-Top Sneaker Collaborations Ever," July 9, 2021, https://www.sneakerfreaker.com/features/the-most-outrageous-over-the-top-sneaker-collaborations-ever.

84 Jeff Staple, "Edson Sabajo and Guillame Schmidt," podcast audio, 26:33, https://hypebeast.com/2020/1/patta-interview-business-of-hype-jeffstaple-episode-60-edson-sabajo-guillaume-schmidt.

85 Erik of Sneakersnstuff recalled that Tier Zero was introduced "since they already had some decent stores in Tier 1. But top it with even more limited runs of sneakers—they created more limited stuff . . . today this all has evolved a bit. TierZero+ (that really should be named TierZero-since it's one level down from Tier Zero) and some other variations . . . I don't think anyone really knows anymore." Erik Fagerlund, "A Tres Bien night in Paris—still back tracking," *sneakererik*, March 22, 2012, https://sneakererik.com/tag/nike-tierzero/.

86 YLI, "quickstrike, hyperstrike, tier 0-what does it all mean?" *Superfuture*, June 8, 2006, https://supertalk.superfuture.com/topic/12029-quickstrike-hyperstrike-tier-0-what-does-it-all-mean/.

87 Justin Sayles, "The Once and Future Sneaker King," *The Ringer*, May 4, 2020, https://www.theringer.com/nba/2020/5/4/21246027/air-jordan-1-nike-michael-jordan-sneaker-king-legacy-the-last-dance.

88 Gary Warnett. "A Lack of Movement," *Hypebeast*, April 29, 2011, https://hypebeast.com/2011/4/a-lack-of-movement-by-gary-warnett.

89 Lisa Chow, "You See Sneakers, These Guys See Hundreds of Millions in Resale Profit," *FiveThirtyEight*, October 17, 2014, https://fivethirtyeight.com/features/you-see-sneakers-these-guys-see-hundreds-of-millions-in-resale-profit/.

90 Riley Jones, "Campless Launched a Stock Market for the Multi-Billion Dollar Sneaker Resell Business," *Complex*, February 8, 2016, https://www.complex.com/sneakers/2016/02/campless-stockx-launch.

91 Tom Huddleston Jr., "The world's most valuable sneakers originally retailed for $60—now they're selling for $90,000 online," CNBC, *Make It*, June 18, 2022, https://www.cnbc.com/2022/06/18/the-worlds-most-valuable-sneakers-from-nike-dunks-to-og-jordans.html.

92 Corral, French, and Kahn, *Sneakers*, 206.

93 Daisuke Wakabayashi, "The Fight for Sneakers," *New York Times*, October 15, 2021, https://www.nytimes.com/interactive/2021/10/15/style/sneaker-bots.html.

94 GameKyuubi, "I AM HODLING," *Bitcoin Talk Forums*, December 18, 2013, https://bitcointalk.org/index.php?topic=375643.0.

95 JesusSkywalkered, "Just Hodl It. (Found on FB)," *Reddit*, September 6, 2017, https://www.reddit.com/r/Bitcoin/comments/6yf179/just_hodl_it_found_on_fb/.

96 Gibson, "My Obsession."

97 https://trends.google.com/trends/explore?q=shoe%20bots&date=all&geo=US; https://trends.google.com/trends/explore?date=all&geo=US&q=nike%20bot,nike%20shoe%20bot; https://trends.google.com/trends/explore?date=all&geo=US&q=sneaker%20bots,sneaker%20bot&hl=en-US; https://trends.google.com/trends/explore?q=sneaker%20bot&date=all&geo=US; https://trends.google.com/trends/explore?date=all&geo=US&q=sneaker%20bots&hl=en-US.

98 Sockjig Sneaker podcast, "Episode 48: Jean-Michel Lemieux, ex-CTO of Shopify," January 27, 2023, https://open.spotify.com/episode/1hqA1cMVVjUlqHFG07G3Xb.

99 Alphalist.CTO podcast, "#15—Jean Michel Lemieux // CTO Shopify," December 3, 2020, https://podcasts.apple.com/us/podcast/15-jean-michel-lemieux-cto-shopify/id1512227295?i=1000501156708.

100 Shopify, Inc., "Systems and Methods for Bot Mitigation," Justia Patents, June 8, 2021, https://patents.justia.com/patent/20220394058.

101 Sockjig Sneaker podcast, "Episode 48: Jean-Michel Lemieux, ex-CTO of Shopify," January 27, 2023, https://open.spotify.com/episode/1hqA1cMVVjUlqHFG07G3Xb.

102 FireDemon216, comment in reply to "NFT's on StockX . . . also I know my phone is about to die lol," *Reddit*, January 19, 2022, https://www.reddit.com/r/Sneakers/comments/s7zh9x/comment/htduckf/?utm_source=share&utm_medium=web2x&context=3.

103 Reddit discussion, "NFTs on StockX," https://www.reddit.com/r/Sneakers/comments/s7zh9x/nfts_on_stockx_also_i_know_my_phone_is_about_to/.

104 Cryptokickers, "NBA Veteran Wilson Chandler Makes History by Signing First-Ever Completely Virtual Shoe Deal," *Cision PR Newswire*, April 20, 2021, https://www.prnewswire.com/news-releases/nba-veteran-wilson-chandler-makes-history-by-signing-first-ever-completely-virtual-shoe-deal-301272253.html.

105 "Nike Acquires RTFKT," Nike press release, December 13, 2021, https://about.nike.com/en/newsroom/releases/nike-acquires-rtfkt.

106 Ernest Kim, "1on1: Wilson Smith," *Kicksology*, May 2, 2003, https://web.archive.org/web/20030711135701/http://www.kicksology.net/inthepaint/oneonone/qa_nike_wilson.html.

107 Thank you to Ernest Kim for the suggestion.

108 Speculation about how Flyknit was created was written in *Knitting Industry*, https://www.knittingindustry.com/nike-flyknit-quantum-leap-for-flat-knitting/.

109 Corral, French, and Kahn, *Sneakers*, 298.

110 adidas, "From Futurecraft to 4DFWD and Beyond: The History of adidas 4D," August 2021, https://www.adidas.com/us/blog/737899-from-futurecraft-to-4dfwd-and-beyond-the-history-of-adidas-4d.

111 Corral, French, and Kahn, *Sneakers*, 298.

112 Matt Burgess, "How Nike used algorithms to help design its latest running shoe," *Wired*, January 25, 2018, https://www.wired.co.uk/article/nike-epic-react-flyknit-price-new-shoe.

113 Burgess, "How Nike used algorithms to help design its latest running shoe."

114 Cajsa Carlson, "'We're recontextualising what a shoe is' says Nike VP Darryl Matthews," *Dezeen*, May 12, 2023, https://www.dezeen.com/2023/05/12/nike-darryl-matthews-interview-ispa-trainers/.

115 Maria Cristina Pavarini, "How Nike is exploring new creative and sustainable paths," *The Spin Off*, April 21, 2023, https://www.the-spin-off.com/news/stories/The-Brands-How-Nike-is-exploring-new-creative-and-sustainable-paths-17171.

116 Carlson, "'We're recontextualising what a shoe is' says Nike VP Darryl Matthews."

117 Carlson, "'We're recontextualising what a shoe is' says Nike VP Darryl Matthews."

118 Driscoll, *The Modem World*, chap. 2.

119 Driscoll, *The Modem World*, chap. 2.

120 Driscoll, *The Modem World*, chap. 2.

121 Brothers, *Nike Park*, April 29, 1999, accessed via the Wayback Machine, https://web.archive.org/web/19990429041027/http://www.nikepark.simplenet.com/picture.html.

122 Giorgio Riello, "Ghost of Fashion Past," Bard Graduate Center, video, November 12, 2013, https://www.youtube.com/watch?v=5jr6CxiDLXI.

123 Wood, *Ultimate Sneaker Book*, 591.

124 Riello, "Ghost of Fashion Past."

125 "The Greatest Mixtape Ever," directed by Chris Robinson (Bristol, CT: ESPN Films, 2022), ESPN+, https://www.espn.com/watch/catalog/18366ee5-6226-410e-80cc-98457cbbebe2/the-greatest-mixtape-ever.

6

Cyborgs vs Skins. Which Will Dominate the Future of Fashion Design?

IDIT BARAK

Introduction

In a world fascinated with technology it is only fitting that fashion designers are eager to explore how emerging technologies—that is, wearable electronics and digital skins—could augment both conceptual and practical aspects of their profession. Currently there are two main expressions of tech dominating the conversation: wearable tech (or "smart fashion") and digital fashion. These two manifestations of technology in fashion offer different scenarios of the future, each with its unique promise but at the same time physical and philosophical pitfalls.

In order to question the viability of one over the other we must first distinguish fashion from clothing, and design from the production of goods. A great example of this can be found in Google's Jacquard project from 2018. The mission statement reads: "Jacquard takes ordinary, familiar objects and enhances them with new digital abilities and experiences, while remaining true to their original purpose—like being your favorite jacket, backpack or a pair of shoes that you love to wear."[1] Although the denim jacket Google developed with Levi's was marketed as smart fashion, not everything we love to wear is fashion. Any fashion designer will tell you that simply sticking tech into ordinary clothes is not design innovation. The same way dressing your avatar in a generic T-shirt wouldn't be hailed as the future of fashion for the metaverse.

So what is fashion? Fashion is about what's new and next. Innovation in fashion, much like in other design fields, is rebellious in nature and an urge to resist old notions and conventions. This is the ideal scenario for fashion; it should be rebellious and forward-thinking. But is this what fashion looks like today? The late Louise Wilson, one of the most influential professors in fashion academia and course director of the MA in Fashion at the prestigious Central Saint Martins, said in reference to fashion design students, "I don't think many of them here today are that interested in fashion. Perhaps it's because there's not much going on. No punk, no reaction to something. I think we are in a waiting period."[2]

The last time such a dramatic revolution occurred in fashion began in the early 1950s and was completed by the 1970s. In these two decades, fashion etiquette was thrown out the window and youth was crowned in charge of deciding what's cool. Fashion was left with very few taboos to break and not much skin left to expose. With that said, it is not surprising that in the decades that followed, Western fashion has focused more on reminiscing and regurgitating. It is not that we haven't seen breathtakingly beautiful creations coming from extremely talented designers, but design innovation has been scarce. Perhaps technology could offer tools that would allow designers to think of fashion in truly innovative ways.

A Profession is Born

Fashion has always been driven by technology. One might even say that fashion design was born as a by-product of the first tech revolution. Before we can consider which technological advances will be the major players in shaping the future of fashion, we must first revisit the origins of fashion design in order to understand the role of fashion in modern life and why keeping us warm is not actually the top priority.

Fashion, or more accurately the act of designing fashion as a documented profession, dates back to the mid-nineteenth century. The event that is often regarded as the birth of modern fashion is when English dressmaker Charles Frederick Worth, for the first time in documented history, sewed a label carrying his name into his designs. This happened a few decades after the end of the Industrial Revolution in which technological innovations enabled the automation of clothing-manufacturing processes. This, in conjunction with the rise of a new bourgeois urban social class, marks the conceptual distinction between clothes and designed fashion.

One might argue that fashion was born when Eve chose a fig leaf over a banana one, proving garments have always had aesthetic importance and were used to communicate class and social affiliations much beyond the merely functional purpose. So why was Worth's label so revolutionary? And why is he considered to be the first fashion designer? Worth's practice marked a shift, from creating clothes as a service for an opinionated customer, to a creative individual offering his personal vision, realized in fabric, to the public. By buying his work, these trusting consumers are no longer looking to royalty for stylistic reign but rather to Worth for aesthetic guidance. Worth and others that soon followed became the authorities on what was right to wear right now. They interpreted cultural sentiment through their own prism; they designed fashion.

These designers took upon themselves to tell our stories through garments. They enable us to show up for life feeling a few inches taller, reinventing ourselves when needed, pushing boundaries, and making political statements all without saying a word.

When we unpack the idea of innovation in reference to fashion, three major aspects of the realization of the product come into play: design, fabrication, and production. In design, innovation is an elusive concept and although we can agree that concepts can be quite avant-garde and forward-thinking, tracking the impact of new technologies on the thought process of designers can be quite tricky. This is why when examining innovation in fashion, the examples will usually fall under the two latter components of the realization of a garment (i.e., fabrication and production). It is important to distinguish between these three aspects because many times the material or production tech can be so exciting, new, and innovative that it overshadows the fact that

Figure 6.1 *Charles Fredrick Worth label. Metropolitan Museum / Costume Institute Archive.*

we are not actually witnessing a truly new way of design thinking. For a designed garment to be truly innovative, all three aspects must be addressed.

Since the Industrial Revolution, advances in fabrication and production processes have been constant and ground breaking. From the invention of the Jacquard loom in 1804 through Lycra in 1958 to the SLA 3D printer in 1987, these innovative technologies and others have had an enormous impact on the fashion industry, but not necessarily on fashion design. In some cases, these advances *have* had a direct impact on fashion design itself, such as in the work of renowned fashion designer Iris Van Herpen. Her work is a great example of how 3D printing technologies can be utilized as a way to rethink the design process and go beyond simply working with new materiality. Her designs offer a completely new dialogue between material and a three-dimensional body in motion, which is crucial for innovation to be realized in fashion design.

Designers must use technological advances to re-examine the way they approach designing fashion. Who are the clients? What is the use case? How can these new tools change the practices and aesthetic conventions rooted in traditions that no longer encompass the complexities of modern life?

Maybe a good place to start is to re-examine the role designer fashion should play in life today so that we can determine where technologies can fit in instead of overshadow. A constant principle, that hasn't changed since Worth opened his atelier, is that fashion must be current. At the time, having a person whose job was to define what was current was in itself revolutionary. Today that alone isn't enough because "current" has become mainstream. And designers should be thinking outside of the consensus, identifying possibilities yet to come by challenging conventions and offering individuals a means of self-expression. In addition, fashion is a platform where designers reflect and react to social, political, and cultural sentiment. Today that translates into addressing concepts like sustainability, gender identity, cultural appropriation, individualism or lack of it, democratization of fashion, and body positivity. These are the burning issues of our time. The designers at the top of the trickle-down conceptual pyramid must know that tackling these subjects is their responsibility in order to balance design that is relevant with economic growth potentials. Last, but certainly not least, fashion should move us and stay coveted and elusive, exuding an allure of cool effortlessness.

A fashion designer's objective is to achieve a form of non-verbal communication, and, much like in language, constant evolution is key. Adding new words to the vocabulary is crucial to achieve a current and relevant conversation. That is why designers and fashion product developers are constantly looking for ways to innovate in an attempt to end that waiting period Wilson was referring to, scrambling for a new syntax to articulate the next big thing in fashion.

Is Smart Fashion a Smart Idea?

Around the early 2000s, with major advances in wireless communication, computational power, and miniaturization of electrical components, the world became fascinated with IOTs (internet of things)—the idea that we could digitally and wirelessly connect people to people, people to things, and things to things was as if science fiction was becoming our reality.

Could wearable devices be the breath of fresh air designer fashion was waiting for—technology that could stir up an industry in stagnation? Could they be a hybrid between clothes and robotics, garments that would be able to collect our data: what we did, where we did it, with whom we did it, and how fast our heart beat in the process. In return, garments would soon be able to shape-shift, change size by sensing body shape, dyes reacting to temperature and changing color like a chameleon—fashion was going to be smarter and more beautiful than ever. All one needed was to integrate microcontrollers (very small and simple computers), conductive materials, tiny sensors, actuators, and slim batteries into textiles. Cynicism aside, integrating electrical components into textiles is a complicated task: for starters, garments need to be washed, and they tend to be in constant movement. Even those two very basic characteristics posed a huge obstacle, since electronics are allergic to water, and wires tend to disconnect when moved. Besides these minor hurdles, the real tough questions were: would these garments be fashionable and, most importantly, how would consumers react? Would they want to wear these creations? Future or fad? The promise sparked the curiosity and creativity of fashion designers who were eager to explore these technologies.

CuteCircuit, co-founded by Francesca Rosella and Ryan Genzopened in 2004, were pioneers in exploring digital interaction and connectivity

Figure 6.2 *Fiber optics hoodie. Design by Noa Sharvit. Photo by Guy Nahum Levy.*

Figure 6.3 *Fiber optics hoodie. Design by Noa Sharvit. Photo by Guy Nahum Levy.*

embedded in garments. Winning *Time* magazine's invention of the year in 2006 for the Hug Shirt™—"a shirt that lets you send hugs over distance! Embedded in the Hug Shirt™ there are actuators that recreate the sensation of touch and the emotion of a hug to the Hug Shirt™ of a distant loved one."[3]

Rosella and Genzopened have collaborated with performers like Katy Perry and U2 as well as fashion brands like Chanel and Converse, and designed speculative uniforms that light up for easyJet airlines. In 2017, CuteCircuit introduced the Twitter Dress—a black evening dress that displayed the wearer's Twitter account activity on the dress via flexible LED panels tucked between layers of Chiffon fabric. This was considered an amazing achievement by fashion folks, since chiffon is known to be the most delicate of fabrics, so being able to hide all these electronic components was hailed as a great success. In an interview with the BBC's Jane Wakefield, Rosella explained that until that point in time the studio mainly designed clothes for the catwalk, and were now focusing on adapting their designs in an attempt to take on the high street. In that interview, Rosella presented two beautifully and classically executed evening dresses and explained, "[I]magine you go out for an evening and you go with your little dress, it just looks like a pretty little dress, it doesn't do anything special. But then if you want to, you just push a button on your remote control and it will light up!"[4]

Was this dress finally the proof that wearable tech was going to catapult fashion design into its next phase? Was hiding the tech in a dress the objective? For Google and Levi's, probably so, but how could this methodology help designer fashion live up to the role we defined earlier? After more than a decade of work, it seemed that CuteCircuit realized that customers were hesitant to embrace the tech's aesthetic outputs (reactive clothing in the form of light displays).

Studio XO, founded by Benjamin Males and Nancy Tilbury, is another example of a fashion and technology company that was pushing the boundaries of fashion innovation. In 2013 the studio received ample media attention for their collaborations with Lady Gaga's TechHaus (the technical division of Haus of Gaga founded in 2012), designing and engineering one-of-a-kind dresses. Two examples are Anemone, a 3D printed white dress featuring an integrated bubble factory; and Volantis, a flying dress designed to carry one person in a controlled hover and directional movement. These were some of the most technically challenging and fashion-forward projects in wearable fashion seen to date. Although they were prototypes, Studio XO's work was exciting because they combined several different technologies and materials to design garments that questioned both aspects of function and form, offering a new aesthetic language. But by 2015 the studio seemed to be shifting focus as well, stating that they believed "generation Z teens want to wear the internet" and that they were the studio's target customer.[5] The studio launched a line of generic-looking hats and backpacks made of fiber optics that synced up with an app, which features a host of modes, including one that makes the lights react to sound, made to be worn at music concerts.

What wearable technology has achieved quite successfully is the ability to collect endless amounts of our personal data, allowing our clothes and accessories, or rather the companies that manufacture them, to know so much about our habits and functions. This might be beneficial for fitness, medical, or other practical uses, although these scenarios were also met with suspicion and criticism. Companies like Fitbit and Jawbone and projects like the Google Glass and Jacquard made no pretense of revolutionizing fashion but were certainly making big promises when it came to the benefits of data collection and analysis. In reality, aside from the Apple watch, most of these products were rejected by consumers.

Smart fashion is smart, but it is not yet fashion design. More than two decades have gone by and still clothing embedded with electronics are either closer to textile art sculptures made to exist in museums or wearable gadgets. The tech is unfortunately not there yet; it is still cumbersome and clunky. Besides serving as an app, sewn into our pocket, streaming our data elsewhere, the aesthetic outputs available now cannot offer that coveted and allusive allure of cool effortlessness that is at the heart of what captivates us in designer fashion. This is by no means due to lack of attempts made by independent fashion design studios such as the ones mentioned above. To achieve innovative garments that would be both "smart" and fashionable is a complex task: time and money are needed for research, testing, prototyping, and iterating.

For wearable technology to truly become part of fashion's future in a way that can offer customers an authentic and meaningful experience, the fashion industry must decide to financially back design-driven innovation that starts with an aesthetic and conceptual vision for which specific tech is developed. If not, we will keep seeing gimmicks, accessories, and garments that are trying so hard to look futuristic they are outdated before they reach mainstream fashion. It is like looking at an episode of the 60s cartoon *The Jetsons* and thinking, "Is that what they really thought the future of fashion would look like?" when in reality we are still aesthetically closer to the Flintstones.

Fashion Crafted of Bits and Bytes

In 2010, while some engineers and fashion designers were doing their very best to make the marriage between clothing and electronics work, others were already setting their sights on another area of technology for inspiration. In digital gaming environments, players were buying skins, clothes, and accessories for their characters to wear. It became clear that people were willing to pay good money for their character to stand out. Granted, these clothes were not fashionable—ranging from archetypes of basic clothing staples, such as T-shirt, jeans, little black dress, and so on, to fantastical creations designed to match a character in a specific game—but maybe they could be? Games were becoming more visually elaborate with advanced computational power while new software was producing realistic, live animations never seen before—and fashion designers were paying attention.

Fast forward to 2016 and the fashion industry was deep in digital. At first, companies embraced digital media as more of a marketing tool, a way of strengthening customer engagement and brand identity. It had been clear for some years that a brand without a strong presence on the web and in social media was practically non-existent, but when designer Alexander Wang stated in a 2014 interview that he was designing his physical fashion by thinking about how it would look on Instagram, it was clear that fashion was changing.[6]

That same year, Trevor McFedries and Sara DeCou from the robotics startup Brud developed the digital influencer Lil Miquela—a 3D avatar that was sharing her life and preferences with followers. What started as an Instagram profile project, quickly gained serious attention from consumers, and fashion brands could not stay indifferent to the phenomenon. This could be dismissed as a marketing gimmick or trend, if not for the fact that today Lil Miquela not only has 3.1 million followers on Instagram, but has collaborated with high-fashion brands like Calvin Klein and Prada as well as paving the way for a second generation of digital influencers.

In the realization of "smart" fashion, one of the biggest hurdles is the amount of hardware development involved versus the fast-paced nature of the fashion market. Digital fashion doesn't suffer from this, due to its nature of not being physical. Most of the hardware needed for creating digital fashion exists in more than half of households worldwide. 3D clothing and fabric simulation software used in the creation of digital fashion like CLO3D and Browzwear, which had been around since the early 2000s and were initially created to cut time-consuming processes in the production of physical fashion, were now being used by fashion designers to create digital garments. This software, combined with 3D modeling ones like Maya and Blender, allowed novice creators to hit the ground running with ample online tutorials, libraries, and communities to work with.

By 2018 one could not help but feel that digital was revolutionizing and reinventing fashion. Independent digital fashion designers were springing up like mushrooms after the rain, not a trivial occurrence considering that in the last twenty years many independent fashion labels had either been bought by conglomerates like LVMH and Kering or closed shop. Digital fashion felt democratic and liberating, with no inventory or showrooms to worry about and no gravity and material constraints stopping designers from experimenting in total conceptual bliss.

The detachment of fashion from a physical human body is at the epicenter of this revolution, naturally odd but exciting at the same time. When studying fashion design, the first thing an aspiring designer is taught is to never forget that carrying their textile fantasies is a 3D living, breathing, human that has to feel comfortable and have freedom to move. Physical fashion is a functional product.

For designers to now think of fashion as the act of designing garments for a virtual body, one that can be augmented by swiping a slider button, was to turn the profession on its head. Designing digital fashion is obviously not the same practice as designing physical fashion. It requires methodological shifts and utilizes a different technical skill set, but maybe digital fashion is a way to return designer fashion to what it used to be? "What it's meant to be" means garments that enable us to show up for life feeling a few inches taller, letting us reinvent ourselves when needed, pushing boundaries and making political statements—all without saying a word.

Roei Derhi, a classically trained fashion designer working for one of the industry's biggest fast-fashion mega brands, opened Placebo digital fashion house in 2019 from his living room. He had dabbled in 3D fashion design software and was always fascinated by how technology could innovate fashion design. I asked him what drew him to digital fashion?

> Initially I was designing digital garments for myself as a creative outlet and a way to create content for my social media presence. I was posting CGI (computer generated imagery), and people were noticing. I realized I was getting the same thrill from my digital wardrobe as I was from my physical one, maybe even more because I couldn't afford to buy or make the kind of fashion I was creating digitally. I was also paying close attention to what was happening on the business side and when I saw Fortnite had made some $50M selling one digital outfit I knew digital fashion was monetizable.[7]

Placebo has since grown into a fully fleshed-out business invited to show collections at physical fashion weeks from LA to Stockholm as well as on the 3D virtual world browser-based platform *Decentraland*, spreading their agenda of bringing fashion into the metaverse and providing individuals with sustainable, ageless, genderless, and highly conceptual and fashionable digital garments.

> [IB] What would you say to those who claim skins or digital fashion is not "real" fashion because there is no physical product?

> [RD] In my digital designs I always make sure to include "real" clothing details like buttonholes and pockets, which may seem peculiar to some since avatars don't use pockets. I believe that preserving the connection to IRL (in real life) fashion is critical; I don't want to lose the heritage and cultural references of fashion and that is why I also believe that when fashion designers create digital garments they have a sense of design integrity and believability that does not exist otherwise. One must know the rules in order to rethink them.[8]

Figure 6.4 *Placebo Meta Genesis collection. Placebo metaverse fashion house / Roei Derhi.*

Figure 6.5 *Placebo Meta Genesis collection. CGI on customer for social media use. Placebo metaverse fashion house / Roei Derhi.*

What Does One Wear to the Metaverse?

What really catapulted digital fashion into wide awareness was the Covid-19 pandemic. When our physical world literally shut down, life went mostly digital and, like every other industry, fashion needed to adapt quickly. Zoom meetings and the metaverse were introduced into everyday jargon. High fashion brands like Gucci, Balenciaga, Valentino, Loewe, and others were holding digital fashion shows and designing digital fashion for customers to buy for their characters to wear in games or wear IRL (in real life) via augmented reality platforms like Snapchat. The growing interest and substantial amount of digital fashion being designed justified the creation of specialized marketplaces like DressX, The Fabricant, and Artisant, where one can try on and buy virtual fashion.

The trauma of the pandemic served as the catalyst that fashion designers needed to embrace these technologies. If we are spending so much time living in digital, why do we need physical fashion? If that new dress that was liked so many times on Instagram was made of fabric or digital mesh, does it matter? For some, "the realness" of the product is a mental hurdle, but digital fashion *is* real. It is made with the same pattern-making techniques that have been used for hundreds of years. Materials are real; they are just not made of fibers but of zeros and ones. Is Kim Kardashian real? Most will never meet her and the image of her that we know is filtered and augmented both digitally and physically. So what is the difference between her and Lil Miquela? Not much in a practical sense, except for how we preserve reality. Fashion is a designed product we carry on our body to help us convey who we are. Today that body is interacted with in several different realities: the physical world, via digital platforms like social media and increasingly in virtual reality where we are represented by an avatar of our choice. It is only fitting that fashion will evolve to serve us in each of these different scenarios.

In October 2021 Mark Zuckerberg, founder of Facebook, announced that the social media platform was changing its name to Meta. Zuckerberg's announcement, in which he presented his avatar changing attire, did a service in mediating the concept of digital fashion to mainstream audiences.

For many digital creators the corporation's move to appropriate the metaverse and its promise of democratic creativity was concerning and many opted out, choosing to offer their creations on platforms that use blockchain technology like Decentraland. SHOWstudio's founder Nick Knight shared a post on Instagram:

This is HUGE !! We at showstudio asked an A.I. (created by creative director and A.I. image-maker @arthur_chance) to predict Daniel Lee's first Burberry collection before Daniel has actually designed it !!! This fundamentally changes the creative process ! The world is opening up new horizons, new frontiers. Artists must be the people creating this new world or it will be created by the military and capitalism. Do you want to live in another world shaped by greed and killing? We have a chance to do something incredible. Don't let fear stop you getting involved? It's a new world ! Live in the moment, not in the past.[9]

Quo Vadis Designer Fashion?

In the spirit of full disclosure, I am a classically trained fashion designer who, after years of designing and teaching womenswear fashion, decided to take a leave of absence and explore what all the buzz was about. At the age of forty-five, studying for a Master's degree in interactive digital media seemed like a daunting task but a necessary one. If I wanted to responsibly shepherd my students through the current "industrial revolution," I needed to evolve as well. Initially, I was absolutely sure my main focus was going to be wearable technology and for the best part of my first year it was. I prototyped shoes that tracked your mood by the skip in your step and accordingly played the appropriate playlist on your mobile device. I created a dress embedded with vibration motors that rang bells in different intensities when touched to convey how much attention is too much and many other fashion-related physical computing projects. These experiments were interesting, but as a fashion designer I felt they were just that: speculative experiments that were more about pushing the tech boundaries than finding a new aesthetic that could be innovative in a fashion scenario.

At the same time, I was introduced to extended reality technologies (augmented, virtual, and mixed) which opened a new and exciting range of possibilities. In my opinion, both conceptually and aesthetically, these technologies afforded a more meaningful exploration of how fashion design can expand its vocabulary and methodologies to be a part of social changes that are happening more rapidly than we realize.

This excerpt from a series of tweets shared by entrepreneur Shaan Puri clearly articulates why digital fashion has become so relevant and a natural progression in fashion:

> What it is, the metaverse, is the moment in time where our digital life is worth more to us than our physical life. Every important part of life is going digital.
>
> Work → from factories to laptops. boardrooms to zooms.
>
> Friends → from neighbors to followers.
>
> Games → more kids play fortnite than basketball & football combined.

Identity → filters are the new makeup. Stories are your personal billboard to broadcast who you are.

If everyone hangs out online all the time, then your flexes need to be digital. [O]ur attention has been sucked from Street to digital. And where attention goes, energy flows. So if you play this forward another 10–20 years—we will cross into the metaverse.[10]

I think Puri makes a strong argument and although his predictions carry obvious concerns, as a designer I can't help but be excited. Digital life and the fashion that will accompany it has all the characteristics of a revolution. The premise of a multi layered reality is new: some people are intrigued, some are hesitant, and others are appalled. These mixed sentiments are what great fashion design is made of—rebellious in nature, with an urge to resist old notions and conventions.

One of the interesting trends in designer fashion is an aesthetic dialogue between physical and digital fashion. Digital fashion is now inspiring physical fashion, as seen in collections by Loewe or designers like Richard Quinn and Demna Gvasalia from Balenciaga that are dressing women in second-skin-like garments that cover the entire body and masking the wearer's identity, even referring to these designs as "avatar attire."

For digital fashion to become a widely used product, computational power needs to advance even further: high quality fabric simulations are so heavy, it is almost impossible to achieve movement in real time while wearing an elaborate designed garment. The game engines usually crash.

It is also essential for all three realms of fashion design—design, fabrication, and production—to work in conjunction. Physical fashion design methodologies are important because tradition and heritage is the foundation, and newness is only viewed as such in perspective. Plus, unless the science fiction "brain-in-a-jar" scenario happens, people are going to need fashion both practically and as a way to express themselves.

Wearable tech has not disappeared and perhaps it is not very "smart" right now, especially from an aesthetic standpoint, but augmented and virtual reality headsets alongside haptic suits, like the Teslasuit produced by VR Electronics, are crucial for digital fashion to reach full potential. If and when wearable tech is able to allow us to physically sense our virtual activity via sensors and actuators, with our data used responsibly and in a transparent manner, with screens moving out of our hands and onto our face—only then will a real multilayered, experiential reality be realized.

Personally, I believe digital media technologies are going to be the ones shaping the future of tech-based fashion design. These tools offer designers a chance to be truly innovative and reclaim the traditional values of our profession that have been lost to fast fashion and clothing manufacturers. Independent designers have accessible tools to gain creative freedom which is revolutionary in itself and which in turn can offer customers one-of-a-kind, customizable, tailor-made fashions that in essence are a continuum of Worth's couture legacy. Stay tuned as fashion design continues to morph in interesting and exciting ways.

Notes

1   Google, "Jacquard," https://atap.google.com/jacquard/.

2   Louise Wilson, "Influential Fashion Educators: 'The Force that Moves Fashion'—Louise Wilson," *1Granary*, May 22, 2014, https://1granary.com/designers-3/schools/fashion-educators/louise-wilson-quotes/.

3   CuteCircuit, "Hugshort," https://cutecircuit.com/hugshirt/.

4   Jane Wakefield, "Who wants hi-tech socks for Christmas?" *BBC News*, December 21, 2012, https://www.bbc.com/news/technology-20529992.

5   James Stables, "Studio XO: Generation Z teens want to wear the internet," *Wareable*, November 17, 2016, https://www.wareable.com/fashion/studio-xo-building-wearables-for-generation-z.

6   Matthew Schneier, "Fashion in the Age of Instagram," *New York Times*, April 9, 2014, https://www.nytimes.com/2014/04/10/fashion/fashion-in-the-age-of-instagram.html.

7   Roei Derhi, conversation with author, March 2023.

8   Derhi, conversation with author.

9   Nick Knight, Instagram post, September 30, 2022, https://www.instagram.com/p/CjIS18lq5wr/?hl=en.

10 Shaan Puri, Twitter post, October 29, 2021, https://twitter.com/ShaanVP/status/1454151241785696256.

7

Digital Fashion Education: Towards a Fluid Transition between the Virtual and Physical Worlds

MINGJING LIN

Introduction: Fashion Gamification and the Fashion Metaverse

Gamification, by definition, refers to transferring elements of gaming and its theory, such as "skills, motivational benefits, creativity, playfulness, engagement, and overall positive growth and happiness," into a broader context of technical, cultural, and social developments in other fields.[1]

Accelerating fashion by engaging with gamification[2] has been adopted enthusiastically by many brands that include both high end and high street names, examples being Gucci, Prada, Balenciaga, and H&M. However, the correlation between fashion and gaming has long been the subject of research experimentation. For example, in 2000, Jane Harris, in her doctoral thesis "Surface Tension: The Aesthetic Fabrication of Digital Textiles," discovered that the use of gaming 3D CG (computer graphics) software can generate innovative imagery and surface decoration for textiles.[3] The sociology researchers Zhigang Cao, Haoyu Gao, Xinglong Qu, Mingmin Yang, and Xiaoguang Yang referenced game theory and its formulations to investigate fashion phenomena through cooperation and social interactions.[4] Researchers such as Chole Luo and Yi Wang have suggested that game theory is an effective marketing strategy for fashion retail companies, looking specifically at H&M.[5]

In a contemporary context, digital platforms and technologies, such as Instagram and game engines, have reinforced the connection between fashion and the digital game industry by enabling various virtual-related social interactions. It is also inevitable that fashion is identified as an important element in social media and video games. Fashion brands are aware of the great potential of fashion gamification and many are endeavoring to "tap generation Z through the 2.7 billion gamers worldwide."[6]

There is a variety of definitions of "the metaverse"—a buzzword in the creative and technical industries[7]—but they consistently include four conditions: "(a) a shared social space with avatars to represent users; (b) a world for the avatars to inhabit and interact with; (c) a space enabling users to own virtual property as they would physical property; and (d) a space enabling users to create their virtual property."[8] The fashion metaverse essentially refers to a digital space in which all the fashion components and their relevant assets are created and presented in digital format, including fabrics, garments, accessories, trims, scenes, models, make-ups, catwalk, performance, animation, and beyond.

Fashion brands and creators look at the opportunities offered by the metaverse to generate additional revenue through selling their products in a parallel, digital world, enabling brands to diversify from purely physical products.[9] Gucci's Executive Vice-President for Branding and Customer Engagement, Robert Triefus, observed that customers have recently become interested in purchasing NFTs and digital collectibles, as well as "having a second life in the metaverse."[10]

Advancing fashion into the digital realm presents two sides of the coin, from a design and production perspective. On the one hand, the cost of physical materials and physical toiling processes can be reduced in the fashion metaverse. Designers can create digital patterns, textiles, and trims, and can even customize avatars entirely so that they remain in a digital form: the cost involved in making these processes and materials is thus minimized. Conventionally, in the context of either a fashion atelier or fast-fashion company, designers and pattern-makers usually put sufficient effort (such as time, money, and materials) into making the prototypes as perfect as possible before sending them out for production. This design and sampling process can now be combined and visualized by digital software, such as CLO3D. The use of the latest software, such as Adobe Substance, Maya, and CLO3D, enables realistic textures and trimming details to be rendered.

An additional benefit of digital making is that creators use digital software to invent surreal designs that they are less likely to be able to create in physical form, in real life. For example, setting up a zero-gravity digital environment in CLO3D allows fringe tassels to float in the air, or can create a material that is semi-transparent in color but has the quality of leather. Designers modify the parameters of different functions of the software to achieve unexpected and often surprisingly high-quality outputs, which demonstrate their creative thinking in breaking the limitations and boundaries associated with making in a physical/real environment.[11]

On the other hand, fashion that exists in a purely digital format has been critiqued for its inability to fully transfer the physicality of the materials and enable a human tactile experience, which includes color, fit, texture, and comfort, all of which are essential criteria for fashion products, especially in the luxury market.[12] Although texture-rendering engines such as ApexFiz, Shima Seiki, Maya, and Unreal Engine enable digital fabrics to be visualized in a very real way, the touch of the hand, sensual tactility, and the sensation of the physical material can never be replaced by digital production. Technologies are advancing, but they are not advanced enough to offer the actual "feeling," the human interaction created by simply touching fabric.[13]

However, should the purpose of inventing new technologies be to merely replace traditional making by hand? Could the aim of digital technologies be to innovate with new approaches rather than offer substitutes for the existing ones? What do the advantages and disadvantages of creating fashion in/for the metaverse mean from a pedagogical perspective? There are questions that remain to be asked of us as fashion educators: how can we facilitate digital fashion education? How can we equip students with the appropriate knowledge to be prepared for a digital future in fashion? And how could we maximize their potential in the creative circumstances of the contemporary world?

Digital Fashion Competences

Digital Fashion Education

The use of digital technology has dramatically changed the fashion industry, from design and communication[14] to production and manufacturing.[15] Emerging technologies, such as blockchain, non-fungible tokens (NFT), artificial intelligence (AI), machine learning (ML), and virtual reality (VR) have promised new directions for luxury fashion companies to recreate their brand images and discover their marketing potential.[16] Researchers, including Kalvaska and Cantoni,[17] have noted that the fashion market and individual companies currently seek highly skilled workers who are competent in using the latest technologies and communication tools. Researchers such as Wang and Ha-Brookshire, in the article "Exploration of digital competency requirements within the fashion supply chain with an anticipation of Industry 4.0,"[18] summarized that digital competency is essential, especially in the early stages of the fashion business cycle, such as design, forecasting, and consumer research. Their study highlighted that nearly 98% of the job advertisements they gathered required employees to be equipped with digital skills, which includes being proficient in the use of Adobe software as a basic requirement.[19]

Recent examples illustrate that renowned fashion companies are collaborating with equally influential game developers to create incredible digital fashion outputs. These cases have illustrated that commercial fashion has already responded to digital fashion effectively with the aim of gaining additional revenue from digital streams. However, the key problem is that gaming technology and creative methods have not yet been fully transformed into solid pedagogical approaches and curricula for digital fashion education.

For example, as of this writing, the MA Digital Fashion course at Leeds Arts University, the Fashion and Textile departments at the University of Portsmouth, and the Digital Technology for Fashion pathway at Ravensbourne University, London, only focus on teaching CLO3D and have not yet engaged with gaming software.

In a systematic literature review of digital fashion marketing and communication, Noris, Nobile, Kalbaska, and Cantoni[20] concluded that the concept of "digital fashion" has recently gained dramatically increasing attention from both practitioners and academics. With the majority of these focused on fashion practice (business, design, communication, and production), digital fashion education has rarely been discussed. Out of a total of 491 publications researched by Noris, Nobile, Kalbaska, and Cantoni, 46.4% discussed the activity conducted by the fashion industry and the digital tools that are enabling better communication and marketing strategies, while 31.6% are about the implementation of digital technologies for design and production, but only 4.5% were related to the discussion of digital fashion education.[16]

If this data and the previous examples indicate that digital fashion is one of the most important markets, and that the fashion industry and companies are already part of a "digital transformation,"[21] are fashion educators ready to equip students with the knowledge and skills they need for the future? In terms of fashion design and innovative practice, the main reason why fashion education seems to be undergoing a digital transformation more slowly compared to the fashion industry is that traditionally fashion and game design have been separate academic departments within an educational institution. Although certain fashion students might be interested in learning/borrowing technologies from other fields, such as game and architectural design, or in collaborating with students in these departments, self-learning and collaboration is often fragmented.

Professor José Teunissen, Dean of the School of Design and Technology at London College of Fashion, one of the leading UK fashion institutions, stated that it is a challenging task for both companies and educators nowadays to recruit emerging talents.[22] This is because many aspects of fashion, including "sustainability, design, product innovation, entrepreneurship, manufacturing, data analysis, management and governance, policy-making, omnichannel, and e-commerce," require digital-driven knowledge and skill sets, as well as interdisciplinary collaboration, by the new generation of talent.[23]

The Erasmus+ funded project FT Alliance (2020–3), powered by European fashion-tech businesses and institutions, aims to enhance students' employability via knowledge exchange and collaboration in the fashion-tech fields.[24] The research data revealed that "the Fashion-Tech industry is asking for a variety of new skillsets" and that "Higher Education Institutions (HEIs) should prepare graduates as hybrid practitioners for an increasingly digital future where the development of the right mindset and mix of soft/er skills— being entrepreneurial, open to change, a team player, etc., is prioritized alongside that of the necessary hard/er skills."[25]

Therefore, it is not too difficult to conclude that the future of digital fashion education requires consolidated multidisciplinary skill-based training and collaborative awareness to be implemented in the curriculum. This collaboration would involve both the embedding of other disciplinary knowledge into fashion education and cooperation with external/industrial partners. As Teunissen states, there is an urgent need for fashion institutions to work with industrial partners to develop educational programs to nurture the development of "hybrid practitioners."

In addressing the gap between industrial development and fashion education, there are existing examples of educational programs that embed either technical training or industrial collaboration into the fashion curriculum with the aim of enhancing employability and students' experience. Research[26] shows that an Integrated Graduate Internship Program (IGIP) at the Arts University Bournemouth is a good model for training students with digital and technological skills in fashion design while they are studying. This project, which exhibited great potential for enhancing the employability of these students after they graduate, focused on embedding digital technology into fashion construction and production—the pattern-cutting process and manufacturing, rather than the design and initial creative processes. Other projects—such as the design competition organized by Lenovo, Stella McCartney, and Central Saint Martins; the commercial capsule sportswear collection "Day Zero" by Puma and Central Saint Martins; the Reshape wearable tech competition project by the Institute for Advanced Architecture of Catalonia, Noumena, and Fab Lab Barcelona—have all contributed to different dimensions of collaboration between the fashion industry and academia. These earlier examples prompted me to explore and identify the learning frameworks that are useful for digital fashion education, and ask, what digital skills creative students need for design processes?

Parametric Thinking 2.0

Speaking from my own experience, I was originally trained as a fashion designer and garment maker. My design and making process focused on hand-making, which indicates my interest in physical entanglement with real/tactile materials. I constantly touched, played with, and manipulated materials in order to sense their quality and comfortability in order to proceed with my design.

This sense of tactility became even stronger when I was conducting my Ph.D. research, which was about body-oriented parametric design for 3D-printed fashion and textiles. When I was experimenting with digital tools, 3D modeling, and parametric design software, I initially anticipated that I would use all the digital means available to model and visualize the design onto a virtual mannequin and send the files to 3D printing production straight away, without prototyping and sampling. However, I found it difficult to imagine how the materials would look in real life and how these materials would interact with a human body or the tactility of the materials and their relation with the human body. Inevitably, I 3D-printed out the physical samples and placed them on the human body to test out their material qualities.

Combining hand-making with digital-making can enable the creation of innovative design outputs. For example, I used textile dip-dye to blur the edges of two different 3D-printed materials (clear resin and black plastic) by adding a gradient color effect to the 3D-printed resin. Here is the story. I made myself an evening gown by using one of the spare samples to wear to the 3D-Printing Industry Awards ceremony. The 3D-printing companies I encountered there were curious about how the materials were made. This is because they had considered 3D printing as an end-product approach, but my way of using textile hand-making on a 3D-printed sample had produced unexpected and innovative outputs, which surprised the 3D printing experts.

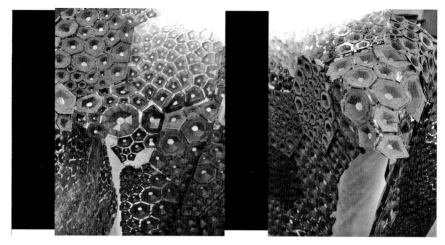

Figure 7.1 *Inter-fashionality Project: Hand-dyed gradient color onto 3D-printed resin, by Dr. Mingjing Lin (2016).*

Through a series of 3D-printed fashion and textile experiments, I eventually developed a new research concept and learning framework, Parametric Thinking 2.0, as one of the key outputs of my Ph.D. research. "Parametric thinking 2.0 is extracted from designing and making algorithm-based and 3D-printed textiles and fashion. It is a thinking that emphasizes the raising of awareness of the human body and its relevance during the design, especially in relation to pattern cutting for fashion construction and structural design for textile development."[27] Parametric Thinking 2.0 highlights the importance of combining physical- and digital-making in the creation process of 3D-printed textiles and fashion. This is because as a fashion and textile practitioner, the tactility of and engagement with the physical materials is always essential for my making. In this sense, introducing hand-making in the 3D printing and 3D modeling processes for fashion and textiles can be unique compared to other disciplines. For example, architects and/or product designers often take advantage of 3D printing and 3D modeling as digital tools to rapidly prototype their ideas, avoiding the necessity to produce physical samples. Since Parametric Thinking 2.0 encourages digital practitioners to think fluidly and to bridge conflicts between hand- and digital-making, I anticipate that this fluid combination between hand- and digital-making will be valuable for artists and designers from other professions, such as architecture and product design.

The second aspect of the learning framework of Parametric Thinking 2.0 is multidisciplinary collaboration. My conclusion from my practice is that multidisciplinary collaboration led to the success of the project. The development of technology contributes to the growth of collaboration, as "individuals are increasingly aware of the limitations to their knowledge and skill in a complex technological and interactive world."[28] 3D printing was not originally designed to be used in fashion and textiles. Although avant-garde practitioners have been experimenting with 3D printing since the 1990s, it is still unusual to find higher education design programs that focus exclusively on designing 3D-printed fashion and textiles, and the co-design approach has still occupied the majority of 3D-printed fashion and textiles practices to date.[29] Neither of the fashion design courses I attended (Tsinghua University and London College of Fashion) included 3D printing as part of their formal curricula.

Thus, my lack of knowledge of 3D printing and 3D modeling in the early stages of my research led me to seek collaborators who were more familiar with these technologies. This is a situation faced by all digital fashion adventurers: all the cases from industry mentioned above adopted the co-creation approach.

Extending the field from 3D printing and parametric design to digital fashion, I anticipated that hand-making and multidisciplinary collaboration were two learning models that could usefully be embedded in future digital fashion education.

Case Study: MA Digital Fashion at UCA

The concept of the MA Digital Fashion (Digital Fashion MA) program at the University for the Creative Arts (UCA) was initiated by Professor Jules Dagonet and the program director, Neil Bottle. In early 2021, a college-wide short workshop was organized at UCA to train fashion, textile, and game-design students in how to use gaming software for virtual garment creation. It soon attracted more than 200 students, who have produced promising digital works.

Led by the demand from students, later in the year UCA launched a unique digital fashion MA aimed at nurturing creative fashion thinkers and designers preparing for a new and exciting digital future.

This brand-new digital fashion course first emphasizes the use of digital and game software, such as Adobe Substance, Daz 3D, Autodesk Maya, and TwinMotion, for advancing fashion design, creation, and presentation; it has also been leading the current debates on connecting fashion with the game industry, by closing the gap between fashion and game design education, which had traditionally been separate departments.

My Ph.D. research made me, as a fashion designer, realize the importance of learning digital skills from other fields, such as architectural design and animation. Experimenting with a new technique, such as parametric Grasshopper software, enabled me to bring my fashion and textile knowledge to digital-making. This hands-on experience helped me create new 3D woven textiles that were less likely to be produced via conventional approaches to weaving.

Figure 7.2 *Fold-the-Interfashionality: 3D-printed woven garment piece by Dr. Mingjing Lin (2017).*

Therefore, following the learning framework of Parametric Thinking 2.0, multidisciplinary training aimed at equipping students with relevant software was the first step and the fundamental goal of the MA Digital Fashion program at UCA. The curriculum focuses intensively on workshops and software learning, while providing students with professional game-design technology and high-spec computers. Beyond that, theoretical studies, contemporary case studies, and research methods and methodologies are briefly introduced to the students, so that they are able to use this knowledge to underpin their practice. Tailored tutorials ensure that students' individual skills and talent reach their maximum potential.

Although digital fashion as a concept has already been welcomed by influential fashion brands, whether the MA Digital Fashion program will nurture the right kind of talent for the current fashion industry remains an unanswered question: for example, is the software we plan to teach relevant to the fashion industry? With the aim of testing out the industrial value of our existing training, and to help enhancement the curriculum, we created a live project for the first MA Digital Fashion intake in September 2021. Collaboration was facilitated between the UCA and a UK-based internationally renowned online luxury retailer.

This live project was scheduled to run from the end of September to the end of December 2021, when the first unit of the MA Digital Fashion curriculum took place. The idea was that while teaching emerging fashion design and visualization software, CLO3D, students would transfer their technical learning from CLO3D into actual designs in the live project. The project brief set out to create a new digital platform and fashion designs for the retail company involved.

Visit to the Company's Headquarters

The first activity was a visit to the company's headquarters, located in London's Old Street, an area noted for its creative vibe and culture. The coordinators of the company briefly introduced all the participating students to the office set-up and directed them to a meeting room where the leaders of the project (from the company) presented the project brief. There was a Q&A session, where students asked questions and exchanged their views with the company.

Students valued this opportunity because they were able to immerse themselves in the company and experience its culture, which was useful for the research and concept development of the project.

Technical Workshops and Training

CLO3D was the main software taught to MA Digital Fashion students simultaneously with their work on the live project. The purpose was for them to use digital means to realize their concept and ideas in a virtual 3D environment. Further to the software training, I arranged pattern-cutting workshops, which were not compulsory, to support students who had limited pattern and 3D garment knowledge. Interestingly, all the MA Digital Fashion students participated in nearly all the workshops and tutorials. Students reported that these physical-making workshops informed their digital-making, and the physical mannequin helped them to better understand the body. They appreciated these hands-on and 3D draping experiments, even though the whole process can be visualized in CLO3D software. Combining physical- and digital-making was thus highlighted as a reflection of the learning/research model of Parametric Thinking 2.0.

Group Collaboration

MA Digital Fashion, MA Printed Textiles, and MA Creative Direction for Fashion at UCA's Rochester campus were involved in the project from the start. There were six students from MA Digital Fashion, ten from MA Printed Textiles, and seven from MA Creative Direction for Fashion. We wanted the students to be able to learn from each other and to apply their different strengths, such as digital fashion design skills in MA Digital Fashion, textile design skills in MA Printed Textiles, and curatorial and presentation skills in MA Creative Direction for Fashion. Thus, we conceived this project as a group collaboration. We used a theme-oriented approach to divide the students into three groups to ensure that these students had common interests and starting points. We provided three topics: a) a one-of-a-kind product, b) ultimate consumer choice, and c) continued trajectory and widespread usage. These topics were extracted from the future market scenarios projected in the

Deloitte report "Apparel ~~2030~~ 2025: What New Business Models Will Emerge?"[30] Each student chose their favorite topic and joined the relevant group. The division of the groups, topics, and numbers of students are detailed below.

Their concepts were developed and narrowed down to more specific fields. The students' presentation topics were refined and made more specific while the live project progressed. The group who took on the topic of ultimate consumer choice developed their project to create a virtual city for digital creators and musicians to meet up, so they could discuss their projects in exciting virtual spaces, while promoting their products to consumers. The one-of-a-kind product project culminated in a concept called "You Create You," which creates a highly customized digital product and experience for consumers, with an awareness of community, diversity, and inclusivity. Individual consumers entered a virtual fitting room as a customized avatar, and selected from a full range of choices: body size, skin tone, garments, fabric pattern, and trims. The final project, continued trajectory and widespread usage, featured NFTs, AI, and social-sharing functions to allow an eco-relationship and interaction between the designer and their customers.

Table 7.1 *Student numbers for the live project*

Group	Topic	Digital Fashion MA	Printed Textiles MA	Creative Direction for Fashion MA	Total number of group members
1	Ultimate consumer choice	2	4	3	9
2	One-of-a-kind product	3	2	2	7
3	Continued trajectory and widespread usage	1	4	2	7
Total participants: 25					

Pitching Ideas

Pitching ideas involved two stages. Students first pitched their presentations and ideas to UCA staff, including their supervisors and the head of the program. Students also pitched their ideas to the project leaders from the company. After the presentations, each group received questions, comments, or feedback on how to improve the project from the attendees. Through this interaction, students were able to practice their communication and presentation skills, gradually becoming more confident about speaking in public.

Tutorials

Tutorials were provided by each department after each pitch presentation to ensure that students understood the feedback and were clear about the next steps.

Final Presentation

The final presentation was delivered online. Two students in the winning group from MA Digital Fashion won first prize and were offered paid, contract-based jobs at the company.

Discussion: Can Parametric Thinking 2.0 Lead Toward a New Learning Model in Digital Fashion in Higher Education?

Reflection 1. Creative Practice and Innovative Pedagogy

From a theoretical perspective, this live project was situated in learning theory as a creative practice and innovative pedagogy,[31] since it helped give students "access to and engagement in authentic instances of practice,"[32] which in our case was the collaboration with a commercial partner. Parametric Thinking 2.0 inspired me to train students in multidisciplinary digital skills. However, the teaching strategy combined technical training in a live project—which gave students a solid direction and background context for their research—with a collaborative approach, in which students exchanged knowledge with their peers and learned from each other.

This live project was beneficial not only to the participating students but also to the academic team, as well as our industrial partner. Specifically, all the participating students gained an opportunity to work with this leading company to discover the commercial potential of digital fashion. They had the opportunity to receive feedback from the company, as well as the academic team. Through the live project, we exposed new talent to the company and promoted their skills to this potential employer. Two students produced exceptional digital design and concepts, and were offered paid contracts to work with the company. This exciting result demonstrates and reinforces the potential of the curriculum of the MA Digital Fashion course, and that the novel skills and training we provided are appealing to the industry and can enhance employability. In addition, we (the staff team) were able to reflect upon our teaching strategies, having a debriefing session after each presentation to review our teaching content and strategies. This project was also a pilot research project on the part of the company, and students generated innovative solutions and creative ideas for the company to consider.

Reflection 2. Challenges

The first challenge we faced was identifying the right time to introduce a live project within a one-year MA course. MA Digital Fashion has three units of study. The first unit focuses on research, technical learning, and concept initialization. The second unit is about developing the research with improved concepts and technical skills. The last unit is the execution and realization of the final outputs in preparation for the MA degree show.

Introducing a live project in Unit 1 immediately excited students. This was because many of the students who had recently progressed from BA study to an MA course had no work experience, so this was the first time they had worked with a commercial company, particularly one that is globally renowned. However, embedding this live project in the first unit was problematical, because most of the students had not yet been trained in advanced 3D software, and thus did not have sufficient skills to realize the concept and ideas. Learning the new 3D software occupied most of their study time.

We concluded that although students could develop interesting concepts from the beginning of the live project, they did not yet have the skills and ability to transfer their concepts into the best possible outputs for this live project. In comparison, the students who already had a higher level of skill in using 3D software, or who had previous experience in other software, such as Blender and Maya, produced more appealing outputs, as they were able to learn CLO3D software more quickly, which left more time for design and making. For the future development of a live project, it is important to discuss with the team whether the live project should be part of Unit 2, when students are more mature and ready for the challenge.

The next challenge we faced was the duration of the project. The original plan was to run the project from early October until the end of December 2021; however, the final presentation was postponed until late January, as both students and the staff felt students' projects were not ready for presentation. Therefore, the overall project took three months and eventually lasted four months, because of the Christmas vacation. At the moment, MA Digital Fashion has been set up as a training and workshop-based course (most of the students signed up for the course for this reason), so it will be important to set a shorter time frame for the next live project, so that it does not interrupt students' technical learning.

Reflection 3. Virtual and Physical Transformations

Although the elements in the fashion metaverse are digital, it is desirable to include hands-on and traditional curricular elements of fashion, such as pattern cutting, to enable students to experience physicality, in digital fashion education. This feature was inspired by the learning model of Parametric Thinking 2.0 and was evident in the live project conducted by students on the first MA in Digital Fashion at UCA, documented above.

Parametric Thinking 2.0 taught us that making by hand and digital-making both have their advantages and are equally important. Digital makers should work towards a fluid and oppositional transition between digital- and hand-making.[33] This is essentially because the MA Digital Fashion opens up avenues for students to access new digital skills, which should add new dimensions to their existing knowledge. On one occasion, a student asked me how to create a glove in CLO3D, and I asked her how she would do that physically. She immediately realized that she could use basic pattern blocks and transfer this process in CLO3D. In other words, it is not the case that as soon as students register for the MA Digital Fashion program they start to erase all their existing hand-making knowledge. Eventually, I hope that the MA Digital Fashion can equip students with the ability to navigate both digital and physical means and move swiftly between the digital and physical worlds.

The increasing oscillation between the physical world and the virtual metaverse is recognized by researchers in the fashion industry,[34] especially after the global pandemic: "for a new generation of consumers who see the online world as essential to their day-to-day lives, the distinction between 'real' versus 'virtual' may be considerably blurrier than older generations might have once anticipated, spurred by a worldwide increase in isolation [brought] about by a global pandemic."[35]

I would also argue that oscillation between the physical and the digital is emerging strongly in many other aspects of digital fashion education, such as blending physical teaching and face-to-face activities with digital teaching; study trips; visits to companies; and face-to-face tutorials and in-person group discussions, which still play an important role in enhancing students' overall learning experience. This virtual and physical transformation needs to be highlighted in the future development of the MA Digital Fashion, and perhaps other disciplines, too, such as product or textile design, which conventionally emphasize hands-on experimentation yet are willing to engage with a new digital era.

I personally have a great belief in the potential of fashion digitalization and gamification, and anticipate that more institutional and industrial partners will work together to facilitate a "post-digital materiality."[36] At the time of writing (September 2022), the first MA Digital Fashion students have completed their studies and have just exhibited their graduate collections at the Rochester campus of the University for the Creative Arts. The students' astonishing work (Figures 7.3–7.7) is a clear reflection of what Neil Bottle

Figure 7.3 *Design by Alana Conlon.*

Figure 7.4 *Design by Lydia Crawshaw.*

Figure 7.5 *Design by Ritambhara Singh Patel.*

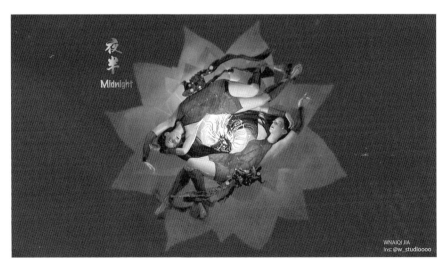

Figure 7.6 *Design by Wanqi Jia.*

Figure 7.7 *Design by Aparna Nair.*

referred to in a recent interview with *Vogue Business*, "[O]ur [MA Digital Fashion] students are so well equipped for the future. When they go for job interviews, they'll likely know more than the people interviewing them."[37]

Notes

1 Juho Hamari, "Gamification," *The Blackwell Encyclopedia of Sociology* (Chichester: Wiley-Blackwell, 2019), 1–3.

2 Catherine Shaer, "The 'gamification' of fashion is accelerating," *Women's Wear Daily*, April 14 2020, https://wwd.com/business-news/technology/tipping-point-the-gamification-fashion-accelerating-egames-1203556945/.

3 Jane Harris, "Surface Tension : The Aesthetic Fabrication of Digital Textiles (The Design and Construction of 3D computer Graphic Animation)," Ph.D. thesis, Royal College of Art, 2000.

4 Zhigang Cao, Haoyu Gao, Xinglong Qu, Mingmin Yang, and Xiaoguang Yang, "Fashion, Cooperation, and Social Interactions," *PLoS ONE* 8, no. 1 (January 31, 2013), https://doi.org/10.1371/journal.pone.0049441.

5 Chloe Luo and Yi Wang, *Game Theory in the Fashion Industry: How Can H&M Use Game Theory to Determine Their Marketing Strategy?*, Lecture Notes in Electrical Engineering, vol. 634 (Singapore: Springer, 2020), 633–8.

6 Lucy Maguire, "Balenciaga launches on Fortnite: what it means for luxury," *Vogue Business*, September 20, 2021, https://www.voguebusiness.com/technology/balenciaga-launches-on-fortnite-what-it-means-for-luxury.

7 Nikhil Malik, Yanhao Wei, Gil Appel, and Lan Luo, "Blockchain technology for creative industries: current state and research opportunities," *International Journal of Research in Marketing* 40, no. 1 (March 2023): 38–48.

8 Annamma Joy, Ying Zhu, Camilo Peña, and Myriam Brouard, "Digital future of luxury brands: metaverse, digital fashion, and non-fungible tokens," *Strategic Change* 31, no. 3 (May 5, 2022): 337–43.

9 Mark Ellwood, "Luxury brands are already making millions in the metaverse," *Bloomberg Business Week*, December 9, 2021, https://www.bloomberg.com/news/articles/2021-12-09/luxury-fashion-brands-are-already-making-millions-in-the-metaverse.

10 Robert Williams, "Gucci's Robert Triefus on testing luxury's Allure in the Metaverse," *The Business of Fashion*, December 7, 2021, https://www.businessoffashion.com/articles/luxury/the-state-of-fashion-2022-bof-mckinsey-gucci-robert-triefus-metaverse-virtual-nft-gaming/.

11 Ellwood, "Luxury brands."

12 Joy, Zhu, Peña and Brourad, "Digital future."

13 Mingjing Lin, "Interfashionality: body-oriented parametric design and parametric thinking 2.0 for 3D-printed textiles and fashion," Ph.D. thesis, Royal College of Art, 2020, https://researchonline.rca.ac.uk/4527/.

14 Tekila Harley Nobile, Alice Noris, Nadzeya Kalbaska, and Lorenzo Cantoni, "A review of digital fashion research: before and beyond communication and marketing," *International Journal of Fashion Design, Technology and Education* 14, no. 3 (2021): 293–301.

15 Karen Ryan, "Digital fashion—exploring the impact of an integrated graduate internship programme in higher education: a UK case study," *International Journal of Fashion Design, Technology and Education* 13, no. 3 (2020): 308–16.

16 Joy, Zhu, Peña, and Brourad, "Digital future."

17 Nadzeya Kalbaska and Lorenzo Cantoni, "Digital fashion competences: market practices and needs," *Business Models and ICT Technologies for the Fashion Supply Chain*, Lecture Notes in Electrical Engineering, vol. 525 (n.p.p.: Springer, 2019), 125–35.

18 Baolu Wang and Jung E. Ha-Brookshire, "Exploration of digital competency requirements within the fashion supply chain with an anticipation of Industry 4.0," *International Journal of Fashion Design, Technology and Education* 11, no. 3 (2018): 333–42.

19 Wang and Ha-Brookshire, "Exploration of digital competency requirements."

20 Alice Noris, Tekila Harley Nobile, Nadzeya Kalbaska, and Lorenzo Cantoni, "Digital fashion: a systematic literature review. A perspective on marketing and communication," *Journal of Global Fashion Marketing* 12, no. 1 (2020): 32–46.

21 Romano Andò, Fabio Corsini, Bianca Terracciano, and Giulia Rossi, "Understanding Fashion Consumption in The Networked Society: A Multidisciplinary Approach," in N. Kalbaska, T. Sádaba, F. Cominelli, and L. Cantoni (eds.), *Fashion Communication in the Digital Age: FACTUM 2019* (New York: Springer, 2019), 3–8, https://link.springer.com/chapter/10.1007/978-3-030-15436-3_1.

22 José Teunissen and Michèle Danjoux, "Fashion-tech: future recruitment strategies and assessment of emerging talent," *16th International Technology, Education and Development Conference*, INTED 22 Proceedings (n.p.p.: n.p., 2022): 8344–53.

23 Teunissen and Danjoux, "Fashion-tech."

24 Teunissen and Danjoux, "Fashion-tech."

25 Teunissen and Danjoux, "Fashion-tech."

26 Ryan, "Digital fashion."

27 Lin, "Interfashionality."

28 Sharon Helmer Poggenpohl, "Practicing Collaboration in Design," *Visual Language* 38, no. 2 (2004): 138–57.

29 Lin, "Interfashionality."

30 Jean-Emmanuel Biondi, Paul Reiner, Karla Martin, Drew Klein, and Kerri Sapp, "Apparel ~~2030~~ 2025: What New Business Models Will Emerge?" *Deloitte Digital*, 2020, https://www.deloittedigital.com/content/dam/deloittedigital/us/documents/blog/blog-20200610-apparel-trends.pdf.

31 Ryan, "Digital fashion."

32 Stephen Billet, *Guidelines for Practice: Integrating Practice-based Experiences* (Sydney: Australian Learning & Teaching Council, 2011), https://stephenbillett.com.au/guidelines-for-practice-integrating-practice-based-experiences/.

33 Lin, "Interfashionality."

34 Joy, Zhu, Peña and Brourad, "Digital future."

35 Joy, Zhu, Peña and Brourad, "Digital future."

36 Elaine Igoe, 2018. "Change matters: theories of postdigital textiles and material design," in C. Storni, K. Leahy, M. McMahon, P. Lloyd, and E. Bohemia (eds.), *Design as a Catalyst for Change—DRS International Conference*, (Limerick, Ireland: DRS, 2018), https://doi.org/10.21606/drs.2018.621.

37 Lucy Maguire, "The digital designers making millions from in-game fashion," *Vogue Business*, May 25, 2022, https://www.voguebusiness.com/technology/the-digital-designers-making-millions-from-in-game-fashion.

Idiat Shiole Interviewed by Michael R. Spicher

Idiat Shiole, based in Nigeria, is the founder of HADEEART ATELIER. In this interview, she explains how and why she made the switch from physical design to digital fashion. Shiole points out that a key difference between the practices of physical and digital fashion is that people do not care what you look like, where you come from, or any of your beliefs, in the digital fashion world. They only care about your creative output—and it needs to stay that way.

Michael Spicher   How did you initially get involved in digital fashion?

Idiat Shiole   It was actually out of curiosity and the lack of employment. When I was coming out of schooling, my course of study did not have a good infrastructure in my country, and the ability to get a job is really very difficult. So, the back story is that I actually went to the university to study medicine. And one way or the other, the accreditation of my school had ceased, so we had to choose other courses. I initially wanted to do food science and engineering, something along the lines of science and technology. But, in my university there were just two Fs: Fine and Applied Arts or Food Science and Engineering. I tried to change my course, but it didn't happen. That's how I became a Fine and Applied Arts student. I did not like the course because I did not have a drawing background. I just had to graduate from this course and from the school and probably have a certificate. So, fast forward to, I think I was in 400-level, we had been taught fashion illustration as a particular course in school. I took interest in it because I like the way we stylize the image. And you're able to think and bring out your own style, create your own mood board.

That was how it started for me. And I got an internship opportunity with a woman who owns Naijafashionista [a fashion design agency that offers services and instruction] in Lagos. It was a bit far from my school, so I had to travel down at times to intern there. After a while, I had to go for my National Youth Service Corps (NYSC), which is a one-year compulsory service to the Nation after your graduation. I wasn't feeling okay with illustration because I felt, is this what I'm going to base my life on? Is this enough to sustain me?

So, I wasn't so confident about it. After that, I tried to work for people as an illustrator, but I got this backlash because I wear a hijab. And people are like, "Oh, can you draw this and that?" It became something I needed to look into. So I thought, what if I add more things to this illustration that I'm doing. It brings me to the forefront of people. And I'm able to get more jobs, thereby I've been employed. And at the same time, this curiosity, I'm looking for how to spice up my fashion illustration. And not just take a pencil and draw random images. These were things I was looking at.

I started researching YouTube and Google, what can a Fine and Applied Arts student do in fashion. Then, one day I came across an article that was talking about Marvelous Designer. Marvelous Designer is a 3D software. Then I started searching for videos on Marvelous Designer. It took a while. All these questions took more than a year because the resources were not readily available yet. I was able to see Marvelous Designer on YouTube. The funniest thing is, I kept getting "marvelous" songs on YouTube because I wasn't inputting the correct phrase or word. Probably things are better now, but then there was nothing to assist me. There was no one to ask.

So, I later found Marvelous Designer on YouTube. I love the way the clothes were simulated together, which is something that was missing in the illustration I was doing. I got access to this software, and I started learning. But one of the things I noticed is these people I walked up to and told them I could do fashion illustration for you, and they looked down on me. What can you do? Like, you've been dressed like this. You can't design anything. So, when I showed them things I had done from Marvelous Designer, the story started to change. It's not like they were willing to pay for it or do it, but the way they responded to it was different. So, I just felt like, a sense that I'm doing something. I started to train people in 3D fashion. I am a self-taught artist, and this is practically how I started. That was how I entered digital illustration from Marvelous Designer to several other softwares that I use now.

So, for me, it was lack of employment, me feeling the insecurity of, "Will I be able to get employment?" And also curiosity. So that is how I started into digital fashion. And from there, I started checking out LinkedIn, which someone introduced to me as a professional platform. So, I started using it, and I found The Fabricant, and I spoke to Kerry Murphy, the founder. I told him what I can do—if you are looking for an intern. But I think they were not taking interns at that time. They told me to check out Facebook to see all the designers. I started seeing amazing stuff, amazing designs. Seeing what others had done, I felt like I needed to do better. So, that's how everything started. I started seeing people's work. I started having more ideas about what digital fashion really is and the possibilities, and how far it can go beyond what I already knew.

Michael Spicher   What were the challenges you experienced in shifting from physical to digital?

Idiat Shiole   One of the challenges was learning, relearning, and unlearning. As I said earlier, I was more of an illustrator than a physical fashion designer. I made dresses up to a point, but not for a very long time. It was while I was in school, and you have to survive. So, I sew for people just to keep up with school. But it was really difficult for me moving from illustration to 3D design because I did not have the assets already available. Number one, I did not have a very good laptop. Number two, the subscriptions, you need to pay for the software. And number three, it was difficult to get the resources. Now, if you go online, you can find tutorials for Marvelous Designer. These were not as readily available then. So, you have to teach yourself some things. So, the skill acquisition part was really challenging because I have to wake up every day and make sure I do something. And you get limited videos online.

When I got exposed to all those designers, I started to think in this digital fashion industry there are lots of things I can do. I can be a designer. I can go into several areas. What do I really want to do? So, one of the main challenges I had was focus. Because at the same time, fashion illustration was bringing in some income. But for 3D fashion, I did not have much resources or needs, but I needed time to learn. And I also need time to make ends meet from the fashion illustration.

So, the learning process was, for me, a big challenge. And after the learning process, me trying to unlearn what I had learned from fashion illustration. So, those stages and steps were challenging for me. You need to balance your energy. When you are moving from one place to another, you need to have a balance, so you can survive. And where you are going to, you need to have more energy.

Michael Spicher   What would you say is the biggest thing you had to unlearn?

Idiat Shiole   Oh, haha! One of the biggest things I had to unlearn is the ability to learn fast. This is a moving industry. Before you finish one stage, you see another technology is out there already. You have to be upping your game. At the same time, you don't have to forget where you're coming from. This is something I wasn't used to. Coming from a more physical background, I was drawing with my hand. So, I'm used to drawing what I see. But going into digital, I have to be able to imagine those things I have seen. And I don't have to stick to one position. In the physical world, I can tell you that I'm a charcoal artist. And that's it. I don't know how to use a pencil; I can just use charcoal. Going to the digital realm, you have to be flexible. So, I think that's the right word, you have to be flexible. So, I had to unlearn my rigidity, so that I could become flexible.

Michael Spicher   Do you ever blend the physical and digital in conception, creation, or other ways?

Idiat Shiole   Yes, I do that a lot because I believe that the physical and digital will definitely come together as one thing at the end of the day. I can't just create anything digital. Most of what I create is from what I have seen or what I've imagined in the physical world. So, those are the things I bring to the digital world. For me, I think they are just one entity in different bodies. I bring both concepts together. For instance, there are times I go to the market, and I see something, like a particular masquerade and the surrounding regalia. And I think this is very cool, so I can get a concept from this thing. Then at home, opening my laptop and going into a space, like Decentraland, I begin to think that I could take elements from what I saw at the market and bring it into this space. So, I pick from both what I see in digital and the physical spaces, and bring them together as one concept. Creativity comes from anywhere, so you don't have to limit yourself. You just have to let it flow. For me, it's where the creativity comes from at the present moment.

Michael Spicher   As technology is constantly changing, in what ways do you see digital fashion changing in the near future?

Idiat Shiole   I think digital fashion will actually change with technology. When it initially started, it was people creating 3D elements and printing out this pattern and using it to create dresses. It moved from that to more immersive ways, like augmented reality and virtual reality. And now we are seeing more uses in AI, though it is still limited. And we don't know the next technology that is coming out. This is just the beginning of digital fashion. Digital fashion only stops when technology stops. And I don't think creation and people inventing things will ever stop. It will continue, and so digital fashion will continue. The changes we would experience may be changes in the way we consume things as humans. The way we see digital fashion. But digital fashion itself would not change. It's just like fashion. To me, fashion has not changed. It only has additional components. Fashion is still fashion. Digital fashion is a new component in fashion. Going forward, we might have new components in digital fashion, but, at the end of the day, everything still boils down to digital fashion. And everything still boils down to fashion itself. So, I don't think technology advancing would really change something. What would change is the way people consume digital fashion.

Michael Spicher   What advice would you give someone considering digital fashion both as a consumer and as a creator?

Idiat Shiole   I believe that, whether you are a creator or a consumer, one of the best ways to try to make good use of something is for you to learn, unlearn, and relearn. Because skill acquisition is one of the things that can really make you successful in life. So, I would say that if you are a consumer and you're not willing to know about physical fashion and you're not willing to learn a new way of consuming fashion (which is digital fashion), you'll remain there. But at the same time, if you're thinking of moving into digital fashion as a creator, and you need to be ready to learn the AR part of things just so you can have a seamless process.

As a consumer, you must be ready to learn all the sectors of digital fashion, so that you can enjoy it to the fullest. And as a creator, you must not limit yourself to designing 3D clothing without learning about AR [augmented reality] and immersive technology; you have to make sure you are valid in every sector of digital fashion. So that you can enjoy it to the fullest. Fashion is not just what we wear; fashion is an art. And you would agree with me that we all want to enjoy art. So, if you want to enjoy an art, then you must be in the artist's mindset. That is for the consumer. You should want to get the full gist of what the artist is trying to pass across to you.

Michael Spicher   Do you have any concerns or cautions about the direction that digital fashion is going in?

Idiat Shiole   Yes, I do. But just a bit because for me I like the decentralized part of digital fashion that we have at the moment. Physical fashion is already fragmented. As I explained, when I was illustrating for people, I would get all this—I don't want to call it racist behavior—but I would get all this backlash about what I could do being dressed like this. In the digital fashion world, there's nothing like that. We are all one big family. Nobody cares who you are. They don't care whether you're black or you're white. Maybe you belong to a particular religion, or you belong to a particular sector. All they care about is the creativity you bring. And that is why digital fashion is able to move fast. My only fear is that things shouldn't change. If all the stakeholders can continue to uphold the decentralized aspect, make things as transparent as we have now, I think digital fashion is ready to be the biggest thing we've ever had in the fashion industry. I really think that the fashion industry is fragmented. There's always a trend that people want to follow in the physical fashion sector. We don't have this in the digital fashion sector. Everybody's allowed to be who they are and what they want to be. Even small designers have a place to grow. But in the physical world, it is a bit different.

My only concern is that this should continue, and we shouldn't experience the centralized version of things. Everything should continue to be decentralized. And this will bring more people into the digital fashion industry and the fashion industry at the same time, and create a more sustainable environment for everyone. Because no one is going to get scared of joining the industry because they are not that rich or whatever else. With the little you have, you can start in the digital fashion industry, unlike the physical fashion industry, which is a bit shaky to start. You have to have a certain amount of money. You have to know a certain amount of people. You have to find a producer that would help you produce your stuff in batches. You have to do more for a fashion show. A creator has to create your dresses. There's a dress fitting. There's a gatekeeper. But in the digital fashion industry, we don't have things like that. It is open to everybody. And everybody can enjoy the goodness of it. So, I really don't want this to change.

Michael Spicher   Digital fashion designers are currently accessible in ways that physical fashion designers are often not. Do you think this sense of community can be maintained as digital fashion continues to grow as an industry? Do you have any specific suggestions?

Idiat Shiole   Number one is the way the door has been open to everybody should continue to be so. And we that are at the forefront of things, we shouldn't start hiding things from people. One of the main reasons why digital fashion is growing so much is because you can easily get tutorials and can easily meet someone online and mention that you're trying to learn something and whether they might assist you. So, if there is a community that works towards education in the digital fashion industry, I think it would also help in decentralizing things. I feel education should be one of the priorities of every industry. And if we can have people dedicated to educating people on digital fashion, it might not be the practical aspect of things, but making people understand that this community you're coming to join is decentralized. Because at the end of the day, when people don't get the necessary education, things start to change. I think educating everybody that is coming to the industry, or coming to this sector of the fashion industry, should be educated and have the appropriate knowledge of how things have been done. Because when people with the knowledge start leaving, or get too old or retire, then the younger ones in the industry will not have this sense of decentralization. And things will start to change. One of my suggestions would be education. We need to educate ourselves, and the people coming after us.

Michael Spicher   Is the practice of digital fashion more inclusive than physical fashion?

Idiat Shiole   Definitely. Digital fashion just cares about your creative process. It does not care about your location. I keep using myself as an example. When I was an illustrator, I was limited because I was a *fashion* illustrator. I had to start learning how to become a general illustrator, so I can make ends meet. You only have a few people you can illustrate for. The fashion designer tells you that you have to come to their show to illustrate for them. And other things like that. So, it's not really that inclusive. But digital fashion is very inclusive. I've worked with brands that I don't even know. I worked with people that I would never have met in ten years of my life, if I had stayed with only physical illustration. So, for me, digital fashion is extremely inclusive. You can be anywhere in the world. You can be anyone in the world. What everyone cares about is the creativity you're bringing on board. It exposes you to people; I can't count the number of people I've met just from putting my work online. Some people don't even know who the person is. I've met a lot of people that use their avatar, so I don't even know who they are or what they look like. But still, I'm able to work with them, and we're able to create nice outfits. Digital fashion is just so inclusive, and that is so sweet.

Michael Spicher   Are there any common misunderstandings from the public when it comes to digital fashion?

Idiat Shiole   Yes. I come from Nigeria. When you try to speak to someone about digital fashion, one of the questions they ask is: why should I invest in something I cannot touch or wear? It's a common thing and you have to explain to them that's not the only thing digital fashion is about. You can still wear digital things. It's still fashion, as I said earlier, but the way we consume it is different. People are stuck to the way they consume fashion, which is physical fashion. So, we kind of have to redirect them to a new way of consuming things. This is where we have a lot of misunderstandings. Because people believe fashion is just about wearable things. You go to the designer, fit your dress, and then put it on. Most people where I come from are really concerned about how they are going to wear this item. It's a big misunderstanding. And some people think digital fashion is just about NFTs, and it's a waste of time and money. I don't know about other places in the world, but this has been my experience.

Michael Spicher   What innovation/change are you most excited about when it comes to digital fashion?

Idiat Shiole   I feel like extended reality will change; we've just started when it comes to extended reality. For one thing—artificial intelligence—I'm looking forward to where that is headed for the digital fashion industry.

Part Three

Issues and Ethics
of Digital Fashion

8

Digital Fashion as the Basis of an Economic Revolution

DANIELLA LOFTUS

Introduction: *Fashion Victims*

Tokyo-based photographer Kyoichi Tsuzuki published his photo series *Happy Victims* in 2008. Described as "a record of the boundless unrequited passions of fashion freaks,"[1] the series depicts Tokyo's brand-obsessed residents in their apartments, surrounded by clothes of ten, fifteen, or even 100 times the value of their homes. When we look at the global fashion industry, Tsuzuki's *Happy Victims* are not just restricted to the Tokyo streets. Responsible for 2% of the world's GDP,[2] bringing in some \$3 trillion annually,[3] ranked alongside the GDP of individual countries, the fashion industry would represent the seventh-largest economy in the world.[4] With the vast quantities of capital the fashion industry generates, one could be led to assume that participants in this economy would be financial beneficiaries. However, taking a closer look, it's clear that the majority of those who engage with fashion—both as producers and consumers—are more akin to "fashion victims," with revenues and profits generated not *for* them, but rather, at their expense.

Digital fashion—defined as any garment created in the digital realm—holds the potential to rewrite this paradigm. It holds the promise to transform fashion into a tool to reward both its consumers and producers. Through the introduction of digitally native technologies, those who engage with fashion can be converted from fashion victims to beneficiaries—with new abilities to sell clothes in digital spaces, program profit, be rewarded for wearing, and benefit from a variety of new incentive structures which form the basis for an economic revolution.

I. Re-production

Fashion employs 12.6% of the 3.4 billion global workforce:[5] an estimated 430 million people.[6] These participants can be broken down into two segments:

1 Producers building their own brands
2 Producers working for the existing brands

Producers Building their Own Brands

A *Forbes* article by Joseph DeAcetis defined fashion as three things: "it's exquisite, it's expensive and it's exclusive."[7] For those looking to break into the fashion industry, at least the final two of these points hold true. In 2021, LVMH and NIKE turned profits of around $20 billion,[8] while non-luxury high street giants such as Inditex (owner of Zara, Pull & Bear, etc.) and H&M Group turned over *c.* $3 billion.[9] These fashion goliaths are described in McKinsey and Co's annual *State of Fashion* report as "super winners,"[10] leveraging their scale and growth to become the industry's dominant players. Alongside the conglomerate titans of Inditex and Kering come the likes of Hermès and Nike as well as sixteen others.

Looking more closely at these "super winners," it's clear that "Goliath" is indeed an apt term. The same McKinsey report that termed these twenty large brands "super winners" also identified the fashion industry as a "value destroyer."[11] It went on to define this term as a state wherein the success of the dominant players came at the expense of their smaller counterparts. Here's where the elements of "expensive" and "exclusive" transform from being characteristics of a brand's allure to instead describing near insurmountable moats.

On the side of the high street players, the deepest moat takes the form of price competitiveness. Though both luxury and high street brands leverage immense economies of scale to forge high margins (Nike boasts 482[12] factories globally and Louis Vuitton, 4,000),[13] the high street competes on cost, while luxury leverages reputation to build a brand that holds more sway than its competitors. Driven by fashion weeks and a global advertising presence (often enabled by celebrities), marketing is crucial. In its heyday, the 2016 Victoria's Secret Show boasted 6.7 million viewers[14] with a show budget of $20 million.[15] Luxury's reputation building allows it to diversify its offerings and capture the hearts of lower income consumers. While a fractional percentage of luxury consumers buy higher value items, diffusion lines and beauty provide the rest with alternative ways to engage with a brand's presence. The result of these factors is that this small cluster of "super winners" generate over 100% of the industry's total economic profit, as was the case in 2020.[16] Therefore, just as DeAcetis unwittingly identified, for an independent creator looking to break into the market it's too . . .

1. *Expensive*

More than 85% of fashion design graduates find full-time employment, but the majority of them will not work as designers.[17] One teacher from *The Startup Club* tells students that "on average, it costs about $10,000 to start a line."[18] For producers trying to break into the industry, these high sunk costs—those of materials, production, and studio space—are often too much of a deterrent. The financial risk of failure is too high to sustain. And where it's near impossible to uphold a financially viable business model that competes with the high street on price, incumbents end up surrendering to the system.

2. *Exclusive*

For those trying to compete on "reputation," the walls are equally high. The allure generated by large luxury brands is extremely costly. Engaging with a "mega influencer" (more than one million followers) can set brands back between $10,000 and $1 million for a single post,[19] whilst a 10–15-minute show at a major fashion week ranges from a minimum of $100,000 to over $1 million.[20] Even if a young designer does achieve these status markers, they still need to find favor with the fashion press. And for the small brands that do manage to break in, the business models favored by the stores that present them to the public are often sources of financial strain. Alternatives, like doing it yourself, are just as tricky.

Finally, shipping costs have been rising over the years, with many small business owners claiming that sending goods is four times higher than costs prior to the Covid-19 pandemic. Smaller businesses believe they are often the hardest hit by higher freight costs and shipping disruption as without the ability to commit to higher volumes, they have lower buying power.[21] Ultimately, without the size and scale of a "super winner," operations in the fashion industry are hard to sustain. Even for those who do break in, attaining financial security in this current model is a constant challenge.

Producers Working for the Existing Brands

You'd expect that the moats which stunt the growth of independent creators would benefit those millions of employees working for "super winning brands." Yet, a glance at the cogs of the fashion machine shows that access to profits is still reserved for those at the top—in this case those leading the companies. While the CEOs of McKinsey's "super winners" make money in the tens of millions of dollars, of the estimated 75 million[22] people who work directly in garment production, many are underpaid and reside in countries that don't facilitate unionization.

Research from the Worker Rights Consortium (WRC) shows that garment workers' average wages have decreased over the past twelve months (year 2022–1) by 21%, from an average of $187 per month to $147.[23] According to Business and Human Rights Resource Center (BHRRC) research, the minimum wage in twelve major apparel-exporting countries is, on average, more than four times less than the amount workers need to live on.[24]

Digital Disruption

Where a lack of accessibility for those looking to break into fashion, and a lack of opportunity for those already employed, can be classed as fashion's ills, digital fashion can be seen as its cure. Providing access and mobility through digital channels, digital fashion makes it not only possible, but lucrative, for fashion producers outside of the "super winners" to thrive across the entire distribution chain by leveraging . . .

Digital Tooling

In the era of digital fashion, long gone are the days where stipends, studio spaces, and first-class fashion degrees were the prerequisites for success. Instead of a degree at Parsons ($53,708 per year for undergraduates)[25] or Central St Martins (£9,250 per year for UK undergraduates, £25,970 for international students),[26] programs like CLO3D and Marvelous Designer (with annual fees of $600[27] and $300[28] respectively) can enable designers to complete collections with little more than a few thousand dollars in the bank.

Algorithmically Generated Exposure

Once clothing has been created, rather than needing a slot at an expensive fashion week to show it, designers have the ability to turn to social media and virtual spaces to find their consumer base. A recent "Metaverse Fashion Week" held on the Decentraland platform saw 108,000 unique attendees[29] watching shows both from luxury brands like Tommy Hilfiger and Dolce & Gabbana and Web3 upstarts like DeadFellaz, The Sevens, and 8SIAN.

Additionally, for those less interested in moving fully virtual, digital technologies such as augmented reality (AR) can still allow physical fashion to generate exposure online and gauge demand before items are produced. Rather than engaging in the costly process of shipping designs to influencers, or overproducing goods, designers can leverage Instagram, TikTok, or Snapchat (2.27 billion daily active users,[30] 1.46 billion daily active users,[31] and 347 million daily active users[32] respectively) for virtual try-on. Digital fashion brand Auroboros saw 2.5 million wears of its digital VenusTrap dress in 2020[33] through a Snapchat filter where users could try the dress in augmented reality. And once a producer has broken down this first set of barriers (manufacturing their collection and getting it seen), digital fashion can reform the ways in which the fashion gets sold, making it simpler for the producer as well as more lucrative.

Novel Routes to the Consumer

As of 2022, gaming company *Roblox* Corporation had over 52.2 million daily active users of *Roblox* games worldwide.[34] Made famous for its user-generated content (UGC) model, *Roblox* publishers do not create the majority of the content themselves. Rather, they revert to their consumer base of "developers" to sell games, wearables, content, and even tools for other creators, all in exchange for their proprietary currency "Robux." During the Covid-19 pandemic, *Roblox* made headlines. These headlines covered both *Roblox's* substantial developer payouts such as the case of creator Arthur Trusov who made close to $848,000 in sales in 2020 and almost $1.4 million in 2021,[35] and *Roblox's* engagement with fashion houses such as Gucci and Hilfiger. A *Roblox* developer earns anywhere between 30% and 70% of a transaction value (depending on whether they are the creator, the seller, or both). In June 2022, 2.7 million developers and creators earned Robux with the platform paying out more than $500 million dollars to its community of developers and creators in the previous year.[36]

Middlemanless Marketplaces

Where the worlds of Roblox offer new and lucrative routes for fashion's independent creators to connect with a consumer base, these platforms still hold restrictions concerning who can sell. Roblox demands "Premium Membership" (ranging from $4.99 to $19.99 at the time of writing) for those looking to sell wider ranges of fashion on its marketplace and have tight curation boards dictating which producers become "fully approved."

Non-fungible tokens (or NFTs) are digital assets stored on the blockchain, which can have specific qualities programmed to automate processes—those of recognition, payment, or transfers—unalterably. These innovations can facilitate full transparency and automated reimbursement, and have given rise to a host of "trustless" marketplaces operating without a middle-man. NFT Platform Opensea, which describes itself as "the world's first and largest Web3 marketplace for NFTs and crypto collectibles,"[37] allows anyone to create and sell digital assets on-chain. With 80 million digital assets on their platform[38] and one million active users[39] (as of 2022), the platform takes only 2.5% on primary sales[40] with no restrictions around who can sell or buy.

Royalties

Royalties are fees provided to creators. When a creator's goods are used or sold, the creator is reimbursed. Previously royalties were best known in the music industry, where those who produced a piece of music received a fee every time that piece of music was used. Leveraging the power of the blockchain, royalties can be programmed into all digital fashion items. Again, this allows creators to be rewarded each time a good is bought, sold, or used (depending on their preference).

For fashion items that become cultural icons (such as the Birkin bag) this can be particularly lucrative for its original creators. What's more, even if a piece was produced in collaboration with numerous creators, each creator would still accrue their equal share of the financial returns—a perfect fit for the fashion market where textile designers, pattern cutters, garment technologists, and many others come together for each step in the creation process.

Immutable IP

The fashion industry has long been chastised for the phenomenon of large brands claiming the work of emerging creators as their own. In June 2022, an American freelance artist, Maggie Stephenson, sued Chinese fast-fashion retailer Shein for $100 million, alleging the company copied her artwork without permission, and whilst few creators end up actually winning these suits, Shein was chastised in the court of public opinion due to previous violations. Digital fashion (when built on blockchain) holds the benefits of immutable provenance. This allows certainty in disputes between creators on originality and further ensuring routes to fair compensation for those involved.

Reductions in Returns

Finally, for those more comfortable with IRL or in-real-life digital fashion (where digital mechanisms are used to create a physical item), virtual clothes can still be a lucrative way to save money and further sales. Consumers can make more considered physical purchases, after experimenting with wearing a digital counterpart, and creators can reach consumers through social media sites like Instagram and Snapchat with no production spend. Ecommerce giant Shopify reported a 40% decrease in product returns from 3D visualization, and Build.com reports that the return rate for shoppers that use their AR product visualization features is 22% lower than non-AR benchmarks.[41]

Conclusion to Re-production

Digital fashion has the potential to expand the categories of who can participate in the fashion system, as well as the ways in which they can benefit. With new routes to exposure and mechanisms for reimbursement the risks for producers are lowered, with greater potential rewards.

II. Re-consumption

A woman will spend an estimated **$125,000** on clothes in her lifetime.[42]
On average these clothes are worn **seven times** before being discarded.[43]

Compiling these statistics, we can paint a picture of the current state of fashion for its buyers; a state characterized by conspicuous consumption and fueled by a synthetic cycle that is not for the benefit of the consumer, but rather at their expense.

The Pathology of Fashion

The phenomenon known as "The Diderot Effect" was defined by French philosopher Denis Diderot in the mid-1700s.[44] A prominent figure during the Age of Enlightenment, the philosopher lived the majority of his life in poverty, until, at the age of fifty-two, Catherine the Great built a library in his honor. According to Diderot, this library was so lavish that he felt ashamed to wear his customary rags within it. He invested in a scarlet robe, to wear while within the space, in order to pay it adequate respect.

When Diderot donned his robe, he finally felt worthy of setting foot in his library. However, in comparison to his other possessions, the robe was so glorious it made everything else he owned seem dirty and insignificant. Diderot concluded that there was "no more coordination, no more unity, no more beauty"[45] in his possessions, seeding the compulsion to buy more in order to achieve alignment. Now defined as the process whereby "obtaining a new possession often creates a spiral of consumption which leads you to acquire more new things," the Diderot Effect forges the foundations for the system known as "the fashion industrial complex," driving consumption in four distinct steps.

Step 1: The First Purchase

In the US alone, $656 million per year[46] is spent on advertising in the apparel and accessories industry. Rather than responding to consumer demand, fashion works by stimulating it. Twice a year, clothes come down the runways of Paris, Milan, New York, and London, and the job of millions of industry professionals—from marketers to salespeople to buyers—is to shift them into consumers' closets. Seemingly simple, there are two inherent challenges that the fashion industry faces when moving these items.

1. Fashion is Created without Responding to the Consumer

The current fashion cycle defies the well-known term "product market fit." Defined as "a first step to building a successful venture in which the company meets early adopters, gathers feedback and gauges interest in its product,"[47] the term was invented by Sequoia Capital founder Don Valentine, to refer to how businesses should first assess if anyone wants to buy their product. Before releasing a product into the market, businesses should confirm that it is meeting a consumer need.

2. Nobody Needs it

Fashion's second challenge relates back to this word "need." If you look at clothes, their most primal function is to keep their wearers warm and protected. Whilst in the twenty-first century this need is still an important one, if consumers were looking to respond to physiology alone they would buy no more than a few items a year. As few purchases as that would not be conducive to a multi-trillion-dollar industry. Thus, instead of dealing with a need for clothes, fashion centers itself on a need for identity. This need is not primal and organic, but rather socially and culturally forged.

These two challenges drive a fashion industry that functions by stimulating consumer demand rather than responding to it. In this way, fashion can be understood to be in the business of creating, and then satiating, consumer needs to transform identity. This cycle is set off from a consumer's very first purchase.

Step 2: The Necessary Realignment

After we've fallen victim to the first hit of transformation, the Diderot Effect (explained above) kicks in. A look at any runway makes clear that fashion is not just composed of a single item, but rather entire "looks." And for real fashion fans who go further than "black is in, red is out," this look comes with a narrative deployed by the designer. If the industry professionals have done their jobs right, this look—and its accompanying narrative—will stand as somehow incompatible with that of last season. One item will not be enough for the consumer. Adopting the new look's identity will demand an entire redefinition of a wardrobe, àla Diderot.

Take the average American woman as a key example of this cycle's effectiveness. Consuming sixty-four new items a year,[48] she burrows down the bi-annual rabbit hole of identity reformation and commits to creating "the new her" when each Spring/Summer and Autumn/Winter rolls around.

Step 3: The Experience of the New

Once the consumer's identity has been reformed, for a brief period, he/she "fits in"—a term known in sociology as "cultural embeddedness." Embeddedness relates to the fact that "an actor's preferences can only be understood and interpreted within relational, institutional, and cultural contexts,"[49] and indeed fashion is creating a new "culture" each time a runway show is complete. By conforming to that new set of aesthetic cultural values, one comes to achieve "embeddedness" inside a wider fashion community and, of course, within the subculture of a brand itself.

Step 4: The Inevitable Churn

As soon as the new season rolls around, the identity that's been constructed by the consumer transitions from a route to achieving embeddedness, to an identifier of the wearer as a cultural outlier. Irish poet and playwright Oscar Wilde termed fashion "a form of ugliness, so intolerable that we have to alter it every six months,"[50] and indeed resparking this reformation of identity—driving the wearer to recommence their cycle of consumption—is an inevitability that the fashion industry depends upon.

To go back to the analogy between fashion and the traditional consumer product, fashion creates consumer needs via advertising, and at the start of the new season works to inspire churn. Just as buyers of an iPhone begin with a set of hardware and software, and need both upgraded on a rolling basis to assure full functionality, the final stage of fashion's cycle aims to inspire consumer dissatisfaction with their original product (their identity), so it too needs to experience an upgrade to the newest model. This pathology, encouraged to further the "fashion-industrial complex," forms a basis for understanding the phenomenon of the $125K lifetime spend, and a garment discarded after just seven wears. However, a second framework is needed in order to understand the ultimate conclusion: one defines fashion goods via expense.

The (literal) Cost of Consumption

According to a McKinsey report, pre-owned watch sales will be about half the size of the market for new retail watches by 2025.[51] Similarly, looking at the art world, the secondary art market accounts for 44% of all sales. On the other hand, in fashion (where the second-hand market is valued at US$27 billion and projected to reach $57 billion by 2025), resale and second-hand fashion only accounts for 3.2% of total sales.[52] What do these figures indicate about fashion? Unlike many other consumer goods, these pieces do not stand as "investments." There are three reasons for this.

1. Expendability

Wear and tear is defined as "the damage that happens to an object in ordinary use during a period of time."[53] Looking at the categories above, "ordinary use" substantially differs in fashion. For art, "ordinary use" takes the form of exhibition, on a wall or within a space. For watches, "ordinary use" is being fastened on the wrist where they sit protected from an array of hazards. For apparel, wear and tear involves fabrics on the body, enduring spills, rips, and consistent washes. The term itself seems defined for this class of consumables, and when viewed through the lens of investments, fashion's value drops with use at an exponential rate.

2. Velocity

Though art and watches respond to trends, many can be considered classics. Of course, galleries and watch sellers operate on cycles, where new creators and models come into vogue, but their sales model is not based on shipping entirely new consumer wants on a bi-yearly basis.

3. Taste (and other tethers)

Finally, the element of taste. Fashion is tethered to a physical body, making it far less reusable than either art or watches. Outside of the purely practical considerations of fit, fashion's utility in helping to express personal identities means that there is no one size fits all (whatever the tags might say). Whereas good art is often dictated by the market, fashion can be thought of as much more subjective, with the multiplicity of styles speaking to the variety in identity expression.

Whose Expense is Greatest?

A final point to note is that within fashion consumers, those on the lower income scale are those who get the least value from what they buy. Mapping this back to the qualities above, cheaper clothes (otherwise defined as "fast fashion') are:

1. More Expendable

The materials are often less durable than their luxury counterparts. A study by Columbia University showed that second-hand accessories demonstrate that high-end goods can be more sustainable than mid-range products because they have a longer life cycle. Instead of being considered a disposable commodity, these luxury pieces are designed and distributed for longevity.[54]

2. *Churned with More Speed*

In Britain, the average woman will amass £22,140 of unworn clothing over the course of her lifetime.[55] Where luxury collections are shown twice a year (excluding resort/capsule collections), fast-fashion retailers produce with a velocity that seems to increase year-on-year. In 2012, Zara claimed that "speed and disposability are the new black,"[56] and living up to their claims produce twenty-four collections a year[57] (> 450 million items). Ultra-fast fashion supplier Shein puts this velocity to shame, offering 700–1,000[58] new styles daily.

3. *Less Timeless*

In relation to the above, it is far harder for the fast-fashion buyer to purchase classics. Though certain items such as a 2010 American Apparel classic hoodie may achieve cult status, the majority of items do not, meaning the money sunk in is considered a loss as the next season approaches.

Digital Disruption

Digital assets can be seen as routes to reform the fashion industry in a way that financially empowers the consumer. While some argue that digital fashion will defy the sociological underpinnings that the fashion industry rests upon (after all, there are no "seasons" in the metaverse!), with gaming giant Fortnite releasing 21 skins per month,[59] it's likely that fashion's foundations in coercing consumers to alter and upgrade their identities will still stand true as we make the digital shift. What changes in a digitally native state is consumers' abilities to monetize both the items they own and the way they engage with them, particularly with the integration of crypto native technologies.

Removing "Wear and Tear"

To begin with an obvious point, wear and tear does not exist for virtual goods, unless programmed in. This gives these items both a longer lifespace, allowing them to benefit from value definers such as provenance, and a resale value not tainted by scuffs and tears. Though in time, in order to integrate stores of value driven by scarcity, we will likely see digital clothing coded to degrade, or expire with the seasons, it's likely that consumers' ordinary use of an item will not impact its value on secondary markets. In fact, it may even do the contrary.

Upgrading Provenance

Provenance defined as "*a record of ownership of a work of art or an antique, used as a guide to authenticity or quality*"[60] is referred to, particularly in the case of the secondary market, as one of the most important markers of an item's worth. Already within the digital fashion space, we've seen instances of goods garnering cultural significance that drives up their value exponentially. Take "Party Hats" in the game *Runescape* as a prime example. In 2001, game developer Jagex gifted guests with virtual crackers at their Christmas party, with some containing gold or silver bars and others producing party hats. Many of these hats were later abandoned. Some were sold on the marketplace or even given out for free—until all party hat production was discontinued. As is common in tales of supply and demand, the moment these objects became scarce, they transformed from discardable items into coveted collectibles. Their price then skyrocketed. Now, twenty years later, the legacy of the party hat lives on, with some hats (often blue ones) going for billions in gold. They are understood as the ultimate symbol of *Runescape* wealth.

What's more, as the digital fashion space evolves, it's plausible that provenance might develop its own digital-specific value. The internet has long been hailed for giving rise to what's known as the "longtail," a theory that the "internet drives demand away from hit products with mass appeal, and directs that demand to more obscure niche offerings."[61] With vast numbers of micro-communities, each with their own cultures, goods can acquire deep significance within smaller consumer groups. Even without mass appeal, these items can hold high value.

Capitalizing on Interactions

The concept of provenance relates to the future of "digital-vintage," where a track record of where an item originated contributes to its increased worth.

But as digital objects store their consumer data within them, further value can be driven based on who wore them and what they did whilst wearing them. Looking to traditional auction houses, the majority of high-ticket apparel items are determined by the cultural significance of the user. Assets such as Dorothy's "Wizard of Oz" dress, Eliza Doolittle's "Ascot Dress" from *My Fair Lady* and Marilyn Monroe's "Happy Birthday" dress sold for $1.6 million,[62] $4.5 million[63] and $4.8 million[64] respectively at auction. Now, with digital clothes, the data of the wearer or their "virtual memories" can be hard-coded in to provide these assets with additional value.

Rewarding Loyalty

This idea of consumer use also finds itself in the idea of loyalty—namely, rewarding consumers for their part in the promotion of goods. As blockchain technology allows digital goods to be fully traceable, creators can see who the original holders are and who utilizes their assets the most—and provide them with subsequent compensation.

Take the brand RTFKT, which made headlines as the first significant acquisition of a digital fashion brand when they sold to Nike in 2021. RTFKT always tries to reward its holders. They do this through airdrops, where they send holders free assets, and with discounts on novel items. Their CLONE X avatars, for example, were sold to those who had been long-term holders of RTFKT assets for the price of 0.05 ethereum (ETH), while others ended up buying them at 2 ETH. If one was looking to buy a CLONE X today, the minimum price would be 9.4 ETH.

Further extrapolating this into a business model, it's easy to foresee a world where terms like "wear-to-earn" become commonplace. Building on the prevalence of influencer marketing, "wear-to-earn" would reward a consumer for their engagement with an item they hold, particularly in places with high volumes of other wearers. On a greater scale, the influencer market, currently worth US$16.4 billion,[65] is known to be moving towards a "micro-influencer model" (working with those content creators with 10,000+ followers who appeal to a niche-longtail). It's easy to envision a world where each one of us as "micro-influencers" can be reimbursed for our effect on brand conversion.

Automating Reimbursement

Finally, at the core of each of the above elements is the idea of automatic reimbursement. Blockchain technology allows for digital goods to have unchangeable sets of attributes programmed in, through protocols known as "smart contracts." Defined as "a computer program or a transaction intended to automatically execute, control, or document relevant events and actions,"[66] smart contracts allow elements such as returns or reimbursement to be automated into a digital fashion piece. Thus, many concerns from those participating in secondary-clothing markets such as rental or resale are completely nullified. The problem of trust is solved, opening more routes to or incentives for engagement.

Conclusion to Re-consumption

Digital fashion can transform fashion items from their traditional positioning as consumer goods into investment pieces that can benefit their buyers. What's more, digital fashion holds the potential to defy the idea that "classic" or culturally significant goods are limited to wealthy consumers. Take Fortnite's collaboration with Balenciaga as an example.

The 2021 Balenciaga Fortnite skins were priced at around $10. Balenciaga's Fortnite merchandise for the real world is much more expensive, with the hoodies from the collaboration originally available for $725. By opening up who can consume luxury fashion, digital fashion not only widens freedom of expression, but heightens the opportunities for all consumers—not just those with thousands of dollars to spend—to make money from their items.

III. Fashioning a New Economic Paradigm

The Basis of a Revolution

Defined as "a challenge to the established political order and the eventual establishment of a new order radically different from the preceding one,"[67] digital fashion is a tool to mend a broken industry. Yet only when we take a closer look at those who engage with the fashion industry, can this revolution be seen as truly impactful. Fashion is one of the few industries that is female dominated. Approximately 80% of the world's garment workers are women,[68] yet only 14% of major brands have female executives.[69] Similarly, women are shown to spend more on clothes than their male counterparts to the measure of three,[70] although they earn just 83 cents for every dollar a man makes.[71]

A digital fashion industry providing increased income as well as access to, and financial returns from, clothing has the power to go some ways in shifting the existing economic system towards those previously underserved. Similar benefits can be reaped for those from lower income brackets. In the case of producers, the fashion industry has made ever more intentional choices to move its labor to low-income countries like Bangladesh, India, China, Vietnam, and the Philippines. While these countries are far from hosting major fashion weeks, with the help of digital design software, they can increasingly access consumers all over the world fully online. With consumers in emerging markets, fashion spends are steadily increasing. By switching consumption to digital fashion, assets that have the potential to reap increased financial rewards, those buyers can become empowered in ways the fast fashion system would never permit.

Some Notes on the Way Forward

Digital fashion is an inevitability. Although the advent of the cohesive virtual world known as "the metaverse" is some way off, more of us are using social media every year. In 2021 alone, 227 million new users joined social media sites. When Facebook declared that they would shift towards becoming avatar' based "Meta," it became clear that our identities would move from curated snippets from our everyday lives to fully virtual existences created from the bottom up.

However, a utopia where fashion becomes a route to financial inclusion should not be taken for granted. Without caution and care, the downfalls of the IRL "fashion-industrial complex" can easily be replicated in digital form. Whilst not always negative, the space could be jeopardized by . . .

1. *Large Brand Entrants*

Over the past few years, every large brand, such as Gucci, Ralph Lauren, and Nike, have made a digital fashion play. Game producer Epic made $50 million from one set of NFT-branded skins.[72]

In December 2021, clothing brand Forever 21 launched *Shop City*, a virtual playground on *Roblox* where users could shop for virtual clothes and curate their own stores. Forever 21's CEO Winnie Park said that this was key to their strategy of engaging younger consumers by creating a presence for the brand in spaces already inhabited by Gen-Z. In the *Shop City Roblox* experience, this creation of brand presence was a success. Forever 21 created a virtual black beanie that proved so popular, the company will physically produce the hat and sell it in their stores. According to Park, the virtual beanie is one of the company's best-selling items of all time, and is on track to sell over 1.5 million units.[73]

While it's inevitable that each and every "super winner" will be establishing themselves in virtual spaces, it's vital that these spaces are not just used to fortify further moats. If the platforms that host these experiences begin to prioritize revenue (the type only large brands can afford) over the creative longtail, then digital fashion could become little more than a route to help large brands retain IRL dominance.

2. *Unfair Creator/Consumer Compensations*

Where the Covid-19 pandemic saw a host of start-ups selling digital fashion items, large traditional entrants participating in what Animoca Brands founder, Yat Siu, terms "Digital Feudalism" are also vying to dominate the space.

The platform formerly known as Facebook, now Meta, is launching a digital clothing store where users can purchase designer outfits for their avatars. A Meta spokesperson said these pieces would be priced between $2.99 and $8.99, much less than the real outfits by those designers (Prada's Matinee ostrich leather bag, for example, sells for $7,500).[74] However, these platforms do not prioritize rewarding either producers or consumers. Though the specifics are complex, Meta will be taking a large cut of what creators sell on their platform, posing a stark contrast to Opensea's 2.5% cut.

Conclusion

Ultimately, a glance at digital fashion shows immense potential for financial revolution; revolution in who can scale barriers to find and benefit from meaningful work as a producer and revolution in who can consume and then benefit from their fashion choices—from the young designer vying to break into the market, to the trend-savvy buyer who consumes early and leverages their communities' clout to help a brand succeed. Yet digital innovations cannot be separated from their creators and users. Only through keeping digital fashion's routes to revolution as a key priority for the industry will this potential revolution take hold.

Notes

1   Kyoichi Tsuzuki, *Happy Victims* (Kyoto: Seigensha Art Publishing, 2008).

2   Júlia Vilaça, "Fashion Industry Statistics: The Fourth Biggest Sector is Way More than Just about Clothing," *Fashion Innovation*, https://fashinnovation.nyc/fashion-industry-statistics/.

3   Vilaça, "Fashion Industry Statistics."

4   Imran Amed et al., *The State of Fashion 2022* (London: BOF & McKinsey & Co, 2022), chap 01.

5   Zippia, "28 Dazzling Fashion Industry Statistics [2023]: How Much Is the Fashion Industry Worth," Zippia.com, June 15, 2023, https://www.zippia.com/advice/fashion-industry-statistics/.

6   Zippia, "28 Dazzling Fashion Industry Statistics."

7   Joseph DeAcetis, "The Perfect Balance: How Luxury Brands Can Maintain Exclusivity And Still Be Relatable Online," *Forbes*, October 25, 2020, https://www.forbes.com/sites/josephdeacetis/2020/10/24/the-perfect-balance-how-luxury-brands-can-maintain-exclusivity-and-still-be-relatable-online/.

8   MacroTrends, "NIKE Gross Profit 2010–2023 | NKE," https://www.macrotrends.net/stocks/charts/NKE/nike/gross-profit.

9   MacroTrends, "NIKE Gross Profit 2010–2023 | NKE."

10 Amed et al., *The State of Fashion 2022*.

11 Amed et al., *The State of Fashion 2022*.

12 Nike, "Nike Sustainability—Interactive Map," https://manufacturingmap.nikeinc. com/.

13 HandbagHolic, "Where Are Louis Vuitton Bags Made?" *Handbagholic* (blog), January 4, 2022, https://www.handbagholic.co.uk/blog/where-are-louis-vuitton-bags-made/.

14 Mary Hanbury, "The Victoria's Secret Fashion Show Saw a Big Drop in Viewership in the Wake of Exec's Controversial Comments about Transgender Models," *Business Insider*, December 3, 2018, https://www.businessinsider.com/victorias-secret-fashion-show-2018-viewership-drops-2018-12.

15 Noah Silverstein, "The 2016 Victoria's Secret Fashion Show Was the Most Expensive Show in History," *Glamour*, December 5, 2016, https://www.glamour.com/story/2016-victorias-secret-fashion-show-most-expensive-in-history.

16 Amed, "The State of Fashion 2020."

17 Imran Amed and Robin Mellery-Pratt, "Is Fashion Education Selling a False Dream?" *The Business of Fashion*, November 18, 2021, https://www.businessoffashion.com/ articles/news-analysis/global-fashion-school-rankings-2015/.

18 Melanie DiSalvo, "How Much Does It Cost To Start A Clothing Line?" *Virtue + Vice*, June 12, 2022, https://shopvirtueandvice.com/blogs/news/how-much-does-it-cost-to-start-a-clothing-line.

19 Chavie Lieber, "Influencer Engagement: How People Can Earn $100,000 per Instagram Post," *Vox*, November 28, 2018, https://www.vox.com/the-goods/2018/11/28/18116875/ influencer-marketing-social-media-engagement-instagram-youtube; BBC Newsround, "How Much Does Kylie Jenner Earn on Instagram?" July 26, 2019, https://www.bbc. co.uk/newsround/49124484.

20 NSS Staff, "How much can a fashion show come to cost?" *NSS Magazine*, May 30, 2022, https://www.nssmag.com/en/fashion/29988/cost-fashion-runway-show.

21 Joanna Partridge, "'Exceptionally Challenging': How Rising Shipping Costs Hit UK Firms," *Guardian*, February 10, 2022, https://www.theguardian.com/business/2022/ feb/10/exceptionally-challenging-how-rising-shipping-costs-hit-uk-firms.

22 World Bank Group, "How Much Do Our Wardrobes Cost to the Environment?" September 23, 2019, https://www.worldbank.org/en/news/feature/2019/09/23/ costo-moda-medio-ambiente.

23 Alysha Khambay and Thulsi Narayanasamy, "Wage theft and pandemic profits," Business & Human Rights Resource Centre, March 11, 2021, https://www.business-humanrights.org/en/from-us/briefings/wage-theft-and-pandemic-profits-the-right-to-a-living-wage-for-garment-workers/.

24 Khambay and Narayanasamy, "Wage theft and pandemic profits."

25 The New School, "Tuition and Fees," https://www.newschool.edu/tuition-fees-billing/ current-tuition/.

26 University of the Arts London, "Undergraduate Tuition Fees," https://www.arts.ac.uk/study-at-ual/fees-and-funding/tuition-fees/undergraduate-tuition-fees.

27 CLO Official Site, "CLO | 3D Fashion Design Software," n.d., https://www.clo3d.com/en/plans.

28 Marvelous Designer Official Site. "Marvelous Designer," n.d., https://marvelousdesigner.com/pricing.

29 Olivia Pinnock, "The Drapers Verdict on Metaverse Fashion Week," *Drapers*, March 29, 2022, https://www.drapersonline.com/product-and-trends/catwalks/drapers-takeaways-from-metaverse-fashion-week.

30 Mansoor Iqbal, "Instagram Revenue and Usage Statistics (2022)," *The Business of Apps*, https://www.businessofapps.com/data/instagram-statistics/.

31 Mansoor Iqbal, "Tiktok Revenue and Usage Statistics (2022)," *The Business of Apps*, https://www.businessofapps.com/data/tik-tok-statistics/.

32 Mansoor Iqbal, "Snapchat Revenue and Usage Statistics (2022)," *The Business of Apps*, https://www.businessofapps.com/data/snapchat-statistics/.

33 Kelly Lim, "How Tech Couture House Auroboros Is Paving the Way for Digital Fashion," *BURO*, October 19, 2022, https://www.buro247.my/fashion/features/auroboros-digital-fashion-interview.html.

34 Statista, 2022.

35 JP Mangalindan, "How a 21-year-old Made Over $1 Million in Sales From Roblox Last Year," *Business Insider*, March 21, 2022,

36 Noah Landsberg, "55 Amazing Roblox Statistics Revenue, Usage & Growth Stats," *Influencer Marketing Hub*, September 14, 2022, https://influencermarketinghub.com/roblox-stats/.

37 OpenSea, "OpenSea, the Largest NFT Marketplace." *OpenSea*, n.d. https://opensea.io/.

38 Rebecca B., "OpenSea: A Guide to One of the Most Important NFT Companies Today," *History-Computer*, December 2, 2022, https://history-computer.com/opensea-history/.

39 Stefan Campbell, "OpenSea Statistics 2023: How Many Users Does OpenSea Have?" *The Small Business Blog*, June 2, 2023, https://thesmallbusinessblog.net/opensea-statistics/.

40 OpenSea, "10. Setting Fees on Secondary Sales," OpenSea Developer Documentation, https://docs.opensea.io/docs/10-setting-fees-on-secondary-sales.

41 Mike Boland, "Does AR Really Reduce ECommerce Returns?" *AR Insider*, November 1, 2021, https://arinsider.co/2021/09/28/does-ar-really-reduce-ecommerce-returns-2/.

42 Futureniyi, "Have You Ever Wondered How Much Women Actually Spend On Clothing & Accessories?—Prisoner Of Class," *Prisoner of Class*, March 15, 2019, https://www.prisonerofclass.com/how-much-women-actually-spend-on-clothing-accessories/.

43 Dana Thomas, "The High Price of Fast Fashion," *Wall Street Journal*, August 29, 2019, https://www.wsj.com/articles/the-high-price-of-fast-fashion-11567096637.

44 Charles T. Wolfe and J. B. Shank, "Denis Diderot," *The Stanford Encyclopedia of Philosophy*, ed. Edward N. Zalta (Stanford, CA: Stanford University Press, 2022), https://plato.stanford.edu/archives/spr2022/entries/diderot/.

45 Wolfe and Shank, "Diderot."

46 Statista, "U.S. Apparel and Accessory Stores Ad Spend 2020–2021," January 6, 2023, https://www.statista.com/statistics/470617/apparel-and-accessory-stores-industry-ad-spend-usa/.

47 Paul O'Brien, "Product/Market Fit Is Backwards," *Linkedin.Com*, January 21, 2022, https://www.linkedin.com/pulse/productmarket-fit-backwards-paul-o-brien/?trk=articles_directory.

48 Steven Bertoni, "How Mixing Data And Fashion Can Make Rent The Runway Tech's Next Billion Dollar Star," *Forbes*, August 20, 2014, https://www.forbes.com/sites/stevenbertoni/2014/08/20/how-mixing-data-and-fashion-can-make-rent-the-runway-techs-next-billion-dollar-star/?utm_campaign=forbestwittersf&utm_source=twitter&utm_medium=social&sh=5cb895551fa0.

49 Anna Schmidt, "Embeddedness | Definition, Theory & Examples," *Encyclopedia Britannica*, April 1, 2013, https://www.britannica.com/topic/embeddedness.

50 Oscar Wilde, "The Philosophy of Dress," *Reading Design*, n.d. https://www.readingdesign.org/philosophy-of-dress.

51 Sabine Becker, Achim Berg, Tyler Harris, and Alexander Thiel, "State of Fashion: Watches and Jewellery," McKinsey & Company, June 14, 2021, https://www.mckinsey.com/industries/retail/our-insights/state-of-fashion-watches-and-jewellery.

52 Business of Fashion and McKinsey & Company, "The State of Fashion," (2022), 90, https://www.mckinsey.com/~/media/mckinsey/industries/retail/our%20insights/state%20of%20fashion/2022/the-state-of-fashion-2022.pdf.

53 *Cambridge Dictionary*, "Wear and tear," https://dictionary.cambridge.org/us/dictionary/english/wear-and-tear.

54 Jennifer J. Sun, Silvia Bellezza, and Neeru Paharia, "Buy Less, Buy Luxury: Understanding and Overcoming Product Durability Neglect for Sustainable Consumption," *Journal of Marketing* 85 (2021): 28–43.

55 Danielle Wightman-StoneRoberts, "Brits amass 32,000 pounds of unworn clothing in a lifetime," *Fashion United*, December 19, 2018, https://fashionunited.uk/news/fashion/brits-amass-32-000-pounds-of-unworn-clothing-in-a-lifetime/2018121940656.

56 Suzanne Jacobs, "The clothing industry is churning out new styles faster and faster," *Grist*, December 16, 2015, https://grist.org/business-technology/the-clothing-industry-is-churning-out-new-styles-faster-and-faster/.

57 Nathalie Remy, Eveline Speelman, and Steven Swartz, "Style that's sustainable: A new fast-fashion formula," *McKinsey Sustainability*, October 20, 2016, https://www.mckinsey.com/capabilities/sustainability/our-insights/style-thats-sustainable-a-new-fast-fashion-formula.

58 Priya Elan, "'Worst of the worst': why is fast fashion retailer Shein launching a reality show?" *Guardian*, August 29, 2021, https://www.theguardian.com/fashion/2021/aug/29/fast-fashion-retailer-shein-design-reality-show.

59 Grant Taylor-Hill, "How Many Skins are in Fortnite?—2023 Update," *Esports.net*, June 5, 2023, https://www.esports.net/news/how-many-skins-are-in-fortnite/.

60 Natalee, "NFT Provenance and How It Will Change Art Forever," *NFT CULTURE*, August 22, 2022, https://www.nftculture.com/guides/nft-provenance-and-how-it-will-change-art-forever/.

61 Staff, Knowledge at Wharton, "Rethinking the Long Tail Theory: How to Define 'Hits' and 'Niches,'" *Knowledge at Wharton*, September 16, 2009, https://knowledge.wharton.upenn.edu/article/rethinking-the-long-tail-theory-how-to-define-hits-and-niches/.

62 Lorenzo Ferrigno, "Dorothy's Dress from 'Wizard of Oz' Sells for a Pretty $1.56 Million," CNN, November 24, 2015, https://edition.cnn.com/2015/11/23/entertainment/dorothy-dress-auction-wizard-of-oz/index.html.

63 Callum Paton For Mailonline, "Eliza Doolittle's Dress, James Bond's Aston Martin and Sam's Piano from Casablanca: the most expensive items of memorabilia from iconic films revealed," *Daily Mail*, March 6, 2015, https://www.dailymail.co.uk/news/article-2982786/Eliza-Doolittle-s-dress-James-Bond-s-Aston-Martin-Sam-s-piano-Casablanca-expensive-items-memorabilia-iconic-films-revealed.html.

64 Chioma Nnadi, "Kim Kardashian Takes Marilyn Monroe's 'Happy Birthday, Mr President' Dress Out For A Spin," *British Vogue*, May 3, 2022, https://www.vogue.co.uk/fashion/article/kim-kardashian-marilyn-monroe-dress-met-gala.

65 Statista, "Topic: Influencer Marketing Worldwide," January 19, 2023, https://www.statista.com/topics/2496/influence-marketing/øpicOverview.

66 Jake Frankenfield, "What Are Smart Contracts on the Blockchain and How They Work," *Investopedia*, May 31, 2023, https://www.investopedia.com/terms/s/smart-contracts.asp.

67 Editors of *Encyclopaedia Britannica*, "Revolution | Causes, Impact & Legacy," *Encyclopedia Britannica*, June 14, 2023, https://www.britannica.com/topic/revolution-politics.

68 Harpreet Kaur, "Low Wages, Unsafe Conditions and Harassment: Fashion Must Do More to Protect Female Workers," *Guardian*, October 19, 2022, https://www.theguardian.com/sustainable-business/2016/mar/08/fashion-industry-protect-women-unsafe-low-wages-harassment.

69 Pamela Brown, Stacey Haas, Sophie Marchessou, and Cyrielle Villepelet, "Shattering the Glass Runway," McKinsey & Company, October 4, 2018, https://www.mckinsey.com/industries/retail/our-insights/shattering-the-glass-runway

70 Brown, Haas, Marchessou, and Villepelet, "Shattering the Glass Runway."

71 Greg Iacurci, "Women Are Still Paid 83 Cents for Every Dollar Men Earn. Here's Why," CNBC, May 19, 2022, https://www.cnbc.com/2022/05/19/women-are-still-paid-83-cents-for-every-dollar-men-earn-heres-why.html.

72 Paul Tassi, "Epic Reveals It Made $50 Million From One Set Of 'Fortnite' Skins," *Forbes*, May 11, 2021, https://www.forbes.com/sites/paultassi/2021/05/11/epic-reveals-it-made-50-million-from-one-set-of-fortnite-skins/?sh=337add039032.

73 Ben Sherry, "Brands Are Already Making Millions in the Metaverse. Here's What Business Owners Need To Know," *Virtual Brand Group*, August 1, 2022, https://www.virtualbrandgroup.com/press/brands-are-already-making-millions-in-the-metaverse-heres-what-business-owners-need-to-know.

74 Katie Paul, "At Avatar Fashion Store, Meta to Sell Virtual Clothes for Real Money," *Reuters*, June 17, 2022, https://www.reuters.com/technology/facebook-owner-meta-launching-high-fashion-clothing-store-avatars-2022-06-17/.

9

Is Digital Fashion Socially Equitable?

SARA EMILIA BERNAT

Introduction

Digital fashion is often praised for its potential to provide sartorial experiences that are more socially sustainable and ethical than their physical counterpart. Claimed to be embracing a wide spectrum of bodies by providing garments of all sizes and shapes, safe experimentation for the LGBTQ community, and easy access to persons with disabilities, digital fashion has been making the headlines. Taking a closer look, however, it is evident that this novel consumer segment is not free from all social barriers and concerns.

To begin with, the metaverse is an extension of the physical world, carrying its historical, philosophical, and pragmatic considerations and residues. Hence, it is vital to understand the evolution of consumption, sustainable discourse, and social stratification as a pathway into this next, and highly anticipated, era. This chapter will critically examine the opportunities, as well as the often-neglected shortcomings of digital fashion, from a consumer-centric viewpoint.

New Fashion Segment on the Rise

The Social Role of Fashion

As we know, fashion is far from being a frivolous pursuit, but rather a central facet of social life. The capability of garments to articulate one's identity and to convey that to another person, who possesses no previous knowledge of the wearer, is not only an important communication stimulus, but one that facilitates social rendering in societies. In other words, before even engaging in a conversation with another person for the first time, they already have an idea about who we are, based on our garments. Clothing is a reflection of class, taste, income, and culture, whether utilized and interpreted consciously or unconsciously. As a mirror to these social constructs, fashion steps in and out of conventions, as a means to adopt or forsake group memberships, while also embracing personal preferences. Adding to this complexity, it is important to note that personal taste is also highly influenced by culturally prescribed characteristics, which are by no means fixed. Fashion, whether physical or virtual, consists of collective symbols that trigger social processes, rendering groups based on taste, and result in hierarchies deeper than it is generally assumed. The access, or lack of it, and choices users may or may not have are deeply consequential and vital to consider as the metaverse is being built. It is important to note that while some of these barriers may be financial in nature, not all of them are. They can be rooted in education, representation, or even access to knowledge and new technologies.

But while discourse frequently focuses on the economic potential of the metaverse, those other social benefits and detriments of virtual fashion are less clear. Part of the reason is rooted in the fact that the social context at hand is novel, and we simply do not have enough information, especially when it comes to the social nooks and echo chambers that do not exist elsewhere. Indeed, the term "metaverse" was only created in 1992 by Neal Stephenson, and did not widely take off until 2020. Metaverse, or persistently occurring virtual worlds, sits at the intersection of the digital and physical worlds. On the one hand, they are created by people and as a result they are highly reflective of "real-life" social constructs. On the other hand, though, the metaverse gives rise to new memberships and social customs that would be unusual, or even forbidden, in the real world. For instance, in real life, jumping from supernatural battles to take part in solving murder mysteries with friends are not only highly difficult, but outright impossible to achieve. At any rate, all these activities require specific looks that correspond to their wearer's identity, allowing them to express who they are, and how they wish to be perceived amongst other users. To put it simply, both social spaces and the bases of social stratification of the metaverse are still in the making and are highly fragmented, leaving much of the discourse to educated guesses.

However, what is clear is that the first wave of the internet, also known as Web1, was a non-interactive read-only universe, failing to involve people in a creative, collaborative manner. Then, Web2 gave rise to apps and social media platforms, bringing on user-generated content, and the foundation of democratic usage. Still, this second generation carried a significant amount of discrimination and bias, as it was largely created and operated by colossal tech companies, with efforts led by a homogenous population: millennial, wealthy, male consumers.[1] Consequently, the digital efforts of this period reflect inclinations to this group, often overlooking needs, sensitivities, and representations of other, more marginal populations. The Web3 emerged as a direct response to this issue, providing a decentralized web with more independent, user-generated content, not only as a consumer, but often as a creator, too, effectively claiming the ability to shape virtual spaces. Those marginal populations that have been overlooked for so long are increasingly central in design, and social sustainability is referenced in the metaverse more than ever before. While the toxic practices of real-life fashion are slowly changing, a complete resolution takes a long time, as already established infrastructures are difficult to shake up in their entirety. Digital fashion is just emerging in the Web3, and this launch offers unprecedented flexibility for newcomers.

Ripe for Reform

Needless to say, exploring social sustainability in this emerging context is vital to ensure a safe and equitable future. In order to do so, we must begin with the very definition. The United Nations defines social sustainability as identifying and managing business impacts on people.[2] In other words, it is an elusive umbrella term for all things business-related that may benefit (or harm) people, both on an individual and societal level. While the intersection of social concerns and business needs may be organically intertwined, allowing entities to tap into social issues as a means to position their brand efforts in a positive light, it is vital to note that impact can arise from many different angles, across the supply chain, leaving certain populations vulnerable to harm. From design through production to consumption and beyond, the fashion system brings together stakeholders of all kinds, setting up a complex and sometimes convoluted backdrop for both policy making and ethical consumer behavior, as well as brand efforts. Furthermore, the objective of considerate processes may be entirely different depending on brand positioning and their value proposition. For instance, some fashion brands may be excellent catalyzers in craft preservation across a culture, but by definition they will be unsuitable candidates to mitigate class-based inequalities. Arguably, direct and indirect effects have never been more complex, and the reason for that can be rooted in our very social fabric.

To understand the proliferation of sustainable efforts in the fashion sector, and the types of initiatives that thrive in the metaverse, it is worth taking a look at the segment's origin and evolution. This is warranted to understand why consumers are turning to this mode of consumption, and the specific residues the fashion system has carried from the past into the present, and possibly to the Web3.

(Un)sustainable fashion has a long history, beginning with the labor practices dictated by the Industrial Revolution. For the sake of conciseness, this segment will focus on the period between the twentieth century and the emergence of the metaverse. The first half of the twentieth century was characterized by the legacy of the late 1800s, namely how manufacturing was dramatically transformed. With the rise of new textile machines, notably the invention of the sewing machine in 1846, prices rapidly fell while the scale of manufacturing rocketed. Factories embraced these novel potentials, and while the working class still made clothes at home and the upper class turned to couturiers, mass-produced garments served a wide range of the middle class.

A distance between production and consumption was established, removing consumers from seeing the manufacturing process altogether. It wasn' t until World War II that fabric restrictions were introduced and functional styles were made necessary. As a result, standardized production and sizing became customary, paving the road to a system that catered to some populations and not to others. This created a residue that was carried into the 2010s, until the body positivity movement demanded a more egalitarian system of measures, which is still in motion, but more about that later.

As the 1960s rolled on, the first wave of post-war baby boom children was coming of age. A vast generation, baby boomers realized the power at hand to reinvent the world around them. Indeed, it was a decade characterized by revolution when it came to music, society, and style. In 1968, Hennes acquired retailer Mauritz Widforss, and set the world's longest running fast-fashion empire in motion: H&M. International acceleration continued, with increasing global production, and by the early 1990s with Zara's arrival, the *New York Times* coined the term "fast fashion," referring to the rapid path from design to the racks. In the early 2000s, fast fashion was celebrated for its "democratic" values and was embraced by icons such as Kate Middleton and Michelle Obama.

It was not until the economic crisis of 2008 that people's liking for fast fashion turned sour. The ensuing era witnessed the loss of wealth and a depletion of welfare, and as a consequence, consumers turned to intrinsic values. Around the same time, in 2012, the Rana Plaza in Bangladesh collapsed, taking 1,134 lives, exploding the underbelly of fast fashion and setting the stage for the next era of fashion, characterized by conspicuous production. Shifting from an emphasis on representation, branding became preoccupied with spirituality, health, and the well being of others. In addition, as social media provided an increased level of transparency and the possibility of participation, a previously racially, physically, and socially homogenous group began to erode, opening up entry to a more diverse and inclusive consumer base.

Nevertheless, while social awareness and its role both in fashion production and consumption grew, under-representation, tokenism, and outright offensive images also remained prevalent in the fashion system. Supporters of the metaverse claim that this new system presents a clean slate, one that is perceived to be body less and which is often seen to challenge the systemic racism, body chauvinism, and exclusion of people with disabilities.

A New, Hopeful Terrain

Induced by the Covid-19 pandemic, the digitalization of the fashion industry has accelerated beyond imagination since 2020. At root, there are oppositional consumer desires: to participate in a more sustainable and equitable system and, at the same time, enjoy the consumerist culture to the fullest. Hence, digital fashion claims to be the perfect synthesis between these two yearnings: a permission to keep consuming while also curbing fashion's footprint. Tapping into two co-existing, but oppositional, areas that have long been brewing, this fusion offers novel solutions and drawbacks across the shopping journey.

The following sections will dissect specific access points, including intimidation as psychosocial obstacle, virtual clothing as an embodied practice, religio-cultural representation, and tangible resources. These concepts underpin status, a misunderstood concept that, contrary to common belief, is not reserved for the rich, but the force that confirms worth in people's eyes. Acquiring status is essential for understanding what really is at stake when discussing the seemingly trivial concept of digital fashion.

Intimidation: Eradicating Apathy from the Fitting Room and Beyond

Social intimidation arises from customs that reinforce already existing power dynamics. While it is often practiced subconsciously, it can still continue to preserve existing exploitation and inequalities, on the basis of class, gender, or physicality. Fashion, an arena ironically often labeled as trivial, is one area of intimidation, where consumers can face fear, anxiety, and unease. When it comes to consumer experience, one of the first areas where shoppers may experience intimidation is the fitting room. Inaccessible to people with disabilities, unsafe for the trans community, and oftentimes humiliating for plus-size shoppers, real-life fashion has failed for a wide segment of society in providing a safe and graceful trial experience.

Virtual trial rooms may serve as a solution by providing entry and ease to a wide array of overlooked consumer groups. Using AR technology, shoppers can try on garments from the comfort of their homes, allowing people with mobility issues or rural consumers with limited access to physical retail space to participate easily. This technology also caters to highly stigmatized social groups, such as the trans community, or plus-size shoppers, who previously felt a high degree of intimidation both on the emotional and physical level. While these experiences can appear mundane on the surface, they often contribute to deep trauma, further exacerbating distress in vulnerable individuals. In other words, for these populations, the digital trying-on experience is not merely a way to simplify shopping by saving time, but to experiment with identities without fear.

Safe spaces in the metaverse must be continuously maintained, even outside the fitting rooms, in shared spaces. Well-defined rules mandated by platforms, culture, and values can help users to feel seen and connected, encouraging participative styles that are aligned, reassuring users of their safety. As fashion is a non-verbal language, it has the capacity to establish and reinforce digital cultures, guiding participants in understanding their prospects and boundaries.

Immaterial Body Considerations

While fashion is about self-expression, it appears as though plural body types are neglected both IRL (in real life) and, to a lesser degree, in digital fashion. This neglect has a long history, and is largely rooted in a binary sizing system. At the time of the Great Depression, fabric prices were very high, but industrial technology was improving. As a result, mass manufactured clothing virtually eliminated made-to-order clothing. Subsequently, the rise of catalogs and advertising solidified this model. While there were attempts to regulate sizing over the course of history, these were mostly concerned with war time uniforms. It was not until 1939 that the US government commissioned statisticians to collect key measurements. Recruiting 15,000 white women, this paid study attracted mostly lower-income clusters who often suffered from malnourishment.[3] In 1958, standard sizing was created, ranging from 8 to 42, combining the earlier statistical result with intuition. Though there was a revision in the 1970s, paving the way for vanity sizing (labeling clothing with sizes smaller to appeal to consumers), these amendments did not result in wider representation. In short, fashion has a long tradition of being systematically designed for tall, slim, cis-gendered bodies. While discourse is increasingly emphasizing a push for inclusivity and diversity, reality hardly caters to these desires. Some 67% of American women wear size 14 or above, but most stores do not carry those sizes.[4] Fashion brands rarely cater for people with disabilities, and adaptive brands that introduce features to make clothing more accessible are few and far between. When it comes to the trans community, it is important to emphasize that while transition therapy does change physicality, it does not result in a change of bone structure, making it difficult for the community to find appropriate clothing, ultimately hindering their ability to experience gender affirmation through fashion.

Digital fashion is able to directly mitigate all these matters, as clothing is essentially a modifiable filter that is meant to be placed on any 2D virtual body. In other words, digital fashion discards the idea of sizing and the practice of dressing altogether, in favor of instant presentation. No longer bound to physicality, digital fashion has the capacity to truly cater to symbolic transformation, removing specific bodies as a prerequisite. Ironically, however, plus-size and disabled bodies are largely missing from virtual boutiques and representation, undermining a great potential and a pathway to an intentionally inclusive system.[5]

Lack of Deep Identities

Body image is not the only aspect of fashion that digital marketers seemed to have missed. In 2021, the Institute of Digital Fashion conducted a comprehensive survey involving 6,000 people with the aim of exploring perceptions of diversity and inclusion in digital fashion.[6] The results showed that about 60% of respondents wished to reflect their IRL identity virtually, as opposed to the

40% who sought a more "surreal style." The analysis emphasized the importance of expression when it comes to foundational identities in real life. Nevertheless, in practice, when it comes to digital skins, representation is still rather binary, lacking choices when it comes to the expression of religion, disability, gender, or age.

Religious clothing, in particular, seems to be lagging. While holy spaces are emerging in the metaverse, including VR church services, Haitian voodoo ceremonies, or Hindu funeral rites, the corresponding religious outfits are scarce. Indeed, it appears as though religious clothing and representation is restricted to Muslim practices, specifically to hijabs, tribal markings, and braided hair, but clothing as a religious expression takes a backseat elsewhere.

The lack of deep identities is not limited to representation. There are other, tangible barriers to those with disabilities. To begin with, session time-outs often lack countdowns, or a way to extend a session, making it difficult for users to complete tasks, including shopping processes. To put it simply, potential consumers can be easily excluded by not getting enough time to choose and check out on their own terms. This oversight completely subverts any attempt to bring garments to populations outside the able-bodied. Furthermore, instructions that are easily readable and audible are still rare, highlighting a flaw in the understanding of representation and inclusion.

Pricing Individuality

Financial capabilities and limitations can also be barriers to users. To begin with, many novel platforms require significant power, demanding expensive and up-to-date computers and smart devices, as well as high-speed internet services. In addition, lower income users may also lack the time to familiarize themselves with the digital terrain. As a result, even if the intention to participate exists, entry without the sufficient funds may be a challenge.

Notwithstanding, digital outfits tend to be significantly less expensive than their physical counterparts. While IRL garments naturally will not cease to exist (physical bodies need to be outfitted), digital outfits can accommodate the hunger to consume and express, at a lower price point. As fashion plays an extraordinary role in impression creation and management, a human experience that is heightened by social media, digital fashion is able to bring the kind of democratic fashion that IRL fast fashion failed to do. While fast fashion provided entry for all, it also came with environmental and social exploitation that not only caused direct harm, but stigmatized their consumers too.

Nevertheless, democratic price points in the metaverse seem to come with a caveat. While digital fashion offers accessible price labels, alarmingly, in December 2021, Bloomberg reported that prices for digital avatars from Cryptopunks, a popular NFT collection on the Ethereum blockchain, have been fluctuating based on race, gender, and skin tone.[7] Mid- and dark-skinned avatars have shown lower prices, as well as female over male. While Cryptopunk investors claim that the price disparity is due to market value, rather than a result of racism or other bias, the results are equally concerning.

Status, an Overlooked Consequence

These insufficiencies are not only a matter of individual irritation, discomfort, or exclusion, but also play into systemic inequality. Fashion is often perceived as a benign, and somewhat trivial, phenomenon, but as discussed earlier, reality could not be more different. Fashion is an indicator of haves and have-nots, and indicates social status, a widely misunderstood concept.

Max Weber's analysis of the origins of inequality has three components: power, resources, and status.[8] While the first two concepts are addressed in academia frequently, the latter is often neglected. The first two ideas cover control over material capital and access, while the latter taps into differences of esteem and respect. Hence, status is essentially who is seen to be better, more deserving. In the branded consumerist context, brands draw narratives around aspirations reflected in their products. In other words, they draw arbitrary, symbolic images in relation to garments, with the aim of persuading consumers that they can reflect their aspirational selves in such garments, thus buying more. By providing a symbolic path from reality to desire, clothes embody values that certain segments of society rate highly, and activate them through rich imagery. This only works if tapping into status. What they do not say is that while they reinforce some ideas, they also undermine others. By reinforcing one status group's values, beliefs, and ideas, they effectively elevate them above those of other groups.

It is essential to examine to what extent these digital garments reflect class fractions, adding another dimension to the current, largely minority-centered, discourse. To sum up, while digital fashion is certainly breaking down barriers that the previous system put up, hindering individuals and groups from entering, this new system has carried over some of those stigmas as well. Fashion, after all, is not conceived in a vacuum. It is shaped by social norms, values, and desires, ultimately culminating in ways of presentation not devoid of stories of success and failure.

Future Considerations

In conclusion, the use of technology is deeply shaped by prevalent social norms and structures, as well as biases carried over from IRL settings. While there are certainly improvements when it comes to product pricing, tailoring, and the shopping experience, fashion in the metaverse is still far from supporting complex identities at large. Digital fashion still requires significant financial resources and education to navigate the system, and has a long way to go to provide for under-represented communities. As we move forward, it remains to be seen whether online communities will be able to reflect a more inclusive and diverse approach in co-existing, or if the metaverse will be just another facet to ultimately cement social inequalities as we know them.

Notes

1   Allison Levitsky, "Diversity in Silicon Valley tech jobs lags the industry nationwide," *Bizwomen*, April 11, 2021, https://www.bizjournals.com/bizwomen/news/latest-news/2021/04/silicon-valley-women-black-latinx-tech-workers.html.

2   United Nations Global Compact, "Social Sustainability," https://www.unglobalcompact.org/what-is-gc/our-work/social.

3   Laura Stampler, "The Bizarre History of Women's Clothing Sizes," *Time*, October 23, 2014, https://time.com/3532014/women-clothing-sizes-history/.

4   Eliana Dockterman, "One Size Fits None: Inside the fight to take back the fitting room," *Time*, https://time.com/how-to-fix-vanity-sizing/.

5   Sara Emilia Bernat and Doris Domoszlai-Lantner explored these socio-historical considerations in their paper, "Digital fashion: Solutions and limitations for the LGBTQIA+ community," *Fashion, Style and Popular Culture*, September 13, 2022, https://doi.org/10.1386/fspc_00146_1.

6   Maghan McDowell, "Shaping Online Avatars: Why Our Digital Identities Differ," *Vogue Business*, October 19, 2021, https://www.voguebusiness.com/technology/shaping-online-avatars-why-our-digital-identities-differ.

7   Misyrlena Egkolfopoulou and Akayla Gardner, "Even in the Metaverse, Not All Identities Are Created Equal," *Bloomberg*, December 6, 2021, https://www.bloomberg.com/news/features/2021-12-06/cryptopunk-nft-prices-suggest-a-diversity-problem-in-the-metaverse.

8   Max Weber, "Class, Status, Party," in *Max Weber: Essays in Sociology*, ed. H. H. Girth, and C. W. Mills (London: Routledge, 1948), 180–95.

10

Fashioning Border Spaces: African Decoloniality and Digital Fashion

ERICA DE GREEF WITH KING DEBS, SIVIWE JAMES, LESIBA MABITSELA, AND SIHLE SOGAULA

"The self is only a threshold, a door, a becoming between multiplicities."[1]

Part 1: Fashioning Digital Encounters at Border Spaces

In this chapter we share eight digital fashion projects that engage with critical fashion thinking and making; they were developed by or in proximity to the African Fashion Research Institute based in South Africa; and they employ digital formats and technologies to explore the *in-between*. As in-between or borderspace[2] projects, they grapple with, straddle, and interrupt the definitions and logics that shape the boundaries of one entity—a discourse, concept, culture, practice, location, and so on—from others. This brief introduction to several South African creatives working at the intersection of decoloniality, fashion, and the affordances of the digital, offers insight into their dialogues, encounters, and projects that manifest *in between* design and academia, making and thinking, art and fashion, self and community, history and memory, local and global, archival and speculative, and the digital and real.

In 2019, Lesiba Mabitsela and Erica de Greef founded the African Fashion Research Institute[3] with the launch of the first virtual fashion exhibition on the continent. Prompted by the need to reclaim access for an African audience, the International Fashion Showcase offered a unique opportunity to bring the work of three African fashion designers back to the continent through digital means. Using Matterport capture, *Fashioning Brave New Worlds: Africa at the International Fashion Showcase 2019*[4] is an immersive 3D digital rendering of the *International Fashion Showcase 2019* exhibition, which was held at Somerset House in London, from February 11 to February 24, 2019 (see Figure 10.1a–d).[5] The digital exhibition highlights—and productively expands—the work of South African designer Thebe Magugu, Kenyan jewelry designer Ami Dosh Shah, and Rwandan fashion artist Cedric Mizero, who shared the bi-annual platform with thirteen other emerging creatives from Lithuania, Brazil, Vietnam, Canada, Italy, Columbia, and more, exploring global issues such as climate change, cultural sustainability, waste, and notions of freedom.

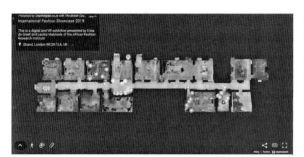

Figure 10.1 a–d Fashioning Brave New Worlds: Africa at the International Fashion Showcase 2019, *detail of digital exhibition, 2019.* ©African Fashion Research Institute.

Between Time and Space

Interviews for the virtual project—inviting the African designers to speak about their work—were conducted by Mabitsela at Somerset House and captured on both stationary and 360 cameras by fellow South African creative King Debs, ensuring that the voices of the creatives were elevated by the additional content.[6] In order to decolonize the online version of the exhibition, the interviews together with additional fashion show reels, websites, and biographies, were embedded in the offering. Creating a digital exhibition dissolved the distance that would have denied access for the majority of viewers from a Global South,[7] which radically shifted the dynamic of an exhibition "celebrating international fashion" in terms of their audience reach and impact.

Photographs and catalogs aim to reproduce the content of exhibitions, but the largely ephemeral nature of exhibitions relies on the immersive experience of space, as embodied context *and* content. The digital overcomes the erasure of the exhibition, by creating its virtual double and ensuring ongoing immersive access that radically diversifies who may (in the future) engage with the curated space. The online exhibition has become an alternative knowledge archive of new, accessible, and alternate historical references to draw on in teaching contexts, where the exclusion of fashion narratives from the Global South continues to haunt fashion textbooks and curricula. In the Global South, creating archives also invokes a future making or future imaginary. Following Achille Mbembe, we pay attention to the absence of those presences that are no longer so, and that one remembers, as well as the absences of those others that are yet to come and are anticipated.[8]

Between Authenticity and Imagination

In "The Power of the Archive and its Limits," Mbembe notes that there cannot be a conceptualization of archival documents without a consideration of the institution or building that holds it.[9] While Mbembe reflects on physical iterations of the archive, his thinking provides necessary scaffolding from which to conceive ideas around the metaphysical and its storehouses. It is from this thinking that the research project Inxili takes its inspiration. Inxili is a small bag that is worn on the body. Yona, kuba iyinto ebalulekileyo, ihlala ithe ngca apha kumnikazi wayo kude kuthiwe 'ngufel'emntwini'. Kuyo, kufakwa izinto ezixabisekileyo nezinto ezibalulekileyo. Singathi umsebenzi wayo ufana nesafe.[10] Inxili does not discriminate, nor does its owner; everything matters. It honors every object it holds.

Inxili informs the archival, collaborative research between Siviwe James and Sihle Sogaula (SiSi), who seek to engender a symbiotic exchange between Xhosa sensibilities and Western materiality. Inxili is a wayfinder, an experiment if you will, one that has at its core a shared interest in the critical imagination of surrogate spaces that can hold, respond to, and engage with Xhosa histories and contexts in the contemporary moment. More broadly, Inxili looks at how acts of archiving, keeping, and repair, as understood through the lens of Xhosa design thinking and cultural sustainability, can manifest in the Afropresent. Xa livulwa elinxili, ndinothi ndibaqa ntoni?[11]

Chos'chosi is an iteration manifesting from the shared research of Inxili. As a place-finding experiment, it explores the abilities and the limits of virtual technologies as a counter-space and the intersection of sustainable fashion and immersive digital creative technologies, developed within the Design Futures Lab (see Figure 10.2).[12] As a storytelling device, Chos'chosi is a core cliché that anchors a sometimes wandering, but always meaningful, narrative in the ancestral. The animated 3D figure is of umntu omdala in a seated position, smoking from a pipe which suggests a storytelling moment; through the use of AR technology, the figure can be placed in any environment. An in-app recording function allows for unique placements to be uploaded onto a shared and publicly accessible archive. As narrator and ethereal guide, umntu omdala invites the app-user to grapple with ideas of the fashioning, mending, and making of indigenous histories. In this way, Chos'chosi is a co-creation and shared speculation on ways of making histories. It flattens the hierarchy of knowledge production and instead emphasizes a shared history-making. As an experiment, the collaborative design process of making the digital interface reveals to SiSi what can be lost in the transmediating of Xhosa sensibilities into the digital.

The use of augmented reality presents a useful metaphor to think through what a symbiotic exchange between Xhosa sensibilities and Western materiality

Figure 10.2 *Chos'chosi, animated 3D figure of umntu omdala smoking a pipe, Design Futures Lab, 2022.* Designed by Sisanda Tech © Siwiwe James and Sihle Sogaula.

can look like. Chos'chosi breaks out of disciplinary boundaries; it crosses borders, shifting between temporalities and languages; it cannot be fixed or contained in one place. It is co-created through encounters as events with memory, as a collective synergy between one mode of being, world, and thinking, and another. It is both nomadic and located. It is the past insisting in the present, with traces of the multiplicity of futures.

Between Memory and Belonging

Erasure and absence have long haunted the writings of fashion, art, and design cultures in the Global South. As such, the histories of countercultures, sartorial resistance, or design innovations from across Africa have been excluded from the largely Western canon of design libraries, universities, museums, and curricula. Fashion, as a rich locus for reading an entangled politics of the city, nation, culture, and enfolded individual subjectivities, can inform and lead archival research on the continent that can redress these lacunae.

Functioning as an open-access research reference focusing on South African popular culture, Between Histories is an Instagram-based social media archive[13] created by Sungano Kanjere as part of her internship with AFRI, with an aim to research, collect, curate, and share pop culture histories post-1994 (see Figure 10.3).[14] Between Histories demonstrates a deep listening into the absence of an archive. The record of popular culture, not only in South Africa but elsewhere on the continent, has been rendered mute by the dominance of the Western canon.[15] The deeply local (often nostalgic) resonances of shared pop culture continue to live on in collective memories. To speak from and for a local popular culture history helps to craft possibilities for belonging, at times in vernaculars that may differ widely from the canon of (predominantly Western) pop culture.

Repairing the wounds of erasure requires seeking, unearthing, at times re-inventing, and re-investing, traces of the past. While the Between Histories public-facing Instagram account presents a curated, continually-evolving visual archive, it is supported by an open access catalog or personal library which houses links to artifacts, readings, related resources, and research

Figure 10.3 *Between Histories, Instagram post, 30 September 2021.* © Sungano Kanjere.

references. Where performance scholar Diana Taylor distinguished between the archive and the repertoire,[16] new digital archival projects, such as Between Histories, draw on the recorded materials of performance *as archive*, using music, dialogue, documentary film, and personal audio-visual content to build new hybrid or multimedia knowledge materials. The bounded halls and walls of knowledge gate-keeping (libraries, museums, and archives with books, objects, and documents) are collapsed through the digital, disrupting the agency of authorship and access, creating fluid, flexible spaces for knowledge collation, curation, and exchange.

Between Vernacular Looking and Belonging

Where archival projects harness the affordances of the digital to redress histories, and propose futures, the digital can also be productive in the present. Used as a way of seeing, of appropriating spaces of power (by interrupting the sites of mediation), and collapsing the geographies of isolation, Bongani Tau's Instagram platform, @Daveyton1520, acts as a discursive portal to the obscured histories, everyday resilience, and forgotten accomplishments of individuals in marginalized township communities (see Figure 10.4). The digital platform performs a metanarrative with new knowledge-making and place-making possibilities.

Daveyton is a township on the East Rand of Johannesburg. It is also the site of struggle, memory, and alternative methods of world- and sense-making.[17] Daveton1520 forms part of a broader project titled Abengoni in which Tau investigates, instigates, and elevates acts of fashioning, as forms of re-existence and resistance against the ongoing dehumanizing effects of apartheid on black bodies, thirty years after the promise of a new democracy. Tau uses the Daveton1520 Instagram platform as a "route to remember," highlighting and visibilizing thoughts about communities in Daveyton as critical archives documenting a black politics of being.

Fashion-as-thinking becomes both a lens and a method, placing fashion in the in-between, spanning a politics of memory and a politics of becoming. Fashion tells others how we think about ourselves in relation to our environment; it positions us in space and across time; it is the fabric of our embodiment. From the position of being the Other—pushed to the urban margins in a kind of liminal space—Daveyton1520 recenters and reimagines

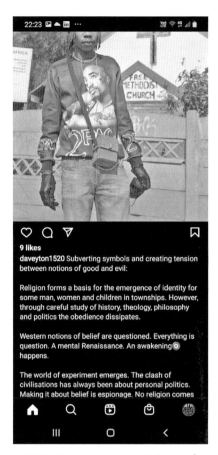

Figure 10.4 *@Daveyton1520, Instagram post, 20 September 2021.* © Bongani Tau.

the place and its people, weaving images and histories into new tapestries of being and belonging. Through the digital, Daveyton becomes a site of tenacity, brilliance, creative ingenuity, communal coalitions, and powerful resilience that flips the script, disrupting the disavowals and difficulties imposed on its residents by the ongoing dehumanizing effects of apartheid on black bodies.

The digital witnessing of alternative narratives makes visible a redefinition of the conceptual colonial borders imposed and inherited by education and history that persist in the minds and lives of many in Daveyton. Fashion becomes the site of creative resistance and critical self-making; its power lies in its capacity to present counter-narratives at borders, and act as a navigating tool for making sense of space, imagination, and experience at the borderscape.[18]

Part 2: Fashioning Afro-futures

In 2020, Dr. heeten bhagat and Erica de Greef developed and launched an online course, "African Fashion (?)."[19] The course challenged the stereotypes problematically associated with fashion from Africa (see Figure 10.5). It also disrupted the gatekeeping that would normally reproduce the violence of who has access to critical knowledge spaces and who does not. Through the digital, equal opportunities to speak and be heard were made possible with participants from the Global North and the Global South, previously separated by their privileges and positionalities.

This discursive online course became a critical contact zone for listening differently, and for hosting other possibilities for thinking, writing, and speaking about fashion from the continent. The digital affords opportunities for very diverse voices to be heard in relation to other voices, creating a kind of decentered politics for disrupting the discourse and prototyping new speculative, curious, audacious, and imaginative opportunities. It offers opportunities for complexity through a discursive multiplicity that evolves from enfolding disparate thoughts in shared dialogues.

Figure 10.5 *"African Fashion (?)." Reflections on the online course, July 2020.* © African Fashion Research Institute.

Between Disruption and Definition

Recent technological advancements have afforded Africans on the continent and in the diaspora new ways in which to consider and manifest their futures, disrupting the restrictive colonial binary of modernity versus primitivism. The growing use of new technologies has seen radical shifts in imaging African futures. While Afrofuturism as a concept has risen in popularity, across literary, artistic, or popular culture platforms, it is both generative and problematic. In his doctoral study, titled "Speculative Indigeneities: The (K)New Now," bhagat teases out the complexities of remembering the past and "dreaming the future" in twenty-first-century Zimbabwe, through a deeper inquiry into the historical and anthropological constructs of indigenousness that continues an, as yet, under-explored ontological terrain with the concept of "indigeneity."[20] In thinking through the concept of "polygeneity," bhagat proposes that it revives the notions of dynamism and creativity that have been dormant since the onset of European colonization in Zimbabwe.[21]

Drawing on the Afro futures imagined in the film *Black Panther*—particularly through the costuming—bhagat shares in the critique of Afrofuturism that Ainehi Edoro points out, suggesting that the film "didn't quite succeed in working out the terms on which Africa could truly inspire a futuristic aesthetics."[22] A key argument about the challenges of Afrofuturism is that it is not only about producing futures, but just as much about re imagining the past. Mbembe reflects on the entangled temporalities in the history of African societies, that, far from being homogenous, "harbor the possibility of a variety of trajectories neither convergent nor divergent but interlocked, paradoxical."[23] Although there are many definitions of Afrofuturism (sharing themes of reclamation, black liberation, a revisioning of the past, and future predictions through a black cultural lens), there are concerns that less utopian voices and alternate visualities are excluded. New iterations that destabilize and complicate the techno-focused aesthetic of Afrofuturism are necessary and emerging.[24] Efforts to reframe and diversify who gets to create, make, or tell these future African narratives are key, especially in the convergences of fashion with technologies.

Between Mythologies and Decolonial Aesthesis

Botho is a Sesotho phrase that can roughly be translated as "the act of carrying the required level of respect for the other, of treating the other with respect; an act achieved through the highest expression of being or humanity."[25] With their shared concept of botho in mind, digital artist King Debs and Lesiba Mabitsela created a digital app as part of the Design Futures Lab (2022) that integrated concepts of the modern, ancient, indigenous, analog, and digital with fashion design, and related technological knowledge systems (see Figure 10.6a–d).[26] Botho, digital natures and possibilities, and ideas around language and visibility were part of two consecutive recorded conversations between Mabitsela and Debs, held on September 19, 2022. Four short excerpts are included here of their two explorations at the convergence of fashion and the digital.

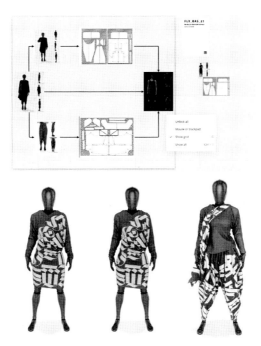

Figure 10.6a–d *Botho, digital app, Design Futures Lab, 2022.* © Lesiba Mabitsela and King Debs.

Conversation One: Botho as Principle
(8:10–14:10)[27]

Lesiba Mabitsela   How were we able to synthesize this ideology of botho into a digital fashion project? I think this is what resonates with me and the project—this idea of botho, and reincarnation and má—and how these different ideologies fed into this project from a perspective of not being eurocentric.[28] Recently I have started to like, look at botho holistically as a design principle, similar to the way that I was looking at Japanese design philosophies, like má. It's looking at botho and seeing how our project helped me to think about my design approach in a way that could be translated as a Sesotho understanding of botho, or you could look at it from the Zulu perspective of ubuntu. I don't know if they mean the same things.

King Debs   They do. They literally mean the same thing.

Lesiba Mabitsela   Do you think then that an understanding of botho is also there in Ghana, or let's say, in the UK? What is the UK version of botho? I don't know whether there is that sort of understanding in the West. Do you know what I mean?

King Debs   Yeah, I honestly can't think if there's words for these. It's one thing to translate the word, but it's another thing to articulate how it works like, with the ideas of "reciprocity," you know what I'm saying.

Lesiba Mabitsela   Mmmm.

King Debs   So, how for me, the way I look at botho, is that it's a very humane quality that transcends language. Like how guests are received, how you know, strangers are communicated to. It's like a certain quality of engaging. But I can't speak about it, in terms of other places that I don't know. Like, how people live in Europe or in the West in terms of botho.

Lesiba Mabitsela   I guess there's this thing of humanity, right. Because, it's too simplistic to say that, the West does not have any sort of design philosophy like that.

Conversation One: The Digital as Nature
(21:00–29:20)

Lesiba Mabitsela   I wanted to put tech—as this idea of a detached, Western, even inorganic, kind of entity—into our description for the project, but you saw tech rather as an inevitable sort of process within human evolution. I wanted to know whether you wanted to elaborate a little bit further on that.

King Debs   Yeah, so you know, part of my gravitation towards using technology as a medium was really organic. I've always felt that there is a misconception of the idea of tech, based on people's perceptions and conditioning. For example, when we think about tech evolution, you know, there's different ideas that come to mind. It's based on what we're exposed to. Often you can think about movies you've seen, these sci-fi flicks. So, when that informs someone's idea of the technological juxtaposition to the human condition it falls into tech being "Other" or external or alien. Whereas, I look at technology as something which is conceived by the human mind, so as a result, it is as organic as us. It's just a tool, like a spoon, it's a space.

My life's work and my relationship with technology is just expanding on that relationship, on how tech takes humanity forward, and how it impacts the human condition. And, all I do is I contextualize tech from my own lived experience, from where I was born, what I went through, and things like that. I basically tie a knot—no, I weave a thread—and I see at what point there are quantum leaps.

I've always existed in the tech space as a minority, as a black guy. And also, as a non-gamer, for example. There are a lot of default things that are attributed to technology that I don't resonate with. Because I have an alternative outlook, I get to work on projects where one can really have a platform that further elaborates on how one works. Like with our project, botho, using tech in this way, is as natural as a tree, because we came up with it. Anything conceived with, within, and by human beings can be seen as natural. It's just shaped differently. It's like metal is based on mining, and extraction and things like that. It's just that the final form, like in tech, is the synthesis, but the original source of it is natural. The final output may feel external, because it's not in the soil, it's not in the ground, it's not in the body, it's around us, because of engineering, because of technology.

Lesiba Mabitsela   Which is kind of weird, because it's opposite to what we would conceive of as the supernatural. Within the African context, the supernatural tends to be, you know, partnered up with what is traditional. If you think about it, like when someone gets twassa'ed or a spiritual calling, the best way to describe that in English is that these kinds of manifestations are seen as supernatural. It's so interesting how we perceive technology away from what we think is organic or traditional, as being on top of what we think is within the lexicon of the "primitive." For instance, mathematics started in Africa. It's started on this continent. The idea that we didn't contribute to this tech, where digital fashion has ended up, the fact that it's never really considered that Africans contributed to that, is a farce.

Conversation Two: What the Digital Allows (2:00–8:20)[29]

King Debs   Commercializing digital experiences have become much more adaptable, like we shifted from Web2 to Web3. Now, the digital space is a more widespread experience. You can draw a lot of user experiences that are marketable, sustainable, quantifiable, predictable, and measurable. We are able to contain and expand much more than we could back then, so that is why there is a gravitation to the digital medium in industries such as fashion and how your world and my world have collided. If you think about it, we have been having this conversation for the better part of a decade, and it's always been about referencing what we find interesting and dope [i.e., cool], and trying to make sense of it. Our two worlds have never been that foreign. It's just that now I would say fashion is much more conventional and the digital has graduated, and becoming more accessible. It's always been there in different ways. As the human evolves, the discipline, the industry, the markets also all evolve.

Lesiba Mabitsela   Maybe, what is interesting is the word "organic" and what is termed low tech and high tech? From what you are saying, all tech is organic, it's natural. Why have we found ourselves in a space of naming certain technologies as low tech and others as high tech? Julia Watson named it Lo-TEK,[30] which is great. But, does it not re inscribe those separations between the modern and primitive? Between the high and low? But the way you are speaking, that it's all tech, it doesn't matter. And it's interesting how that relates to decoloniality, because it's coloniality that makes us think of the divide between the modern and primitive. It's coloniality that divides high from low tech. It's coloniality that also ascribes ideas of blackness, and what a black person should be doing, and not just the dynamics between race, but also the distinction between cultures, and between class. Like you shouldn't be perceived as someone who should be playing with technology.

King Debs   Hundred percent! That's how I feel every second of the day. Because that is what it is. Every milestone I reach, you feel this sense of solitude. Like I'm on my own in this.

Conversation Two: African-ness Through Language (32:00–40:00)

Lesiba Mabitsela   Your work speaks to language. Language is one of the oldest connective tissues we have that still remains with us, that would group us as Sotho speakers. So, botho comes from a Sotho heritage. I don't know if you want to elaborate on spirituality, in terms of your work and how it applied to the project that we did together? And maybe that language is another instance of spirituality in the work, beyond the shape I created, and your artwork is in itself also an expression of that. You know, how we were saying it would be great to have an aspect of this app being spoken in Setswana.

King Debs   Yeah, man. It's a great extension to what you are speaking on. When we are speaking about language—about Tswana or Sotho—we are speaking about spirit. For me, it's important for my work to speak to me in a language that is what I was birthed to speak. Because what happens is that when the public engages with the language in the work, then very interesting conversations come out of that because language invokes ancient spirits in people that they may feel some form of resonance with. I say resonance as opposed to understanding the language, because language is interconnected.

Just having an indigenous language being synthesized in these technological applications that we are working with invokes an evolution of the spirit, even if someone is Venda or Shangaan, or they speak Shona.[31] We are growing as beings all the time, and we are engaging with spaces and scenarios that our ancestors weren't necessarily able to. We are "doing" tech, and we're having conversations in that way.

When you were speaking, like the perception of African spirituality in the Western sense, and how it can be homogenized into this super-serious thing all the time, it mirrors the tension I have with technology. On your end, you are working with fabrics and things, and having a larger conversation that can, and should, evolve. But it's almost like there's a force that is trying to contain it within, or homogenize it within, something, that you are maybe trying to not just solely focus on. So, that is the parallel that I would see in terms of the work, what we were expressing. And that's why botho is in an indigenous language, because it's important for us to make that mark.

Lesiba Mabitsela   I want to ask if you would explain the phrase that you put on the garment?

King Debs   The phrase I used on the garment is *Ditau ga di a dimane meno—Batlhabani ga ba adimanwe*. It is a Tswana proverb that is meant to instill a sense of mindfulness and awareness. It means that one must constantly be alert and be prepared for conflict resolution by any means necessary.

Between Language and Memory

As a Tswana-speaking South African, much of Debs' work is inspired by reimagining (and reimaging) his own heritage. In a work titled *Ritual Dance 0001*, Debs created a fictional avatar named Lerato, after his cousin. The work features Lerato as a young Tswana Queen draped in a crimson-and-black garment worn exclusively for ritual practices (see Figure 10.7). The 32-seconds-long CGI film, about a dance that channels the Bantu ancestors, is fully computer-generated, including the song that plays along with it. In an ever-expanding information era, Debs developed a visual language as a highly

Figure 10.7 Ritual Dance 0001, *3D CGI video still, 2018.* © King Debs.

original, hybrid form of graffiti and calligraphy, that encapsulates his ideas about empathy and humility, and explores new meanings of, and with, his ancestry as an African creative. The calligraphy in the background of *Ritual Dance 0001* is a placeholder for prayer, supplementing the dance. The digital work blurs the boundaries between the real and the imagined, between ideas of heritage and the speculative, folding and twisting a multiplicity of meanings, symbols, and senses to (in)form and manifest new rituals.

Another project advanced through the digital, is one Mabitsela's ongoing enquiries into the construction of notions of Western masculinity encoded and enacted in the three-piece suit. In the Cuttingroom Project, Mabitsela interrogates the encoding of colonial ideology shared between the architecture of a clothing factory in Cape Town, Rex Trueform, and the suits that were produced in the building (see Figure 10.8a–b).[32] The building, dilapidated now, is seeking regeneration as a heritage site, and offers an opportunity to insert overlooked histories, voices, and stories of a divided past. Mabitsela's virtual rendering of the space was visually modeled on the aesthetic templates of a tailored suit pattern and the architectural blueprints of the Rex Trueform building to function as both a storyboard and interactive mind-map. Now, haunted by the recorded memories of workers and seamstresses, the digital Cuttingroom Project makes possible other relations and understandings of

Figure 10.8a–b *The Cuttingroom Project, Deconstructing the Suit Pattern, 2021.*
© Lesiba Mabitsela.

our apartheid past. Mabitsela explored the entanglements of coloniality and modernity, of gender and power, and of looks and labor in his contributions towards building a new digital archive in the form of interviews, a fashion film, and a mapping of the silenced racial and spatial divides. Aimed at bringing forth forgotten stories as possibilities for redress, remembering and rewriting histories, the project draws attention to the unfinished political and cultural reparations in a post-apartheid South Africa.

Conclusion

The eight case studies briefly shared in this chapter employ the generative affordances of both fashion and the digital at their convergence(s). As Mbembe describes it, the affordances of technology witness the entanglement of the deep past with notions of present and future imaginaries, and particularly through the fluidity and malleability of the digital technologies, that these forms "speak powerfully to African pre-colonial cultures and to ways of working with representation and mediation, of folding realities."[33]

The digital becomes less a destination and more a tool that navigates, troubles, or engages the borderspaces of temporalities, identities, geographies, histories, and imaginaries. The need to rethink, reimagine, and rescript the role and place of borders in the changing technological, cultural, and political environment of the twenty-first century points to the critical work made possible in these borderscapes Dina Krichker describes a borderscape as a fluid, mobile, open zone of differentiated encounters—a border zone without borders.[34]

Creatives working digitally with fashion in these transcendent and transit spaces draw on the entangled relations of fashion as both social process and product. The capacity to interrogate forms of multiplicity, authenticity, belonging, language, looking, mythology, and decoloniality means that the new subjectivity forms are both being remembered and remade, towards new African futurisms, where space, imagination, and experience lead the way.

Notes

1   Gilles Deleuze and Félix Guattari, *A Thousand Plateaus: Capitalism and Schizophrenia*, trans. Brian Massumi (Minneapolis: University of Minnesota Press, 1987), 249.

2   Drawing on recent decolonial and feminist attention to the productive and fertile affordances of concepts such as border thinking, border time, and borderscapes, this chapter employs the concept of border spaces to loosely cohere a selection of projects navigating the dynamic tensions, contestations, and opportunities that exist in these in-between spaces.

3   African Fashion Research Institute, https://afri.digital/.

4   *Fashioning Brave New Worlds*, http://bit.ly/FashioningBraveNewWorlds-AfricaIFS2019 DigitalExhibition.

5   The project was funded by the British Council, with support from the London College of Fashion, British Fashion Council, and Zeitz Museum of Contemporary African Art.

6   See AFRI YouTube Channel, https://www.youtube.com/@afri_digital5427.

7 It is important to note that these efforts towards ensuring greater and more diverse access are still hindered by limited internet coverage in less accessible geographical locations.

8 Achille Mbembe, "Decolonising Knowledge and the Question of the Archive," lecture text (University of Witwatersrand, unpublished, 2018). See https://wiser.wits.ac.za/system/files/Achille%20Mbembe%20-%20Decolonizing%20Knowledge%20and%20the%20Question%20of%20the%20Archive.pdf.

9 Achille Mbembe, "The Power of the Archive and its Limits," in C. Hamilton, V. Harris, M. Pickover, G. Reid, J. Taylor, and R. Saleh (eds.), *Refiguring the Archive* (Dordrecht: Springer, 2002), 19–27.

10 "*It [the bag] is said to be an object of importance that remains fixed on the owner. Inside of it you will find items of value and objects of importance. We could say that its main prerogative is to act as a safe.* As practitioners, we have chosen to center Xhosa sensibilities in our works in order to present isiXhosa in ways that counter the denialist approach of modernity's universalism. Our work comes to trouble 'modernity's affirmation of "the real" and coloniality's denial of existence,' and so isiXhosa is written into texts, spoken into spaces in ways that visibilize it where it once would have been viewed as 'other.'" Rolando Vázquez, "Towards a Decolonial Critique of Modernity: Buen Vivir, Relationality and the Task of Listening," in Raúl Fornet-Betancourt (ed.), *Capital, Poverty, Development, Denktraditionen im Dialog: Studien zur Befreiung und interkulturalität*, vol. 33 (Aachen: Wissenschaftsverlag Mainz, 2012), 241–52. See https://www.prismaweb.org/nl/wp-content/uploads/2017/07/Towards-a-decolonial-critique-of-modernity-Buen-vivir-relationality-and-the-task-of-listening%E2%94%82Rolando-V%C3%A1zquez%E2%94%822012.pdf.

11 Provocation: *When we open this bag/this safe—what would I find?*

12 Design Futures Lab was funded by the British Council, Crossover Labs, Twyg, and Electric South. See https://www.electricsouth.org/workshop_item/2022-design-futures-lab/.

13 Between Histories, Instagram, https://www.instagram.com/betweenhistoriesarchive/?hl=en.

14 A new South African democracy was voted in with the first free and fair elections held in 1994.

15 Similar challenges are addressed by researchers Chao Tayaiana Maina and Molemo Moiloa in their podcast *Access for Who?*, as they interrogate the colonial violence of existing archives and whose voice is presented, for whom and by whom. See https://soundcloud.com/user-756417433-541306775.

16 Diane Taylor, *The Archive and the Repertoire: Performing Cultural Memory in the Americas* (Durham, NC, and London: Duke University Press, 2003).

17 The Daveyton1520 instagram research project was first presented in a paper, "Fashioning Counterpublics: The umBlaselo as Urban Archive," by Bongani Tau and Dr Erica de Greef at the Urban Archives of the International EWIS conference, July 6–9, 2022.

18 Dina Krichker explores the power of imagination and space-making as a way in which to navigate complex and ever-shifting contemporary borderspaces. Dina Krichker, "Making Sense of Borderscapes: Space, Imagination and Experience," *Geopolitics* 26, no. 4 (2019), 1224–42.

19 African Fashion Research Institute, "African Fashion (?) Why do these stereotypes exist and persist?" https://afri.digital/african-fashion-why-do-these-stereotypes-exist-and-persist/.

20 heeten bhagat, "Speculative Indigeneities: The (K)New Now," PhD thesis, Department of Theatre, Dance and Performance Studies, University of Cape Town, 2019.

21 bhagat, "Speculative Indigeneities," 194.

22 Ainehi Edoro, "The New Image of Africa in Black Panther," *Perspective Africa* (2018): 8, https://za.boell.org/en/2018/12/04/new-image-africa-black-panther.

23 Achille Mbembe, *On the Postcolony* (Berkeley: University of California Press, 2001), 16.

24 Artist and curator Phatismo Sunstrum describes this need as follows: "It means neither staying in the box, nor thinking outside of the box, nor yelling at the box, but transcending the box entirely," in Tegan Bristow, "We Want the Funk: What is Afro-Futurism for Africa?" in N. J. Keith, T. Bristow, and Z. Whitly (eds.), *The Shadows Took Shape* (New York: Harlem Studio Museum, 2013).

25 This is a translation of Botho developed by Lesiba Mabitsela and King Debs *towards a definition* in preparation for their Design Futures Lab collaboration in 2022.

26 Electric South, "2022 Design Futures Lab," https://www.electricsouth.org/workshop_item/2022-design-futures-lab/.

27 Zoom recording no. 1, September 19, 2022.

28 Mabitsela has incorporated these principles in many of his creative projects. Lesiba Mabitsela, "*Reinstitute*: Performing methods of undress, *má* and decolonial aestheSis," *Critical Studies in Men's Fashion* (2021), https://doi.org/10.1386/csmf_00032_1.

29 Zoom recording no. 2, September 19, 2022.

30 Julia Watson, *Lo-TEK: Design by Radical Indigenism* (Cologne: Taschen, 2020).

31 South Africa is a multilingual country and Section 6 of the Constitution of the Republic of South Africa, 1996 granted official language status to eleven languages. See: https://www.gov.za/sites/default/files/gcis_document/201703/40733gen244.pdf.

32 The Cuttingroom Project was part of the Institute for Creative Arts Online Fellowship program in 2020, University of Cape Town. See: https://icaonline.net/artwork/lesiba-mabitsela/.

33 Achille Mbembe, "Knowledge Futures and the State of the Humanities," African Studies Association, video, 2016, https://www.youtube.com/watch?v=J6p8pUU_VH0.

34 Krichker, "Making Sense of Borderscapes," 3.

11

(Im)possible Digital Fashion Dreams: Who Can Deliver on Accessible and Sustainable Digital Fashion?

BEATA WILCZEK

Introduction

The question "How can digital fashion transform the fashion industry?" has triggered both excitement and confusion among many fashion workers since 2019. Such inquiry immediately triggers a chain of parallel questions: "What is digital fashion?" and "What can it actually do?" In this chapter, my aim is to respond to these questions, while it remains essential for the reader to recognize that this work primarily serves as a reflection on fashion from the spring of 2023. I am convinced that the rapid advancement of digital technology in our everyday life, encompassing such fashion activities as dressing, designing, and shopping, will add further complexity to this subject matter over the next few years and beyond. My objective is to reflect on the occurrence and development of digital fashion and its sustainable claims at this point in time, thereby painting a current and critical depiction of the landscape, and hopefully contributing to new scenarios and tangible alternatives.

The Novelty of Digital Fashion: From New Commodities to Digital Literacy

From the new products, such as digital assets and phygitals,[1] and e-commerce to new design tools and social platforms, the speed of fashion's adaptation to all things digital opened up many new avenues for creators and brands during the Covid-19 pandemic. This has been visible across all industry segments: in luxury houses, sport brands, and newly established digital fashion houses. Prada in December 2019 launched "Prada Crypted"—the NFT area and community server (Discord), focusing on regular drops of new virtual or phygital products.[2] Sports brand Nike acquired digital brand RTFKT, specializing in virtual sneakers and artist collaborations and launched NFT platform Swoosh, focusing on creating, collecting, trading, flexing, and wearing virtual products in games and immersive experiences.[3] Apart from popular brands, a new category of digital-only, independent fashion houses, like The Fabricant, began to produce virtual-only garments and explore the landscape of platforms and co-creation, inviting everyone to digitally customize their designs. Similar to Tribute Brand and Auroboros, these new fashion houses are establishing new business models and are more like start-ups rather than small clothing brands.

The three examples provided clearly demonstrate how digital fashion introduces new products that build upon a brand's legacy. It also decentralizes communication, engaging its clients (often referred to as a "community" rather than as "users" or "target audiences") through social media platforms like Discord or collaborative design processes. Apart from its potential business and engagement value, the design process itself encapsulates a paradigm shift. The creation of digital fashion is linked to various programs, in particular CLO3D and Browzwear. These industry-standard softwares are used to create virtual clothes and digital patterns. Additionally, there are numerous other software solutions, native to 3D modeling or gaming, such as Blender or Unreel

Engine. Incorporating these tools into the design workflow requires different sets of skills. These skills can be categorized as follows: (1) digital proficiency, enabling the learning and use of various softwares; (2) the ability to understand emerging technologies and their application to fashion; and last but not least, (3) the ability to contextualize fashion within the digital cultural landscape, essential for comprehending its complexities and impact. Taken together, these different skills emphasize the importance of digital literacy in the fashion industry.

The first category is tied to the growing popularity of the aforementioned 3D software, which is becoming part of the curriculum at many fashion design schools.[4] The second category is inherently linked to the concept of digital fashion as a space where fashion integrates emerging technologies such as blockchain, token economics, virtual reality (VR), augmented reality (AR), extended reality (XR), and artificial intelligence (AI). This integration introduces immersive, spatial, and gaming experiences, redefining the contours of fashion's traditional spaces and expanding its vocabulary. The third category is about situating digital fashion in a cultural, social, and ethical context. Here, debates revolving around sustainability and responsibility in digital fashion find their place.

Digital fashion is central to the ongoing discussions on sustainable and responsible fashion, as it can be instrumental in supporting the circular economy and achieving sustainable development goals. Such assertions have been proclaimed by different stakeholders, ranging from digital fashion start-ups such as DressX, the digital fashion marketplace, to leading sustainability organizations such as Ellen McArthur Foundation, the charity specializing in circular economy. This debate emerges as both a response to and an outcome of the twin digital and green transitions. On the one hand, it emphasizes technology's role as a solution, while on the other, it points to technology as part of the problem due to its substantial environmental footprint that conflicts with the goals of the green transition. The European Green Deal, a set of proposals by the European Commission aiming at carbon neutrality in the European Union by 2050, stresses the importance of reliability, comparability, and verifiability of the environmental labels and initiatives on the environmental performance of products and companies, against the practice of greenwashing.[5] That is why digital fashion's practices and their supporting claims should be explored, in order to test, ground, and further examine their potential. It is particularly important in the context of undoing fashion's harm, its social impact, and the climate crisis. And as fashion is becoming more and more entangled with digital design and social media, unlocking new possibilities for surveillance and data extraction, it is vital to examine its ethical stances, values, and capacity for change. Next, I explore some of the key promises of digital fashion: accessibility and sustainability.

Accessibility versus Digital Divide

Accessibility in fashion can be associated with ease of experiencing and purchasing, which has already been transformed by Web2, the current iteration of the internet, with e-commerce platforms, digital media, micro-blogging, and the streaming of fashion shows. Its antonym, exclusivity, is integral to the luxury sector, where the higher price point, scarcity, and uniqueness are some of the most important signifiers of the product's value. But what if exclusive goods and highly-priced products could become available at a much lower price point? Digital fashion aims to embrace this duality. Since 2019, luxury fashion houses have been exploring different virtual goods and digital asset strategies, at various price points, from zero up to US$500,000 per digital asset,[6] and different edition numbers, from one-off, unique pieces to infinite supplies. The concept of "digital affordable luxury" has been explored by tech giant Meta, where users can dress their avatars in Balenciaga, Prada, and Thom Browne, by purchasing in-app virtual clothes in the US$3 to US$9 price range.[7] Other social platforms and luxury houses explored such opportunities taking resale into account. On *Roblox*, users could purchase the virtual-only Gucci "Queen Bee Dionysus" bag for US$5.50,[8] later resold for US$4,115. In times of looming recession, multiplying limitations, and rising costs in clothes manufacturing, virtual-only luxury fashion could become a viable revenue stream for companies.

Nevertheless, exclusivity in fashion extends beyond the product. The ruthless work conditions and the elitist education are considered an industry standard and a never-ending rite of passage to join the creative fashion workforce in the Global North. Their expectations of students and employees are known to be insatiable, unreachable, and exploitative.[9] Free labor is marketed as desirable, and mandatory internships, as well as high annual tuition fees reaching tens of thousands of dollars,[10] render access to the industry unattainable for most. Participating professionally in digital fashion is easier, as it requires only the following resources to become a digital fashion designer:

1 digital tools, such as computers and subscriptions to digital fashion software such as CLO3D or Browzwear;

2 stable access to the internet; and

3 the time necessary for learning and practicing.

Of course, fashion schools develop other skills, such as creative, critical, and strategic thinking, yet digital fashion makes it much more straightforward, thanks to the removal of costly design school fees and abundant amounts of textiles. It creates access for those who could not actively participate in fashion and design education before. By doing so, digital fashion contributes to the decentralization of fashion, allowing for new, global practices to become visible, beyond the eurocentric hegemony of fashion trends and cycles. Yet for access and active contribution to this global digital fashion-making, we need to ask who has access to the necessary resources.

In 2022 the global population reached 8 billion, according to the United Nations,[11] out of which only 63% have access to the internet.[12] In other words, more than 3 billion people do not have access to the internet. As fashion will become more and more digital, transforming design, production, education, labor, and commerce, it will also contribute to the digital divide, this deepening gap between those who have and those who do not have access to computers and the internet.[13] This divide has a significant impact on education, employment, and the overall quality of life. While efforts are being made to bridge this divide, it is still a major issue in many parts of the world. In the future, it is crucial that more resources are allocated to closing the digital divide, in order to ensure equal access for all to the benefits of technology. This also includes fashion: design, production, and consumption. Education and access to learning materials will also become essential to minimize the gaps in knowledge.

There is no doubt that more people will be able to access digital fashion, both as makers and wearers, but it is vital for fashion brands and groups to address how they contribute to the digital divide and strive to have their products and services remove barriers, instead of creating new ones—especially when digital fashion and its new products can create new revenue streams for them.

Sustainability versus New Products

The claim that "digital fashion can make the fashion industry more sustainable" is one of the key narratives contributing to the ongoing conversation about responsible and sustainable fashion. There is currently very little reliable data on the topic from independent entities, compared to data from within the industry. On the one hand, digital fashion is seen as a tool supporting a circular economy and sustainable goals, while on the other hand, questions about high energy consumption related to blockchain technology are being raised.[14] I argue that the impact and sustainability of digital fashion needs to be investigated holistically, especially by the policymakers and researchers.

Currently, there are four strategies through which digital fashion can facilitate the fashion industry's transition to sustainability:[15]

1   virtual sampling, where traditional textile samples are replaced with digital, making the process more efficient, less wasteful, and generating less environmental impact;[16]

2   traceability and authentication, supported by tokenizing products on the blockchain and providing access to information about products' authenticity, origin, design, and certifications;

3   enabling production on-demand to help resolve the problem of overproduction;[17] and

4   introducing new, virtual-only products.

Virtual-only fashion products, such as filters, lenses, and wearables, can be purchased in apps and/or on dedicated digital fashion marketplaces. These digital assets can be also sold as NFTs, which raises environmental challenges, as not all blockchains are created equal, and not all NFTs have the same impact. It is crucial to differentiate between different consensus mechanisms, which are used to achieve agreement, trust, and security across a decentralized computer network. The most common ones are Proof-of-Stake and Proof of Work. Proof of Work (PoW) is the first consensus mechanism used in blockchain, and its electricity consumption and carbon footprint remain significant.[18] According to Crypto Carbon Ratings Institute, blockchain networks based on alternative consensus mechanisms such as Proof of Stake (PoS) consume significantly less energy, making it more sustainable from an environmental perspective.[19] There are many other points of differentiation between PoW and PoS, such as security and centralization, but when discussing digital and environmental sustainability, energy consumption and efficiency become key factors.

In order to avoid extra emissions, brands and creators planning to put their products on-chain should avoid PoW blockchain and look for lightweight blockchain running on PoS, such as Ethereum or Polygon. Tracking and measuring these new products should also be embraced and reflected in the CSR or ESG reporting. Most importantly, the questions behind blockchains and other new technologies' environmental impact should be always addressed. Every garment, digital or not, poses environmental challenges.

Digitization can bring efficiency in production and diversify brands' portfolios, but also raises new questions that need to be looked at holistically. Both industry and consumers need to learn and understand all these new developments. It is also particularly important that we address cultural and social sustainability (see Chapter 9), against cultural appropriation and workers' exploitation in digital fashion.[20] There is a lot of space for researchers and policymakers in this field, as many questions remain unanswered and with progressing adoption new ones will soon be raised. Creating interdisciplinary research teams, where different partners contribute knowledge from such fields as environmental studies, tech, and fashion, could support more thorough answers. Advocates and activists, fighting for more ethical fashion futures, should also join the conversation in order to provide new and radical perspectives.

Stop Overproduction versus Digital Hoarding

Overproduction contributes to the fashion waste problem. The unsold product ends its life cycle on a landfill or is incinerated, emitting high amounts of carbon dioxide into the atmosphere, negatively impacting the environment. Digital ownership in fashion claims to be an answer to overproduction in the fashion industry, as it can potentially reduce the number of produced textile goods. In this optimistic scenario, consumers will choose digital-only clothes, decreasing the demand for textile clothes. Smaller demand could lead to fewer garments being produced.

Specifically, regarding production, digital fashion can contribute to developing production on demand, bringing back bespoke and local manufacturing. If on-demand physical production is heavily reliant on distribution logistics and access to technological infrastructure, such as distributed printing facilities, then digital on-demand relies on the emerging consumer behavior of "buy only digital."

If we adhere to the assumption that digital products can be bought as a replacement for physical ones, we become trapped in one-to-one comparisons between essentially different fashion products. I believe that these products should be approached differently, especially when discussing sustainability. Digital products shouldn't be compared using only methods and metrics applicable to textile products. Assessing digital and textile products with a singular mindset might lead to reductionism, miscalculating the potential benefits and disadvantages of digital fashion, by trying to have it fit already existing categories. In other creative industries, such as architecture or music, where digitization was adopted earlier, there were not such literal comparisons. Virtual houses weren't juxtaposed with penthouses, nor were MP3 files compared with live shows. Similarly, and this is my favorite example, playing football on a grass field was not equated to playing a computer game. This also hints at an ontological shift in fashion, as we start to consider a virtual dress as an object or product, just like other garments. The virtual dress becomes yet another fashion good. This might be a consequence of the ongoing blurring of frontiers in our hybrid lives and the growing importance of one's online virtual body representation.

In the dystopian scenario, digital fashion can have the opposite effect, by pairing every fashion garment with its digital twin. Imagine such e-commerce platforms as Asos or brands like Shein introducing a digital double for every physical garment they already offer. This could lead to the doubling of the already oversaturated market, unlocking new digital fast fashion business models, where current sweatshops could be replaced by digital sweatshops. Drawing the parallel with sweatshops in the clothing industry, a factory or workshop, where workers are paid poorly and work in strenuous conditions for many hours, against fair and ethical labor standards, digital sweatshops could become a dystopian reality, where sewing machines are replaced with computers, mimicking the working conditions of tech content moderators. This also raises many questions about digital fashion labor, its regulations and codes of conduct, and the amount of digital goods being produced. If digital fashion becomes overproduced, what type of waste does it bring to the fashion industry?

The debates on overproduction run in parallel with overconsumption, where consumers are blamed for abundant purchases. From a consumer perspective, digital hoarding is an already-known phenomenon, where computer files, emails, and photos are being kept for the sake of keeping and in case of potential future use. In gaming, this can relate to collecting powers, upgrades, or items in quantities unjustifiable for the purpose of the game—for example, stuffing the Sims' house with furniture. Once digital fashion becomes more popular and accessible, it could also become accumulated in vast numbers on smart devices and drives, leading to overconsumption. As one of the leading digital fashion e-commerce platforms claims, "Don't shop less, shop digital fashion."

Hence, digital ownership and emerging consumer behavior should be studied in more detail, especially in gaming. Since digital fashion is native to gaming, it can also be a rich field to learn from, allowing the prediction of emerging scenarios. This could be particularly suitable for cultural anthropologists. It is also crucial for emerging businesses to plan at scale and predict plausible scenarios and their impact. As I have shown, digital abundance is already deployed as a marketing argument, so it is important for marketing teams to make sure their claims are not contradictory, as claiming sustainability and promoting overconsumption definitely are.

Conclusion

As we face rapid digitization in fashion, it is the right time to challenge many aspects of what we consider sustainable and accessible. And as we challenge them, we should do it in a collective effort, creating alliances and cross-disciplinary teams. The fashion system is becoming more complex and if we want its new digital arm not to perpetrate past mistakes, we need new tools and frameworks. There is a legitimate claim that digital fashion can change the fashion industry, but what kind of change it will be, remains open to debate. There are many examples indicating that it can support a more sustainable and accessible fashion system, though there is very little data to substantiate such a projection. That is why digital fashion is uncharted territory for researchers, designers, and policymakers. Activists and advocates should also contribute to this debate, by providing alternative and challenging perspectives. Brands and marketing teams should be careful not to promote misleading claims and not to greenwash, especially in light of emerging regulations.[21] It is their duty to educate internally and externally, as well as to inform on their approach towards new digital products and their energy consumption.

To conclude, digital fashion is a new limb of the fashion system, a new territory for the progressing digitization of everyday life. It proposes a world where people own phygital or virtual-only products and dress their virtual body representations. This world is being shaped by many, and it is up to them to make it not only profitable but also harmless and responsible.

Notes

1   "Phygital" relates here to products which merge the physical and the digital.

2   Prada, "Prada Crypted," https://www.prada.com/prada-crypted/.

3   Nike, "Swoosh," https://www.swoosh.nike/.

4   Noorin Khamisani and Beata Wilczek, "The Digital Shift: Evolution and rapid digitisation of fashion design education during the Covid-19 pandemic," "Can Fashion Save The World?" The Responsible Fashion Series, (forthcoming), 2024.

5   ESMA, European Securities and Markets Authority, "ESAs launch joint Call for Evidence on greenwashing," November 15, 2022, https://www.esma.europa.eu/press-news/esma-news/esas-launch-joint-call-evidence-greenwashing.

6   Dana Thomas, "Dolce & Gabbana Just Set a $6 Million Record for Fashion NFTs," *New York Times*, October 4, 2021, https://www.nytimes.com/2021/10/04/style/dolce-gabbana-nft.html.

7   Steff Yotka, "Balenciaga, Prada, and Thom Browne Will Dress Your Meta Avatar," *Vogue*, June 17, 2022, https://www.vogue.com/article/balenciaga-prada-thom-browne-meta-instagram-avatar.

8   Dylan Kelly, "A Virtual Gucci Bag Sold For More Money on Roblox Than The Actual Bag," *Hypebeast*, May 26, 2021, https://hypebeast.com/2021/5/virtual-gucci-bag-roblox-resale.

9   Giulia Mensitieri, *The Most Beautiful Job in the World* (London, Bloomsbury Publishing, 2020).

10 Daphne Milner, "Is Fashion School Still Worth the Money?" *Business of Fashion*, September 15, 2020, https://www.businessoffashion.com/articles/news-analysis/fashion-school-remote-teaching-coronavirus-racism-classism-design-creative/.

11 United Nations, "Day of Eight Billion," https://www.un.org/en/dayof8billion.

12 Statista, "Digital Population Worldwide," https://www.statista.com/statistics/617136/digital-population-worldwide/.

13 Jan A. G. M. van Dijk, "Digital divide research, achievements and shortcomings," *Poetics* 34 (2006): 221–35, doi:10.1016/j.poetic.2006.05.004.

14 Gregory Barber, "NFTs Are Hot. So Is Their Effect on the Earth's Climate," *Wired*, March 6, 2021, https://www.wired.com/story/nfts-hot-effect-earth-climate/.

15 Beata Wilczek, "The Sustainability Pathway In Digital Fashion With Beata Wilczek," *Sustainable Digital Design*, October 16, 2022, https://sustainabledigitaldesign.com/community/the-sustainability-pathway-in-digital-fashion-with-beata-wilczek/.

16 Yihan Xiong, "The comparative LCA of digital fashion and existing fashion system: is digital fashion a better fashion system for reducing environmental impacts?" Master's dissertation, Centre for Environmental Policy, Imperial College London, 2020, https://static1.squarespace.com/static/5a6ba105f14aa1d81bd5b971/t/5fa3da036d618612a18b5703/1604573714045/RAW+Report_v2.pdf.

17 Ronen Samuel, "On-Demand Production is the Sustainable Future of Fashion and Textiles," *Forbes*, January 17, 2023, https://www.forbes.com/sites/forbesbusinesscouncil/2023/01/17/on-demand-production-is-the-sustainable-future-of-fashion-and-textiles/.

18 Ulrich Gallersdörfer, Lena Klaaßen, and Christian Stoll, "Energy Efficiency and Carbon Footprint of PoS Blockchain Protocols," Crypto Carbon Ratings Institute, January 2022, https://carbon-ratings.com/dl/pos-report-2022.

19 Gallersdörfer, Klaaßen, and Stoll, "Energy Efficiency and Carbon Footprint of PoS Blockchain Protocols."

20 Wilczek, "The Sustainability Pathway."

21 European Commission, "Initiative on substantiating green claims," https://ec.europa.eu/environment/eussd/smgp/initiative_on_green_claims.htm.

Jonathan Michael Square Interviewed by Sara Emilia Bernat

From social to economic inequality, digital fashion touches on some of the most crucial questions with which contemporary societies struggle. Part Three of this book explored some of these matters and offered possible future scenarios. Jonathan Michael Square is a New York City-based writer and historian specializing in fashion and the visual culture of the African diaspora. In this interview, he talks about "digital slavery," cultural appropriation in the metaverse, and the capitalist residues of digital fashion.

Sara Emilia Bernat What are some digital fashion initiatives that you especially like these days?

Jonathan Square There's a few digital influencers that I follow that I'm a big fan of. I really like the Instagrammer and YouTuber Hautelemode. Fashion media, by and large, has a cozy relationship with commerce. In that setting it is difficult to yield a really critical voice because a lot of people are driven solely by sales. A lot of the photo shoots and editorial content is funded by brands, so it is very difficult to maintain independence. YouTubers tend to be more independent, although they also have a tight relationship to sponsorships, something which we can talk about later. At any rate, these digital makers tend to have a more genuine voice. There is another Instagram-based journalist, named Pam Boy, who is very active on that platform. His real name is Pierre A. M'Pelé, he is based in France, and is the director of digital content at *GQ*, though for a long time he worked as a freelancer. He is very smart, very sharp. I like journalists who just happen to be on Instagram. Robin Ghivan, for instance, is a really important fashion voice. She's just really smart and sharp, and I love her writing. In terms of publications, I think *Business of Fashion* provides good content when it comes to fashion. And I'm also a really big fan of fashionista.com. I think those two platforms are not as entangled with other media outlets. But there is still a lot of room for independent voices and criticism, and to be honest, I am not the biggest fan of social media. I like that it's free and everyone has access to it, but along the experience we are also becoming products ourselves, without realizing it. We unknowingly give away our data, preferences, shopping habits. Our impulses are sort of recorded, cataloged, and then marketed to companies. That's a problem. On the flip side, though, social media gives space and voice to marginalized people, and gives them power.

Sara Emilia Bernat   What is it about independent voices specifically that are so important?

Jonathan Square   My answer probably won' t surprise you. There are so many issues that brands fail to address fearing that they would hurt the bottom line. It's all about making more money and meeting investors' expectations. It's part of the reason why I like smaller brands to whom money isn' t necessarily the end goal. Sometimes it's creativity. Sometimes it's speaking to their communities. Sometimes it's proposing more sustainable methods of engaging in the fashion system. Sometimes it's creating space for people with different stories, different bodies, just different gender identities and sexualities. So I would say that's what larger mainstream brands are missing out on: instead of pushing forward new conversations and addressing some of the intractable problems within society, their aim is to be making more money. And when they do attempt to address issues like race, inclusion, diversity, sustainability—insert issue—it's often for marketing to attract customers like you and me who care about these things. Their initiatives end up in greenwashing, in a sort of lip service that does not yield change.

Sara Emilia Bernat   Do you think there are groups that are currently left off from this digital revolution? What can be done to improve their inclusivity?

Jonathan Square   Digital fashion has a potential to be more inclusive, but it's not always the case. There is a lot that needs to be done, especially when it comes to body inclusivity, but the changes needed are more cultural than structural in nature. I think we need to shift how we think: who should be included in fashion spaces, who needs to be on the cover of magazines, who deserves a fashion spread. Who's beautiful, essentially. There are more conversations happening around race, gender, and sexuality, but little talk of ageism.

Sara Emilia Bernat   Can brands push these ideas forward at all while avoiding greenwashing?

Jonathan Square   It's a hard question for me because I'm a low-key Marxist, and I believe that in the capitalist structure the goal is always to make more money. You can't really push for change because it's gonna hurt your bottom line. And so you're not going to include the 70+ model because people don't wanna see that. That's why I said, in order to create more inclusive environments digitally, we need to change culturally and socially first. Brands will be brands, and capitalism will be capitalism. That said, this lets brands off the hook, plus there are brands that I think are genuine in trying to make change. Mara Hoffman, I believe, genuinely cares about wanting to be sustainable and inclusive. Eileen Fisher is another good example. But again, it's the people behind the company, the ones who run the company who make it a point to position these issues as central tenets. I've also done work with Greg Lauren who is behind another brand that I think is genuinely interested in advocating for change.

Sara Emilia Bernat   How do you think cultural appropriation may take place in the digital space, and what is it that brands and consumers may do to avoid this kind of exploitation?

Jonathan Square   I think digital platforms make cultural appropriation easier. At the same time, they also make it easier for us to call out. In the 80s and 90s there was rampant cultural appropriation happening, and we didn't really see fashion shows until the next day, at the quickest, or depending on where you lived, and what your access to media was, even weeks or months. So, it was really hard to call out the cultural appropriation. Now we see it instantly through social media, and respond to it immediately. That's one of the great things about the current digital age.

Sara Emilia Bernat   Speaking of exploitation, you have recently written a piece about "digital slavery" for another Bloomsbury publication. Could you please explain what the term means?

Jonathan Square   You know, I'm still working through the definition myself. I wrote an article on digital slavery, and I was referring to CGI models online, like Lil' Miquela. But when I came up with the term "digital slavery," I wasn't referring to their enslavement. This is arguable, but I don't think an object can be enslaved. Some scholars would disagree with that actually. I'm not saying that it's the truth but my interpretation, and it is up to debate. In the article, I was referring to our enslavement, and by "our," I mean consumers of digital media. People who follow Lil' Miquela, and who may not be aware that these models are created on computers. It goes back to the idea of "Uncanny Valley," and the fact that you cannot be sure whether they are real or not. I think the creators of these CGI models really benefit from this ambiguity.

Digital slavery refers to our enslavement to digital media. These platforms don't tell us how their algorithms work. They don't tell us what they're doing with the information that they're collecting about us. I do think it's interesting that a lot of people who work at these companies don't allow their children on these platforms. It is as if they know something that we don't. Um, so that's what digital slavery is. It's not the enslavement of CGI models, but our slavish relationship to digital media. These CGI models are merely tools that make it easier to sell products. Us humans are more complicated. We have bad days. We have good days. Sometimes we break out with pimples. Sometimes we have crazy political ideas. Some days we don't feel like posting. Sometimes we get pregnant. Sometimes we get sick, you know, we're human beings, but with CGI models, they don't have to go through all the human things that human beings go through. So there's a reliability to them. This makes them a good marketing tool, really good to push products.

Sara Emilia Bernat   Do you believe that there is space for non-capitalist fashion in the metaverse?

Jonathan Square   I have to think so, I'm a fashion lover. I love beautiful things, I appreciate makers, and I want them to be paid for it fairly. The problem happens when there is exploitation and oppression in the supply chain. Good things happen when people make clothes for themselves, have relationships with tailors, seamstresses, and dressmakers, who are artists.

Sara Emilia Bernat   How do you see digital fashion evolving in the next five years? In the next ten years?

Jonathan Square   It is not going away. Digital fashion on social media is going to accelerate, and it will look very different. You know, when we first started using social media, we were basically posting images, alongside texts. And that was essentially what social media was. I think digital fashion and digital media are going to be more about moving images in the coming years. I noticed the popularity of TikTok, and now other platforms are following suit. YouTube has shorts; Instagram and Facebook have reels. Exploitation of user-generated media will continue to happen. I know I am a little cynical about it, because I'm a big fan of long-form content. I love a long documentary that really impacts an issue. Sometimes I think software content and social media doesn't leave any room for nuance; everything needs to be extreme. It's not about sort of unpacking something and revealing complexity but explaining ideas in the most extreme possible way. I find myself really leaning into that too. Sometimes the way I like to write a caption or the way I describe something is done in a way to grab people's attention. I don't think it's going anywhere, though.

I also worry about the effects that digital platforms and fashion have on our self-esteem. I think sometimes people forget that a comment is read by a human being, and so the way you treat someone online should be the same way you treat them face to face. Human-to-human connection is really important, and there are ways to approximate that. I mean, we're doing it right now. We've never met in person, but I mean we're interacting with each other respectfully, and I think that's really important. But that often doesn't happen on social media. So that's one of my worries as a low-key Marxist. This late capitalist era that we're living in worries me; I worry about the Earth, issues such as racial inclusivity, body inclusivity, class, representation: those things are very important to me. So I have a lot of concerns when it comes to the future of digital fashion.

Sara Emilia Bernat   Yes, many of these topics still don't get enough attention. Neither does the idea of what happens to these concerns in a space where you get the freedom to rebuild your entire body and identity based on your likings.

Jonathan Square   Yeah. Can we talk about it right now though?

Sara Emilia Bernat   Would love to hear your thoughts!

Jonathan Square   Sometimes I am a little disturbed by the metaverse. I wonder what the real dangers are if we are all made to become avatars. I have met people who feel as if their realest self is their online self. Like their personal self doesn't feel as their real self. They feel more themselves through their online second life. And so I don't want to impose ideas of normalcy onto everybody, but I think that many of us feel healthiest, most like ourselves, most embodied, through our IRL selves. And so, the metaverse is disturbing for some people. Like you said, it forces us to restructure our bodies. There was a moment on Facebook where people were choosing avatars for themselves. And I felt deeply uncomfortable with that; I just wanted to be myself. Which, of course, brings up the issue of filters, with which I am much more comfortable. I'm using a beauty filter right now!

I think about the conversations that people were having a few months ago about hair texture and how a lot of these digital avatars don't really replicate more curly or textured hair. How does someone represent themselves if they don't like the way their hair looks as an avatar? A lot of these avatars are extremely thin. I've never seen curvy or fat people represented very well in the metaverse. So that's another issue as well.

Sara Emilia Bernat   Is there anything that is currently not talked about in the digital fashion and inclusivity discourse that you would like people to consider?

Jonathan Square   Sometimes when there is a new innovation, or digital shift, people have the impression that these issues are new, but these are conversations that have been happening for centuries. It's just that the medium is different. Conversations about racial diversity, body inclusivity, sexuality, gender, et cetera. Photos have always been filtered since the advent of photographic technology. People have been filtering their photos, but not digitally—they used other means. What I'm saying is that I think conversations about digital fashion are just new iterations of old discussions. That said, I actually think digital fashion does have a lot of potential in inducing inclusivity, and I think to a certain degree it's already happening. I do think power is shifting. People are using social media in radical ways as much as they can. Of course, like I said, these for-profit entities have complete control over preliminary platforms, and they can impose their mandates on audiences easily. But I do think social media and digital platforms have already shifted power in important ways. My hope is that digital fashion will keep throwing wrenches into structures of power.

Part Four

Looking to and Hoping for the Future of Digital Fashion

12

New Definitions for the Future of Fashion

LESLIE HOLDEN

Introduction

The digital transformation of fashion is challenging the industry's status quo. It not only has the potential to impact the design and production process, but the entire supply chain and the people involved in it. Digital fashion is a wide and varied topic and covers more than just the metaverse and Web3 technology, and although the metaverse has had all the bandwidth hype, there are many developments in the digitalization of the traditional fashion industry.

These developments may ensure a cleaner, greener, and more transparent industry.[1] A phygital approach has the power to transform the fashion industry for a circular future. Sustainability can be considered at the core for the innovations in digital fashion enabling zero waste processes and on-demand production. Digitalization can also open major possibilities to empower fashion designers to better direct and oversee their creative workflow from concept to product presentation, making it easier for them to validate their ideas and protect their work. Blockchain can also enable the designer to protect work with NFT certificates. Over the last decade, the digital transformation of fashion has been largely focused on digitization, that is taking the analog and making it digital—for example, scanning a photograph and turning it into a pdf—but this focus was with no real urgency to change the business model of the fashion industry. Since the Covid-19 pandemic, digitalization has taken center stage in meeting the needs of a circular future.

During the Covid-19 pandemic, companies accelerated the digitization of their customer and supply-chain interactions, and their internal operations, by three to four years. Thus, the share of digital or digitally-enabled products in their portfolios was accelerated by a shocking seven years.[2] Digitalization is about process, the work flow, and what one does with the data; it has encouraged companies to remodel their operations and embrace entirely new concepts such as non-fungible tokens (NFTs) and the metaverse, to sell and promote their wares and services. Basically, the metaverse is a concept of connected, digital spaces where people can meet to work and to socialize. It is a combination of social media, virtual reality, video conferencing, and cryptocurrencies, where 3D avatars can spend money, play games, and conduct business. Mark Zuckerberg referred to it as "the next frontier."[3] The metaverse is closely interconnected with the concept of "Web3," which is based around public blockchains and decentralized technology.

Crypto and the technology behind it form the backbone of the metaverse, with the currencies underpinning buying and owning, while blockchain systems enable apps for activities like shopping and gaming and NFTs which are non-fungible, meaning they are immutable and cannot be replaced by something else. The metaverse and Web3 are changing (and can change) the way we understand and engage with fashion. It will become normal to move freely between different virtual worlds and communities, with the help of virtual and augmented reality, changing our definition of reality. Luxury brands have been at the forefront of embracing the possibilities of the metaverse. Many brands have collaborated with gaming companies, such as Balenciaga and Ralph Lauren with *Fortnite*, Gucci with *Roblox,* Bulgari with *Zepeto*, Burberry with *Minecraft*, and Balmain with *Need for Speed*. One may say this opens a possible re definition of the meaning of craft and luxury, and it is certainly a shift in the principles of luxury marketing and product placement.[4] Strategist Cathy Hackl has noted that "younger generations want to be authentically themselves in the physical and digital realms and part of that is who they are virtually so direct to avatar will be important for fashion brands."[5] One could argue that the promise of a fully functioning metaverse could transform not only the ways we engage with clothing but reimagine society in all ways connected to cultural and social interaction. But to be clear, the metaverse does not exist, yet. Technology is currently not developed enough to realize these new virtual worlds at scale.

For brands and manufacturers, digitalizing is a time-consuming and expensive process which involves not only a shift in mindset but also a rethinking of the entire workflow processes involving staff skills and factory investments. There are still significant skills gaps between digitally native designers and the vast majority of manufacturing units which don't have the resources to engage with 3D. The Director of Accessories and Technical Development Apparel at Puma notes that:

> For 3D, on the apparel side, we have tried to implement an end to end process … People need to get used to the change and their new responsibilities. All of a sudden people are excited but wait a minute the product manager still needs to have physical samples in the showroom. People still want to touch and feel, and we have manufacturers who say, "okay we have invested (in the technology), now where are the sample reductions."[6]

In February 2022, Kering announced that it had created a team fully dedicated to Web3 and the metaverse, as well as individual teams for their subsidiaries, Gucci and Balenciaga.[7] They pointed out three potential metaverse opportunities for luxury: (1) NFTs linked to physical products; (2) digital products; and (3) smart contracts that generate revenue from secondary sales. Among luxury brands, Gucci has been a leading early adopter of metaverse technologies, and they are collaborating with other brands in the digital space such as Sandbox, adidas, and more recently the digital retailer 10KTF. The Gucci Dionysus bag costs about $3,400 in real life; a digital version of the same bag was resold in 2022 on *Roblox* for $4,115.[8]

By and large, however, most digital designs are not yet big earners compared to physical clothing, yet the fashion world certainly sees the metaverse as a potentially lucrative new market. The digital fashion industry could be worth $50 billion by 2030, but to put this into context, according to Statista, the physical fashion industry will be worth $2 trillion by 2026.[9] Kerry Murphy, the

CEO of The Fabricant, acknowledged that what is needed to realize the digitalization of fashion is a fusion of different craftsmanship. Traditional physical designing, making, and manufacturing has to be connected to 3D design and then placed on a blockchain. As Murphy explains, the challenge is to establish a common language and understanding: "With the fashion in the foreground, with 3D being the enabler of visualizing in high quality, and the blockchain being, let's say, the foundational layer that gives you the ownership and the provenance around it."[10]

The future of fashion is the communication between traditional design and technology, but it will take a while to get there. Murphy also explains that for digital fashion to evolve and scale, a number of things have to happen. First Web3 must embrace Web2. The language of Web3 must be more accessible to all. And then:

> We actually need the PFP [personal profile pictures] or the avatars to take off first. Everybody needs to have 20 different PFPs or 20 different avatars. Because at that point they're gonna start asking themselves, "how am I gonna dress them?"; "What am I gonna put on them?"; and "how am I gonna create my narrative?" And again, coming to the scalability of digital fashion, people are not gonna just have one body anymore, they're gonna have 20 or 30 different representations of themselves on all of the social media channels, on the game stuff they play, on the virtual platforms that they hang out, their WhatsApp picture, or whatever, wherever they have a virtual existence.[11]

Phygital and On-demand

The fashion industry is one of the largest polluting industries on the planet. Only 1% of clothing is recycled, and every second the equivalent of a truckload of textile waste is sent to landfill or burnt.[12] According to the European Parliament Research Service, textile production alone is responsible for 10% of global greenhouse gas emissions.[13] Despite efforts to reduce emissions, McKinsey points out in their report, "Fashion on Climate," that the industry is on a trajectory that will exceed its 2030 targets set out in the 2015 Paris Agreement by a billion tonnes.[14] Digital fashion can mitigate some of these concerns. "There are three main archetypes of digital circular business models: blockchain-based supply chain, the service-based model, and on-demand manufacturing."[15] Of these, on-demand, or customized, production has the potential to overhaul the economy from scales to scopes, and change the entire process of how fashion items are forecasted, produced, and used.

Phygital is quite simply the blending of the physical and digital, and is a new reality for supply chains in which brands design, produce, merchandise, and sell fashion. Phygital can be considered from a circular perspective as the clothes are designed, produced, and promoted to not only last but also be reused. Digital transformation and a phygital approach have the potential to reimagine fashion as a true "force for good" for the planet and humankind. Phygital is the basis of a digitally driven on-demand manufacturing model. A collection is designed, prototyped, sampled, and sold, fully digitally. Only when the orders are placed does the company organize the manufacturing for the corresponding physical goods. Once the collection is manufactured, the company returns to the digital for online retail.

This approach answers the needs for a more sustainable fashion industry and has increased and normalized the interest in blockchain technologies and solutions, such as NFTs and digital passports which can share product information concerning transparency, sustainability, and circular authenticity. Physical garments are paired with NFTs as digital twins, and consumers then have access to information regarding their garments' supply chain journey. The digital twins or NFTs facilitate access to the metaverse. Traditionally, the fashion industry has no system to follow products after the point of sale, but a phygital approach can boost the products value, longevity, and material value, supporting a circular economy. "The data gathered helps to improve quality and recycling processes by maintaining a connection with the product after it leaves the store, and digital twins allow brands to also earn royalties and secondary sales."[16] Digital solutions are not only useful for being competitive and providing better value to customers, but "are also key to making our economy greener and European businesses more resilient to future shocks."[17]

Case Study

PlatformE, based in Porto, Portugal, is a technology company founded in 2015, which includes Farfetch's CEO José Neves and Net-A-Porter founder Natalie Massenet among its founders and investors. Between 2019 and 2020, they launched DIGGITT, a digital agency specializing in 3D creation and animation, and SKINVADERS, a next-generation platform for at-scale, in-game branded skins and digital assets, that is connecting brands with the metaverse. In recent years, they also built a network of digital-savvy factories ready to produce on-demand in record time. In addition, they have partnered with Houspring to build a factory of the future in Portugal.

The Digital Fashion Group conducted an interview with the CEO and Founder of PlatformE, Gonçalo Cruz, who described the concept of on-demand and its link to digitalization:

> The traditional business model of the fashion industry is a negative working capital model; money is invested in producing stock inventory which is then pushed into the market. Digital Product Creation and digital selling can ensure that garments only require manufacturing once they are sold, so the money comes up-front. This means the traditional "push system" is transformed into a "pull system" or just-in-time, on-demand, made-to-order manufacturing ensuring a sustainable approach and a positive working capital process.[18]

To achieve the on-demand, pull system, which Cruz identifies, brands as well as manufacturers need to work with 3D software which can be used as a real-time feedback and communication platform.

Therefore, apart from training their design team to use the software, brands will also need to bring their manufacturers and partners onboard to ensure interoperability through and throughout their supply and value chain. A brand's ultimate goal is to create 3D models of such high quality that tech packs can be eliminated altogether, allowing their manufacturers to cut and sew products using only the 3D models as input. This could potentially lead to a "first-time right" approach, eliminating the production of prototypes and samples entirely, creating efficiencies and benefits for all the supply chain partners. PlatformE has recently developed a new collection, Valaclava, which is a case study for phygital fashion and answers the needs Murphy points out concerning Web3 embracing Web2. Valaclava is a physical brand engaging with the metaverse through sustainable approaches; although they focus on how NFTs are employed to enhance the user experience, their purchasing process is a recognizable e-commerce one. When the customer buys a garment, they receive the NFT of the digital twin version in their inbox. During manufacturing, the digital twin is linked to a physical tag on the garment.

In an interview for the Digital Fashion Group, Lui Iarocheski, PlatformE's VP of Marketing and New Ventures, described Valaclava's aim to make the onboarding user-friendly for customers who are outside the NFT or web space. There is no minting and there is no necessity to log on with a crypto wallet. Valaclava's objective is to make this transition to phygital as smooth as possible, especially for the gaming audience, who are still skeptical about NFTs, according to Iarocheski.[19]

Another key benefit of working with NFTs and blockchain technology for fashion brands is the prospect of a digital product passport. In May 2023, the European Commission introduced a program that provides funds for businesses to test out these passports, which are effectively a new form of care label that not only includes information about materials and care, but traceability and provenance as well. By using and storing a garment's data on the blockchain, a company can also remove much of the manual authentication processes that many luxury brands have. An NFT is unhackable and is linked to the garment by a physical NFC (near field communication) tag on the garment or the accessory. PlatformE acknowledges that a phygital approach still needs considerable work in solution designing and process technology development to ensure the best system to distribute digital fashion and activate on-demand manufacturing upstream. As Cruz states, "one thing is clear, one without the other will not work. There is no point having great 3D assets, if nothing changes down the line."[20]

Conclusion

Valaclava provides a good example of one vision of the future for the fashion industry and in what ways the metaverse can integrate with physical fashion, and physical with virtual. But there must be considerable technological development and consumer onboarding before the promise of the metaverse becomes a reality and digital fashion in general can scale. Kerry Murphy explains:

> AR is a big unlock; it's been getting bigger. However, I do believe that we need a hardware innovation for it to go into the next step. And with the hardware innovation that everybody is super excited about . . . the AR Apple glasses that are gonna come out. Everyone is expecting Apple to, you know, do something so amazing that it's gonna revolutionize everything. I don't know if that's possible, especially when it comes down to AR. But that's what we need, we need these glasses that you and I, Brian, are wearing right now, to have this digital layer in them. And through that, you're gonna start thinking about "Well, how do I make this experience a little bit richer?" How do I start seeing virtual jewelry, virtual tattoos, virtual makeup, as a tool?[21]

Once the innovation in hardware moves to the next step, one may imagine that it will blur the lines between the real and digital worlds, a point in time when we begin to live more in the digital world than we do in the physical one. We will go into a store, and only see the prices if we are wearing smart glasses. Avatars will guide us to products which match our buying profile. Soon, some company will make smart glasses that sit in front of our eyes all day. We will go from paying only part of our attention, to nearly all of it, to our screens in the future. Our virtual life will become more important than our real life. And this is when the metaverse will truly begin.

Notes

1   Jussi S. Jauhiainen, Claudia Krohn, and Johanna Junnila, "Metaverse and Sustainability: Systematic Review of Scientific Publications until 2022 and Beyond," *Sustainability* 15, no. 1 (2023): 346, https://doi.org/10.3390/su15010346.

2   McKinsey & Company, "Covid-19 Implications for Business 2020," December 16, 2020, https://www.mckinsey.com/capabilities/risk-and-resilience/our-insights/covid-19-implications-for-business-2020.

3   Mark Zuckerberg, "The Founders Letter 2021," *Meta*, October 28, 2021, https://about.fb.com/news/2021/10/founders-letter/.

4   Yogesh K. Dwivedi et al., "Metaverse Beyond The Hype: Multidisciplinary perspectives on emerging challenges, opportunities and agenda for research practice and policy," *International Journal of Information Management* 66 (October 2022).

5   Maghan McDowell, "Meta's new digital fashion marketplace will sell Prada, Balenciaga and Thom Browne," *Vogue Business*, June 17, 2022, https://www.voguebusiness.com/technology/metas-new-digital-fashion-marketplace-will-sell-prada-balenciaga-and-thom-browne.

6   Bernd Sauer, Director of Accessories and Technical Development Apparel at Puma, personal communication, interview conducted June 2, 2023.

7   Laure Guilbault, "Gucci owner Kering says crypto 'no longer niche' wants to be Web3 'pioneers,'" *Vogue Business*, June 10, 2022, https://www.voguebusiness.com/technology/gucci-owner-kering-says-crypto-no-longer-niche-wants-to-be-web3-pioneers.

8   Jake Silbert, "Gucci's Purses Are Worth More in Roblox Than IRL," *Highsnobiety*, May 2021, https://www.highsnobiety.com/p/gucci-virtual-purse-roblox-resale/.

9   P. Smith, "Global revenue of the apparel market 2014–2027," *Statista*, June 28, 2023, https://www.statista.com/forecasts/821415/value-of-the-global-apparel-market.

10 Andrew Steinwold, Brian Leiberman, and Kerry Murphy, "Digital Fashion Is the Future," *Metaverse Live* (EP 7), video, 47:50, February 7, 2023, https://www.youtube.com/watch?v=Qm4c-75vneY.

11 Steinwold, Leiberman, and Murphy, "Digital Fashion Is the Future," 26:14.

12 Ellen MacArthur Foundation, "Redesigning the Future of Fashion," https://ellenmacarthurfoundation.org/topics/fashion/overview.

13 European Parliament, "The impact of textile production and waste on the environment," https://www.europarl.europa.eu/news/en/headlines/society/20201208STO93327/the-impact-of-textile-production-and-waste-on-the-environment-infographic.

14 McKinsey & Company, "Fashion on climate," 2020, https://www.mckinsey.com/~/media/mckinsey/industries/retail/our%20insights/fashion%20on%20climate/fashion-on-climate-full-report.pdf.

15 Leslie Holden and Digital Fashion Group, "On-demand a phygital reality," *The Interline*, January 5, 2023, https://www.theinterline.com/2023/01/05/phygital-fashion-on-demand/.

16 Holden and Digital Fashion Group, "On-demand a phygital reality."

17 Antonio Grasso, "Leveraging the potential of innovative SMEs and start-ups to make Europe sustainable and resilient," *European Digital Alliance News—General Assembly*, November 24, 2022, https://www.digitalsme.eu/leveraging-the-potential-of-innovative-smes-and-start-ups-to-make-europe-sustainable-and-resilient/.

18 Digital Fashion Group 2021, "Digital Fashion 101," Unit 4, https://www.thedigitalfashiongroup.academy/.

19 Holden and Digital Fashion Group, "On-demand a phygital reality."

20 Digital Fashion Group "Digital Fashion 101" Unit 4.

21 Steinwold, Lieberman, and Murphy, "Digital Fashion Is the Future," 31:20.

Matthew Drinkwater Interviewed
by Sara Emilia Bernat

Matthew Drinkwater is the head of Fashion Innovation Agency, an innovation hub at the London College of Fashion dedicated to emerging technologies that disrupt existing practices and norms in fashion and retail industries. In this interview, he talks about the rise and lure of digital fashion, and what is needed for it to fully take off.

Sara Emilia Bernat   Covid-19 has accelerated digital fashion, a concept that previously existed marginally. What do you think has happened?

Matthew Drinkwater   Covid-19 accelerated the acceptance of digital fashion. Technologically speaking, there were no new advancements. What we have seen is the much greater acceptance of virtual experiences built into our lives, and becoming more connected through virtual experiences. Just like everything, it was a question of timing, a true convergence: technology was good enough, culturally the moment was correct, and hundreds of million people were trying to understand how to represent themselves best within virtual spaces. This is really what we were doing every single day during lockdown! I think suddenly there was a recognition that you could behave a little bit differently within virtual space. All these strands coming together is behind the acceleration.

That said, there is probably another driver which is commerce, and the explosion of interest in cryptocurrencies. This is what has pushed many brands to explore the potential of digital fashion as a revenue stream—which we always said it would be, back in 2017–18, when we would be talking about it. But suddenly when you see digital artists making millions of dollars out of NFT sales, and those headlines appearing day after day after day, the recognition and the pressure that brands were facing—physical stores were closed—that beyond commerce there was potentially something else they could explore. It's all of those elements coming together at the same time, but all of those were spurred by the pandemic. That was the spark that lit the fire. I think it was the pandemic which finally forced more of a mindset change around these things.

Sara Emilia Bernat   Speaking of commerce, do you have a favorite digital fashion brand or project?

Matthew Drinkwater   That's a hard one. There are a number of brands that were more prepared internally to build capabilities around technologies. For example, Burberry already had an existing 3D team. They were already beginning to understand the importance of creating within a 3D space, and preparing for when digital fashion was ready to take off. Then, there were brands who started to become far more experimental. For instance, Gucci has been extremely experimental. We spent many years as a team preaching brands, particularly luxury brands, to be more experimental in the space. So, to see an established brand like Gucci beginning to execute in many areas, within the space of sometimes weeks of each other, was encouraging, exciting, and almost set a standard for what a new area could be, where brands didn't have to play by the same rules, and keep to marketing calendars that they used to before. Those, for me, are the things we need to encourage. Infrastructurally, brands need to prepare themselves for what's coming, but they also have to be willing to be very experimental in what they are planning to do.

Sara Emilia Bernat   How do you think brands can prepare the best?

Matthew Drinkwater   Start recruiting, start shifting, and start experimenting—it's all of those together. There is going to be a war for 3D talent. 3D designers, 3D animators, and game engineers will be fundamental for virtual worlds that are much more immersive. Anyone who has those skill sets will be massively in demand, as they are right now; they will be fundamental to what brands will create in the future. If they are not already doing it now, if the last two years did not teach them anything, then they will fall deep behind the curve.

Sara Emilia Bernat   Is there a confusion regarding digital fashion that you frequently encounter?

Matthew Drinkwater   We need to see what really good design could look like. I think there has been resistance to digital fashion, and probably quite reasonably so, because some of the activations have perhaps not aesthetically looked as slick as luxury brands and the fashion world are used to seeing. I think a lot of that stems from where the software came from, but the software is improving year after year. A lot of the people working in the original, first wave of digital fashion come from a pattern-cutting background, and less of a design background. The early days of digital fashion were characterized by a certain aesthetic: lots of metallic, lots of very shiny, very similar looking design—something that made consumers feel a little bit uncomfortable. We are beginning to form a new narrative around digital design and digital couture. There are so many incredibly talented people working in digital fashion beginning to find their own voice, but it will take a long time to be able to understand what good looks like, and what is exceptional in 3D design. These are things that are just beginning to emerge.

Sara Emilia Bernat   Let's dive deeper into this! How do you think aesthetics will change?

Matthew Drinkwater   I think it is a massive talking point as it can be the very reason for resistance around digital fashion. I would point to the reaction around Metaverse Fashion Week, where a huge amount of PR and marketing was pushed to draw in a wider audience. But when people saw the low poly, block-y aesthetic, they found it very jarring.

There are many platforms on which digital fashion can exist. Whether it's *Roblox*, *Minecraft*, or *Animal Crossing*, all of these places can have a look and aesthetics that can be very successful—to a very specific audience. When we talk about aesthetics, it will be a conversation about who you are designing for. You wouldn't be designing a couture dress for somebody on the high street. There needs to be a beginning to understanding what we are creating, and for whom. It is vital to understand how specific platforms can deliver to specific audiences. At the higher end, CG visual effects come into play, resulting in a cinematic quality where I think luxury will shift towards. That doesn't mean that a brand cannot exist within *Roblox* and elsewhere that is created on Unreal Engine. But those will have different audiences, and there will be different aspirations for them. I think in general what we need to see is pushing the limits of where creative design can go with the tools that we have available. When you talk about *Decentraland*, all of those activations are typically taking a CLO file, and then compressing them massively, until under 10 MB. It means that you are taking a multi gig, and then compressing it massively, or downgrading what you created. That's not what fashion is about. We want to create something that is inspirational, showing it at its peak, when it's the most aspirational, in a way. Those tools exist now, we should use them to create "wow" moments.

Sara Emilia Bernat   Does this all mean that craftsmanship will go through a change?

Matthew Drinkwater   I wouldn't say that. It's a change, it's beginning to create acceptance of *savoir faire* or craftsmanship within the digital space which for so long was regarded as . . . well, none of those things. If you created in digital, then you were a programmer or coder. There wasn't an artistry attached to that. That's not always been the case if you look at cinema. And yet, we are using those tools and beginning to apply them to the fashion industry. So that shift in mindset needed to happen from executives, from brands, to accept digital as a form of communication to the industry.

Sara Emilia Bernat   You touched upon the need to understand different kinds of audiences. What kinds of groups are engaging in digital fashion currently, and how can they be expanded upon?

Matthew Drinkwater   I would say the places where you see the most digital fashion is in gaming. When you have platforms like *Fortnite* which now has about 300 million monthly active users with a turnover of their item shop of $5–6 billion a year, it's making them one of the biggest digital fashion brands in the world, even though perhaps they wouldn't be perceived as that. You have a captive audience, you have a place to use it, a place to express yourself. Those ecosystems exist, and they exist for hundreds of millions of people. Those represent the opportunity now. I think there is a perception that gaming is an overwhelmingly male-dominated area, but it's not. I think the latest stats show 55–45% distribution between men and women, and it shifts dramatically on mobile in favor of women. There is already a really big audience purchasing purely virtual goods. The other audience that is really erupting in the last eighteen months are the cryptocurrency and NFT collectors who have started to be part of the digital fashion scene as well. While their numbers are relatively small, they drive large volumes, headline numbers, and artifacts. That is a new type of fashion consumer, probably largely male—as the sphere of cryptocurrency is overwhelmingly male.

To grow an audience there are a few things that need to happen: we need to increase accessibility. The longer-term vision is that there will be a headset or a pair of glasses to put on and watch somebody wearing digital fashion in real time. Body tracking is improving dramatically every year, but there is still space to evolve. There is still not a headset available on the market that would allow affordable access and lightness so that you could wear it for a longer period of time. Improvements in machine learning, body tracking, and hardware will allow us to deliver to a wider audience. Then, I think our clothes could become canvas for digital experiences: everything we wear, the accessories that we carry, can become a potential canvas for digital fashion that we can lay visual effects and computer graphics onto in real time. We are heading in this direction, it is just a question of computer power and time.

Sara Emilia Bernat　　Are there any talking points in digital fashion that are only hypes?

Matthew Drinkwater　　There is huge talk about being able to carry skins from one digital environment to another. For example, if you buy a skin on *Roblox* and then you want to go to *Fortnite*, or want to go into a VR chat room, that digital asset that you bought will adapt automatically. I understand the need to move your purchased skins within digital environments, but there are massive barriers, and not just from a technical perspective. Currently there is little incentive for these platforms to have goods moving around. Although the formation of the Metaverse Standards Council is a positive step which will look at how that could happen. There is massive hype around this topic, and a lot of people think they can deliver it.

Sara Emilia Bernat   How do you see digital fashion evolving in the next five or ten years?

Matthew Drinkwater   I wish I knew that! In five years' time, there will be much greater acceptance. One of the things that we need to overcome in the next five to ten years is the uncanny value of digital fashion. It's like looking at a digital human when you know it's not real. We'll make it a much more natural, realistic type of experience when you can put it on and go "wow it looks awesome," as opposed to "eh, it is a bit junky, does not move in a way you want it to move." I know we draw a parallel around face filters, and how those dramatically improved over the years. It's clearly a lot easier to do something to your face which is fixed in position rather than garments that need to move as they do in the real world, or the realm of fantasy. Tracking the body will be essential to a more realistic experience. Five years from now, we will see quite big jumps, and I am confident that a lot of adoption from Snapchat, Tiktok, or whatever new social platform there will be—because there is bound to be another one—will look at these technologies to make experiences more seamless.

Also, a sense of fun is often forgotten when we discuss digital fashion. Digital fashion can be a ton of fun, and facilitating emotional connections will make people want to be part of it. Joy will be really crucial.

Sara Emilia Bernat   Huh! Emotional connections are not something you often hear about when discussing this topic! Do you think digital fashion has space outside of capitalism?

Matthew Drinkwater   I would like to say "yes" because I think the tools for creation are now widely available. I think there is an exciting core group of creatives who are doing very innovative things slightly under the radar. I meet so many young people who are looking to build their businesses. Many of the designers I have worked with have not viewed their work as commerce or as a business. They did it because it's art to them. But to me, this is where it's going to create more opportunities. In the past, you always utilized certain types of business models to solve problems. For example, you used fashion week to build a fashion business. Those rules are going to go; they are gone;

they were gone a long time ago; it's just the rest of the industry forgot to take notice of that. But the available tools will allow a new generation of creatives to express their art in a very different way, which will create value. I do believe that we can see a renaissance in creativity. The tools are there, and they are widely available. There is such an opportunity beyond what we have seen before.

Sara Emilia Bernat   What excites you the most in terms of the future of digital fashion?

Matthew Drinkwater   There are a lot. First and foremost, the fact that we are having this conversation, and we are having it because you are writing a book about it. This means that there is wider interest in it. Three years ago, four years ago, five years ago, six years ago—however long we want to go back to when we were looking at this being an opportunity—there was always fascination but there was always skepticism around it. I was in Paris six weeks ago talking to a room full of luxury brands at *WWD* about the metaverse. That I was doing that is quite surreal to me. Three years ago, there wouldn't have been buyers for it, or the belief that this is a real thing. Today that belief exists and will create enormous opportunities. That is number one: the belief is there. And that is going to allow us to really move forward.

Beyond that, computer graphics and visual effects can enhance the world that we see today. We are building possibilities for that, and there has been such a massive shift in where VC money is going, where all investment is going. There are hundreds of millions and billions of dollars going into research. This will become a reality. And again, for all of us creatives in the sector, this represents a massive opportunity to do exciting and extraordinary things. We are going to be able to redefine what people thought of as fashion to create a new sector. Not replace it—well maybe a little bit—which would be good because I think everyone knows we consume too many physical products. If there is a way that we can begin to challenge that consumption pattern, possibly we will open up a new area that is complementary to everything that exists. This industry is about emotion. It's a sense of falling in love, your heart is racing when you are at fashion week, and you see a show that is exciting . . . All those things we will do in digital forms in ways that we never experienced before. We can create a level of excitement and emotional pull that exists in the physical world; we will also do it in the digital world. New brands are already emerging, and there will be hundreds more, and we are just at the very beginning of it. Who wouldn't want to be part of that? That's an exciting place to be.

Sara Emilia Bernat   What should we be concerned about when it comes to digital fashion, and its future?

Matthew Drinkwater   I think it's the same with any emerging technology. We should always tread carefully towards a place that is equitable and fair. It is increasingly easy to use machine learning to generate new designs, which are perhaps using somebody else's design. I am sure you have seen DALL-E or Midjourney on the internet, where just by typing a few words into your browser you can generate imagery at a fairly reasonable standard. There are reasons to be cautious around some of those things. Optimistically, I think they represent really big opportunities.

One of the other areas in which digital fashion was always lauded is the impact that it will have on the consumption of physical products. Which I think it definitely has the potential to do. It becomes easy to create and download digital garments, so that at the push of the button you can buy something new. One of the things that we must be really cautious about is that, while you can change what you wear every minute of every day, we don't fuel a new way of consumption, which we don't yet know how will affect behavior in the physical world. When I presented a pre-pandemic talk to students at a college, someone put up their hand and asked me that question: "Are you teaching us to be hyper consumers?" This leads into a potential issue: are we increasing the pressure on creators to design huge numbers of digital fashion because it's so easy to simply download? We talk about pressuring fashion designers into hamster wheels, but is this what we' re ushering digital creatives to do too?

Sara Emilia Bernat   Is there anything that is currently not talked about in the digital fashion discourse, and which you would like people to know about or consider?

Matthew Drinkwater   A lot of what has been happening in the space is excitement around digital fashion. As with any new field, there is a rush to get involved, but there is not a lot of technical knowledge on how to create and what good looks are. There is a lot of opportunity for people to create who perhaps haven't got the experience. I think we need to focus on core skills. Education remains massively important—not just for creatives coming through learning skill sets, but for people consuming and becoming part of the digital fashion ecosystem. Standards need to arrive, just like in any sector in the creative industries. Those things will come about in time, but I think it is a concern with so many people rushing to a new space that it becomes a little Wild West-like, and I think I see a little bit of that at the moment.

Afterword

Trends and technology impacting digital fashion develop and shift quickly, which may cause people to wonder about the future of this intriguing field. There was a boon in the sales volume of NFTs in 2021, yet the next year the market nearly collapsed.[1] The metaverse became a popular buzzword in tech culture and beyond, but then it was declared "dead" by several cultural commentators in 2023.[2] These downfalls may rightfully induce concerns about whether digital fashion will survive, or whether it is merely a fad, awaiting its final bow. To make any absolute declaration at this moment, however, seems premature. For example, Google ended their Glass project in 2015, leading to speculation that the development of glasses like these were over; but a new version was subsequently created, and was quickly shuttered again in 2023.[3] Despite these two setbacks, it still doesn't look like Google has completely abandoned development on this project. Other companies are certainly continuing to work on developing wearable glasses or goggles, as exemplified by Apple's 2023 announcement of the Apple Vision Pro, which will become available in 2024. Apple markets this device as being the first spatial computer, as it blends the physical world with the digital. Needless to say, eyewear such as these have already aided and can continue to aid in the use and omni-virtual wear of digital fashion on XR platforms. Time will reveal the success of this type of product, but many technologies experience some ups and downs in their beginning, which does not mean they are completely gone.

Digital fashion, however, sits in a better position than these other technologies and programs. That is not to say that it is impervious to a downfall; but overall, it rests on a more secure foundation. Even though digital fashion has become entangled with talk about the metaverse—for example, with events like Metaverse Fashion Week—digital fashion existed before all the hype of the metaverse launched into popular culture. As long as video games continue to exist, which seems fairly inevitable, then people will want to clothe their avatars and characters in those games. Digital samples of garments will also likely continue to be made in the production process of physical clothing; in fact, more and more brands are leaning towards completely removing physical samples and relying only on digital ones in an effort to reduce their environmental impact. It is therefore likely that some subset of digital fashion will continue to exist, even if a fully immersive internet fails to become a reality soon.

As showcased in this book, digital fashion encompasses a wider application than just the metaverse or any one digital context. It has the fully digital aspect of clothing worn by avatars, but it also assists creators, consumers, and goals, like sustainability and equitability. The way we use, consume, and think about digital fashion will surely change in the near future—perhaps even drastically. This is the reason why we sought to present ideas and issues about digital fashion from a wide spectrum of disciplines and professions. Digital fashion possesses the potential to spark a fashion revolution, altering the practices of creation and consumption. But if it will be successful, then we need conversations and collaborations from multiple perspectives beyond practitioners; we also need theorists to shape the future of this industry.

Digital fashion is an incredibly dynamic segment of the fashion system that is continually being molded through developments by individual consumers as well as industry players both big and small; no matter the size, any action has the potential to greatly alter the course of digital fashion history. On the software end, Browzwear succeeded in raising $35 million in funding in 2021 to further develop their 3D design software.[4] Digital fashion retailer DRESSX has achieved similar successes: in 2022 they secured a $3.3 million partnership investment, topping that in 2023 by raising $15 million in Series A funding.[5] Yet, even with a boon in finances and innovation in some parts of the system, other segments seem to be struggling. With multiple lawsuits by major brands like Nike and Hermès, which are vying to stake a claim to trademarks and rights in the digital fashion landscape, we can get a glimpse of how the idealistic interpretation of the metaverse could easily just replicate the ills of the current physical fashion system. Global market leaders tend to have a disproportionate influence on current events and industry. As such, we are yet to see what the effects will be as a result of Meta ending their support and development of NFTs on their Instagram and Facebook platforms, not long after declaring 2023 to be their "year of efficiency" for reevaluating and restructuring their initiatives.[6] By comparison, custom content created by independent artists for games like *The Sims* impact digital fashion on a micro level on a regular basis. Ultimately, meeting consumers' demands will be the deciding factor in digital fashion's future. The large companies have invested a lot of money and effort into the metaverse and digital fashion, but it is up to us as consumers to shape the future of these tools.

This book set out to show the scope of digital fashion without pushing a rigid definition, in theory or practice, but by allowing the different approaches to create a range of possibilities. By spanning disciplines (like history and philosophy), practices (like education and sneaker culture), and issues (like equitability and decoloniality), we strove to illustrate the far-reaching impact that digital fashion can and does possess. But as it is only one facet of the overall fashion industry, digital fashion serves to complement the other aspects. It may serve to teach physical fashion how to be more sustainable; it may help creators experiment in new ways; and it may help consumers make wiser decisions through virtual try-ons and other technologies. But it won't happen magically. Ultimately, people control their actions, and digital fashion is just one tool that people can use to accomplish a variety of goals. While digital fashion occasionally feels like an aspect of science fiction, it is also a useful tool through which we can engage in critical conversations and topics, such as those presented in this book.

Michael R. Spicher
Sara Emilia Bernat
Doris Domoszlai-Lantner
June 2023

Notes

1   Shanti Escalante-De Mattei, "After 2022's Crypto Crash, the Future Vision of NFTs Is Looking Far More Banal," *ARTnews*, December 27, 2022, https://www.artnews.com/art-news/news/future-of-nfts-2022-opensea-royalties-1234651990/.

2   Ed Zitron, "RIP Metaverse: An obituary for the latest fad to join the tech graveyard," *Insider*, May 8, 2023, https://www.businessinsider.com/metaverse-dead-obituary-facebook-mark-zuckerberg-tech-fad-ai-chatgpt-2023-5.

3   Rob Thubron, "Google Glass killed off for a second time," *Techspot*, March 16, 2023, https://www.techspot.com/news/97956-google-kills-off-google-glass-second-time.html

4   "Fashion design software venture Browzwear raises $35m," *Retail Technology Innovation Hub*, August 13, 2021, https://retailtechinnovationhub.com/home/2021/8/17/fashion-design-software-venture-browzwear-raises-35m.

5   Roxanne Robinson, "DressX raises 15 million USD in latest round of funding," *Fashion Network*, March 14, 2023, https://ww.fashionnetwork.com/news/Dressx-raises-15-million-usd-in-latest-round-of-funding,1496221.html.

6   Jay Peters, "Meta gives up on NFTs for Facebook and Instagram," The Verge, March 13, 2023, https://www.theverge.com/2023/3/13/23638572/instagram-nft-meta-facebook-quits-digital-collectibles.

Index